D0302230

The Treaty of Amsterdam

Text and Commentary

Edited by Andrew Duff

WITHDRAWN

FEDERAL TRUST

337.142

Treaty of Amsterdam

Copy 3

2 8045 00076 0663

The Federal Trust

The Federal Trust works through research and education towards the widening and deepening of the European Union as well as to enhance the European policy of the United Kingdom

The Trust conducts enquiries, promotes seminars and conferences and publishes reports.

Its current work programme includes studies of long-term change in Europe, the development of the European social model, civic education in Europe, the introduction of the single currency, and the future of the European Parliament. Up-to-date information about the Trust can be found on the internet at www.fedtrust.co.uk.

Recent Federal Trust publications include:

Harry Cowie (rapporteur), *Private Partnerships and Public Networks in Europe* (1996).

Graham Bishop, José Pérez and Sammy van Tuyll (eds), *User Guide to the Euro* (1996).

Andrew Duff, *Reforming the European Union*, (1997).

Federal Trust publications are available through Sweet & Maxwell Ltd. Orders can be placed by telephone from the UK on 01264 342899, and from overseas on + 44 1264 342828.

The Federal Trust is the UK member of TEPSA (the Trans-European Policy Studies Association).

The Trust is a registered charity and expresses no political view of its own.

Published by the Federal Trust

Dean Bradley House

52 Horseferry Road

London SW1P 2AF

© Federal Trust for Education and Research 1997

ISBN 0 90157367 1 (HARDBACK)

ISBN 0 90157365 5 (SOFTBACK)

The Federal Trust is a Registered Charity

Marketing and Distribution by Sweet & Maxwell Ltd

Printed in the European Union

WITHDRAWN

The Treaty of Amsterdam

Text and Commentary

Table of Contents

Foreword by Lamberto Dini
The European Union after Amsterdam

Essay by Andrew Duff
Supranational institutions for postnational Europe

PART ONE
TEXT AND COMMENTARY ON THE TREATY OF AMSTERDAM

SECTION ONE
FREEDOM, SECURITY AND JUSTICE

FUNDAMENTAL RIGHTS AND NON-DISCRIMINATION
GENERAL PRINCIPLES UNDERLYING THE UNION

ACTION IN THE EVENT OF A BREACH BY A MEMBER STATE OF
THE PRINCIPLES ON WHICH THE UNION IS FOUNDED

RESPECT BY ANY STATE APPLYING TO JOIN FOR THE
FUNDAMENTAL PRINCIPLES

STATUS OF CHURCHES

SECTION TWO
THE UNION AND THE CITIZEN

EMPLOYMENT

SOCIAL POLICY

SECTION THREE
AN EFFECTIVE AND COHERENT EXTERNAL POLICY

THE COMMON FOREIGN AND SECURITY POLICY

SECTION FOUR
THE UNION'S INSTITUTIONS

ENLARGEMENT

THE EUROPEAN PARLIAMENT

SIMPLIFICATION OF THE CO-DECISION PROCEDURE

ORGANISATION AND COMPOSITION OF THE EUROPEAN PARLIAMENT

COMMENTARY

THE COUNCIL
QUALIFIED MAJORITY VOTING

New Treaty provisions

Existing Treaty provisions

COMMENTARY

THE COMMISSION

THE COURT OF JUSTICE

OTHER INSTITUTIONAL ISSUES

SECTION FIVE
CLOSER COOPERATION — OR 'FLEXIBILITY'

SECTION SIX
SIMPLIFICATION AND CONSOLIDATION OF THE
TREATIES

SECTION SEVEN
ECONOMIC POLICY

PART TWO
TREATY OF AMSTERDAM AMENDING THE TREATY ON EUROPEAN UNION AND THE TREATY ESTABLISHING THE EUROPEAN COMMUNITY

DECLARATIONS

F. Declaration relating to the Treaty of Amsterdam

Declarations of which the Conference took note

Preface

This book is not the definitive work on the Treaty of Amsterdam. The time and opportunity for that will be well after the Treaty has come into force, and when we know how adaptable the European Union has proved to be in the face of the dual challenge of enlargement and economic and monetary union.

The purpose of this book is to help with the process of ratification by easing understanding of this complex Treaty and its sometimes less than clear provisions.

The text of the Treaty used here is that of late July 1997 (CONF 4004/97). It is three versions different from that initialled by the heads of state or government in Amsterdam in the early hours of 18 June. After further treatment by the lawyers and linguists the final version to be signed in October will be different still — but neither substantively nor substantially so.

Structure

Our commentary in Part One follows the Treaty more or less in the order, policy sector by policy sector, that the heads of state and government themselves dealt with the draft at the Amsterdam conference on 16-17 June 1997. We repeat the most important provisions where necessary to ease access and comprehension. For convenience, and to add context, we reprint the EMU Stability Pact, also agreed by the European Council at Amsterdam. Footnotes appear at the end of each section.

In Part Two we reproduce the latest version of the Treaty. In both Parts we omit the technical parts of the Treaty as they effect the Coal and Steel and Atomic Energy Communities, as well as the provisions on the simplification of the Treaties. We publish a table of equivalences that relates the ordering and numbering here to that which will eventually prevail after the Treaty comes into force. Simple it is not, but rational it may be. (The extensive table of contents is a guide.)

As ever, the Federal Trust would welcome the views of our readers about our publications.

Acknowledgments

Although the commentary is largely mine, I draw on the collective work of the Federal Trust in following the institutional development of the European Union for many years and, pertinently, under a Round Table chaired by Lord Jenkins of Hillhead which from 1994-96 studied the

Intergovernmental Conference that was spawned at Maastricht and terminated in Amsterdam.

The Italian Foreign Minister, Lamberto Dini, has been generous in offering a foreword in which he gives his reactions to his experience at Amsterdam.

The Federal Trust is grateful as always for the support it receives from the European Commission.

Many people have offered their advice and encouragement in this enterprise — particularly Nigel Haigh, Jean-Victor Louis, Jörg Monar, William Nicoll, Simon Nuttall and, as ever, John Pinder. Thanks too to Richard Blackman, research officer, and to Harry Cowie, Susie Symes and Judy Keep at the Trust.

Andrew Duff
London
August 1997

Foreword by Lamberto Dini

The European Union after Amsterdam

The long night of Amsterdam closed on a note of bitter disappointment. We would not be honest with ourselves or with the others if we did not admit this.

We cannot, of course, ignore the progress that was made in the process of permanent negotiation that the European Union has now become. Fundamental rights, guarantees for citizens, the role of the European Parliament, social and employment policy, the transfer to Community level of matters concerning justice and home affairs, the strengthening of intergovernmental cooperation on security, majority voting on foreign policy, and flexibility, all contribute to the making of a more equilibrated Europe — a Europe that has been enriched in terms of solidarity, liberty and participation.

But choices that will nonetheless have to be made one day were put off again. It proved impossible to provide monetary supranationalism with an equally authoritative political interlocutor; to give immediacy to the creation of a space within which EU citizens can move with security; to equip ourselves with a foreign policy that is not only consultative but also able to act; or to deploy force.

We had foreseen this risk, above all that the focus would be exclusively on monetary union and enlargement. It is certainly important that the fracture regarding the steps leading to the euro was healed in Amsterdam, and that a clash between the political and economic approaches to virtuous finance was avoided. The single currency project, the last great challenge the Community has embarked on, is proceeding on its course. And there are grounds for hoping, since such events have a force of their own, that the introduction of the euro will help to create and consolidate some form of government of the economy, whose determination, although it was discussed in Amsterdam, remains entrusted to the future. Indeed, after Amsterdam there is a more credible prospect of a European currency that will be strong, stable and attractive to investors and not merely a means of achieving an easy consensus among the EU partners.

But in other respects, in Amsterdam we saw a Europe that was all too often opaque, inclined to procrastination and ambiguity, a prisoner of interests sometimes more nationalistic than national. Right up to the end, with a frankness and tenacity widely perceived inside and outside the meeting, the Italian delegation sought to ensure that reasonable ambitions would prevail, in order to prevent Europe from being totally unprepared in the face of the two great challenges of the euro and enlargement. We are convinced that the single currency cannot be constructed in a political desert.

Alas, the majority of our partners preferred to give priority to the timetable rather than the content of the Conference, to put off once more the difficult choices, in particular those concerning the Union's institutions, security and defence. We could have asked for the proceedings to be suspended, and we pondered on this possibility at length with Prime Minister Romano Prodi. The conditions, at that late hour, were better suited to an agricultural marathon than to negotiations on Europe's constitution.

Italy's tenacity and intransigence on security and defence, and on the Union's institutions, will at least have helped to prevent the fabrication of ambiguous solutions that would have supported only cosmetically the load of a larger Europe. It appeared to us better to wait for a more propitious day, for a hopefully more favourable political conjuncture, after the appointment with the single currency and before proceeding with enlargement. Everything considered, this was the original aim of institutional reform and the time has not yet run out. On the contrary, the new Treaty can be seen as embodying this sequence of priorities, which will not prevent the membership negotiations from starting as planned.

As I have said, we could have blocked everything in Amsterdam. We refrained from doing so because a pause for reflection would not have sufficed to overcome the stalemate constituted by the present configuration of forces, vetoes, mismatched priorities, and rigidities that at times appeared obtuse. It seemed better to wait for a more propitious moment in order to avoid making European integration appear an ordeal, capable of bringing down governments or causing majorities to vacillate. Better to adopt the disappointed but lucid attitude suggested by Altiero Spinelli after the Single Act — to consolidate what we have obtained and set sail again for the next objective.

The stages of this journey must be clear: incorporate the progress made in Amsterdam by ratifying the Treaty; open the enlargement negotiations in January 1998; decide on the euro in the spring of 1998; make the institutional adaptations needed for an enlarged Europe that is not a pale shadow of that envisaged by the founding fathers; and, lastly, join together the two halves of Europe with the entry of the first group of new member states.

In each of these stages we will have the opportunity, together with others, to clarify and promote the Europe we want. Not a Europe that is preparing to make a leap in the dark, into an institutional void, but a Europe proceeding on a rational course. In this way we shall still be masters of the European construction — especially if others, after more mature reflection than was possible in the agitated hours of the Amsterdam wake, assess the risks of an invertebrate Europe. Our continent no longer hinges on the Carolingian axis around which it was born. There is a price to be paid if we are to extend a grand design to a larger and less homogeneous area. What some want, and what others only pretend to want, must be clearly distinguished. The advent of the single currency and the imminence of the Union's enlargement are bound to bring about a salutary clarification.

Our disappointment must not leave us without a rational and far-sighted strategy. As in the past, we must build on the results achieved, however unsatisfactory they may be. According to a German Enlightenment philosopher, Moses Mendelsshon, throughout Europe's history, even in the darkest moments, there has always been enough light to illuminate the next step. This remains the key to European integration after Amsterdam.

I know that this Federal Trust report on the Treaty of Amsterdam will surely help us find the right road forward. I welcome its timely publication.

Essay by Andrew Duff

Supranational institutions for postnational Europe

The Intergovernmental Conference, which opened in 1996, was bequeathed a clutch of difficult, left-over issues by the Treaty of Maastricht (1992). The official purpose of the 1996 IGC was to revise the European Treaties 'with the aim of ensuring the effectiveness of the mechanisms and the institutions of the Community'. The formal agenda was prescribed as follows:

1. To consider a report on the future security and defence arrangements of the Union, including the future of Western European Union (WEU);

2. To reappraise the 'three pillar' structure of the Union whereby the original European Community does not deal with either internal or external security policy;

3. To consider widening the scope of the co-decision procedure whereby the Parliament shares legislative power with the Council;

4. To revisit the question of the classification of European laws by their gravity, nature and purpose;

5. To consider the introduction to the Treaty of specific clauses in the fields of civil protection, energy and tourism.

These unavoidable commitments and the overriding imperative to complete Economic and Monetary Union (EMU) had been supplemented, in June 1994, by the necessity to prepare for a further bout of enlargement to Central and Eastern Europe. There was much alarmist talk at that time, most of it idle, of the Union within a decade being made up of 25 to 30 member states, and of the drastic institutional reforms required to accommodate them.

Gradually, however, realism prevailed. A Group of Reflection was set up in 1995 to prepare the IGC, but made little headway. When synthesised, the final ambitions of the IGC boiled down to resolving some of the worst anomalies of Maastricht; making the institutions more efficient; trying to improve the democratic legitimacy of the Union.

After the Group of Reflection had reported and the institutions had delivered their official opinions, the official mandate of the IGC was set in March 1996 by the European Council in Turin, under the presidency of Mr Dini. The agenda had three main themes.

Setting the agenda

First, a 'Union closer to its citizens', where the IGC was called upon to produce 'adequate results' in about one year on the following issues:

- within the framework of defined objectives, better methods and instruments;

- ensuring better protection of the citizen from international crime;

- developing coherent and effective visa, asylum and immigration policies;

- resolving divergent views on jurisdictional and parliamentary control of EU decisions in the field of justice and home affairs.

The IGC was also asked to consider as a priority how the EU could better coordinate national employment policies. Other items were:

- the role of competition policy in providing universal access to essential services;

- the status of peripheral and island regions of the Union, as well as its overseas territories;

- the strengthening of environmental protection policies;

- a better application of the principle of subsidiarity, improving openness and transparency, and an attempt to simplify and consolidate the EU Treaties.

The second theme was more democratic and efficient institutions, especially in the context of future enlargement. The IGC was asked to examine:

- simplifying and clarifying legislative procedures;

- widening the scope of the legislative co-decision procedure between the Council of ministers and the European Parliament;

- the wider role of the European Parliament, including its composition and electoral procedure;

- the contribution of national parliaments to the Union.

With regard to the Council, items to be tackled were the scope of Qualified Majority Voting (QMV), the threshold for a qualified majority and the weighting of votes between member states.

With regard to the European Commission, the task was to achieve greater efficiency, taking account of its composition and representativeness.

The IGC was asked to examine the roles of the European Court of Justice and the Court of Auditors, especially in combating fraud.

Notably, the Conference was instructed to consider the question of strengthened cooperation by a certain number of member states that would be open to all, compatible with the acquis communautaire (or patrimony) and the objectives of the Union, avoid distortions to competition and respect the institutions.

The third theme of the IGC was to strengthen the Union's capacity for external action, including making more coherent the Union's performance as the European Community (the 'first pillar' of the Treaty) — mainly external economic relations — and its work under the 'second pillar' — common foreign and security policy. The IGC was asked to:

- identify the principles and areas of common foreign policy;
- define the actions needed to promote the EU's interests;
- set up efficient and expedient procedures, including that of how the Union was to present itself to the outside world;
- agree on their financing.

With regard to asserting 'the European identity in matters of security and defence', the Union's relationship with the Western European Union would have to be clarified, especially in respect of the 'Petersberg Tasks'. The IGC might also examine closer cooperation in the area of armaments. [1]

Intractable problems

In the event, many of the problems raised on this ambitious agenda proved intractable. Some, such as the scope of the co-decision procedure, exposed the tension between those of a federalist persuasion, such as Germany and Benelux, and those, led by France, who wished to achieve a deepening of European integration without much reinforcement of the powers of the EU institutions. Others, such as the size of the Commission and the weighting of votes in the Council, betrayed a widening cleavage between the interests of the more and less populated states.

A third area of contention concerned the social dimension to the single market, where there emerged a clear difference of opinion between those, like the Dutch, who adopted a liberal approach and those, like the Swedes, who did not. This dialogue was sharpened by the quickening pace of structural reform forced on the member states by their obligation to meet the EMU deadlines, as well as by the economic consequences of the recession and of German unification.

The Conference sought to achieve 'adequate results' in these areas without being able either to inculcate or draw upon a sense of historical moment. Unlike Maastricht, there was no one central, driving project such as EMU and no dramatic external impulsion such as the Gulf War or the collapse of Soviet Europe. And unlike the Single European Act, there was no desire for a mass of new legislation or spending at the EU level. On the contrary, subsidiarity was in vogue, and the long economic recession had induced many fears about the state of public finance. General government debt had grown from 56% of GDP at the time of Maastricht in 1991 to 73% in 1996.

The Amsterdam IGC, therefore, was in contrast to its predecessors rather inchoate. Public opinion remained underwhelmed by the whole thing. Eurobarometer surveys conducted in 1996 showed those expressing general support for the EU falling to below the halfway mark; and a large majority admitted to feeling ill-informed about the EU.

Besides, despite the protracted labour of the Group of Reflection, the IGC could make very little substantive progress until after the defeat of the Conservative government in the UK. That the IGC was concluded at Amsterdam barely six weeks later is evidence of a strong desire to move on from the minutiae of the institutional debate.

What Amsterdam achieved

What did the IGC accomplish? First, and at the risk of over-simplification, on the positive side.

The Treaty of Amsterdam moves common visa, immigration and asylum policy from the intergovernmental third pillar of Maastricht to the first pillar of the European Community. We may welcome this because:

- it extends the democratic procedures of the European Commission, Council and Parliament as well as the jurisdiction of the Court of Justice to legislation in this sensitive area;

- it improves the prospect of making a reality of the principle of freedom of movement of people within the European Union.

The Treaty of Amsterdam also glues on to the Treaty on European Union the Schengen Agreement. Schengen was devised by most of the mainland member states to by-pass British opposition to the removal of the EU's internal borders.

Despite the fact that the development of EU common immigration policy will only be phased and gradual, the new British government has insisted on a UK opt-out from the new 'area of freedom, security and justice' and from the Schengen acquis. It claims that its island geography compels it to maintain external border controls in the interests of civility and racial harmony and to combat international terrorism and drug trafficking. Some — including the Irish, who are trapped by the UK into a similar derogation — may take a jaundiced view about that.

Post-modern anti-discrimination provisions are written into the Treaty; and respect for human rights is made an explicit criterion for membership of the Union. Among the most powerful aspects of the Treaty of Rome have been the prohibition of discrimination on the grounds of nationality and on the basis of gender in terms of pay. Now we can anticipate positive results from the involvement of the EU in a wide range of equal opportunities matters.

In the remaining third pillar — now renamed unadvisedly Police and Judicial Cooperation in Criminal Matters — the cumbersome decision-making procedure is somewhat lightened: conventions shall come into force once adopted by only half the member states within those states concerned. And the European Commission has won the important right of co-initiative with the Council in order to provide some impetus.

A high level of employment has always been an objective of the Union, but the addition of a whole new chapter on employment policy gives the objective more status and may make ratification of the Treaty more palatable in those member states that have yet to tackle their problems of structural unemployment. But we should not forget to remind the citizen that employment remains in greater part the responsibility not of the EU but of member state governments.

Amsterdam also reached agreement on the stability pact and ERM 2. This is a decisive step towards the birth, on time, of the single currency; it strengthens EU surveillance of member states' economies and makes the euro regime much more credible despite the fact that EMU is likely to begin on a broader basis than many had anticipated. If the Amsterdam European Council had faltered over the stability pact, there would have been no successful conclusion of the IGC.

That the new French socialist-communist government was prepared to sign up to the euro makes the indecisiveness of the new British government all the more surprising. With Amsterdam behind us, may we expect a definitive announcement that sterling will be part of the euro, an announcement that in itself will have the immediate effect of reducing the pound's exchange rate?

As it had promised, the new UK government conceded the Social Protocol of Maastricht. This means that it will now be a full player in all aspects of social policy development at the EU level. If that means that liberal forces are strengthened we should welcome the reform.

The concept of sustainable development is now written into the Treaty in a useful manner. And those member states, such as Denmark, that wish to apply higher environmental standards than others are guaranteed a right to do so as long as trade and competition rules are respected.

Progress was made in prescribing stiffer rules of open government, especially where it really matters, for the Council. Press and parliamentary scrutiny of the work of ministers in Brussels should now be more practicable.

The existing rules concerning the application of the principle of subsidiarity were written into the Treaty as a Protocol — although this will make no practical difference unless governments are prepared to deploy the argument properly, for example in the field of social policy. The UK's insistence on a clause for animal welfare does not necessarily bode well in this regard.

In the field of foreign and security policy, a common unit for analysis and planning is created and new responsibilities are given to the secretary-general of the Council. The WEU Petersberg Tasks — crisis management, humanitarian and peace-keeping — are written into the Treaty on European Union, but the WEU is not (yet) subsumed. The essentially civilian character of the EU is preserved.

On institutional matters, the new Treaty extends the scope of co-decision into some significant sectors (fifteen old competences and eight new) as well as simplifying and shortening the actual procedure. This is a great bonus for the European Parliament which emerges as the main beneficiary of Amsterdam. The cooperation procedure is all but abolished, reducing the number of basic procedures to three: co-decision, assent and consultation.

The right of initiative of the European Commission in legislative matters is protected, and in internal security matters extended. The President of the Commission is given more power over the other members and its internal organisation, and his appointment will be subject to the consent of the European Parliament.

The goal of the uniform electoral procedure for the European Parliament moves appreciably closer. The new Article 138(3) allows for the electoral system to be based on common principles — such as regionalism and proportionality — without having to achieve complete uniformity.

The possibilities of judicial review by the Court of Justice within the Union have been reinforced to cover fundamental rights, the common policy areas concerning visas, refugees and asylum-seekers, as well as civil proceedings.

John Major's government had provoked its partners into devising methods of 'flexibility' or 'enhanced cooperation' whereby a federal core of member states could integrate more deeply, leaving the UK behind. In the event, and given the demise of the Tories, the flexibility clauses of Amsterdam are so qualified to make their deployment in practice against the wishes of the UK virtually impossible.

There had been much talk at the IGC, mostly stimulated by the French but supported by the British, about a formal role for national parliaments in the law-making processes of the Union and in second-guessing the EU institutions over the application of subsidiarity. No such reform was agreed, however, and Amsterdam was probably the high-water mark of the more naive aspirations of national parliamentarians with regard to their role in dealing with the EU's democratic deficit. What needs now to happen is a coordinated attempt by national parliaments in the second and third pillar areas acting on a pragmatic basis — and the continuing development of the European Parliament into full partnership with the Council.

What remains to be done

As the Foreword by Lamberto Dini reminds us, many staunch Europeans are as disappointed by the results of Amsterdam as they were by Maastricht and the Single Act before it. It is true that even by its own standards — or, more accurately, according to the mandate set for it by the European Council — the IGC fell somewhat short of complete success. Certainly, much still remains to be done in order to achieve the federal constitutional settlement of the Union we seek, so that people will know how they are governed, by whom and from where. The agreement to hold another IGC in around 2000 holds out some hope.

In some order of importance, the shortcomings of Amsterdam are as follows:

- qualified majority vote is extended not as widely as the scope of the co-decision procedure, creating more anomalies, and there has been no reform of the weighting of votes in the Council to rebalance QMV between the larger and smaller states;

- the question of the size of the Commission has once again been put off, pending enlargement;

- the jurisdiction of the Court of Justice still remains incomplete in matters directly concerning the citizen, such as Europol;

- the derogations for the UK, Ireland and Denmark over free movement weakens the integrity of the European Union and will confuse the citizen;

- the Commission's right to negotiate for the Union in services and intellectual property is still restricted (Article 113);

- the European Parliament has rights to be consulted in the third pillar area but not the right of assent to legislation;

- the European Parliament has no right of assent to the new Treaty;

- the simplification of the mound of EU Treaties was barely started, and the radical reclassification of EU law by type and status ducked;

- the attempted fusion of Schengen into the EU will prove to have been botched and will need repair;

- the European Union (as opposed to the Community) was not given legal competence.

Ratification and after

All in all, the importance of the Treaty of Amsterdam is that it marks the first step in the reconciliation between the UK and its EU partners. It continues the Maastricht process and in some important ways moderates it. It allows enlargement negotiations to begin. And it holds out the promise of more political and institutional reform of the Union in the near future.

During the ratification process, the European Parliament, especially, can be expected to level a number of criticisms at the authors of the Treaty of Amsterdam — not least in the failure to reform the way that Treaty amendment itself is undertaken. What must be unacceptable is that the citizens and their parliamentary representatives are so far absent from the constituent process of the European Union.

The EU agenda must now move on too: to getting the single currency going on a sound basis as early as possible, to reform the food, farm and fisheries policies, the EU budget and the structural funds — and to learning to live with and exploit enlargement for the sake of all Europe and of Europe's place in world affairs. The Commission's *Agenda 2000*, published in July 1997, makes a good start towards reform.

Postnational Europe

We would be wise, however, to consider more deep-seated and long-term problems of European unity before we face enlargement.

The traditional process of European integration, now half a century old, seeks to build a Europe fit to replace the ineffective and reduced nation states with a union of member states. Sometimes the development of the European Union has been propelled by leaps forward in the federal direction; generally it has been sustained by functionalist integration, sector by sector, as a pooling of sovereignty in one sector spills over naturally enough into a related one. The difficulty has been to find the right system of supranational governance to manage this process efficiently and democratically, and to exploit its results for the greater good.

The paradigms of the process might be portrayed as in the accompanying table. The Treaty of Amsterdam, and before it Maastricht and the earlier Treaties, have sought to deepen the Union and widen its membership. They have pulled inside the triangle sector by sector, function by function and state by state in an attempt to make coherent and to bring under the rule of supranational law what would otherwise be spasmodic and fickle. Treaty change and institution building are a terribly important part of this centripetal process because they serve to clarify issues, resolve differences and forge pacts.

But the way the Union amends its Treaties is faulty. Chief players in the current and weighty system of the Intergovernmental Conference are precisely those ministers, parliaments, parties and officials of the old, nation state Europe who, more or less wittingly, are obliged to concede powers that their predecessors once took for granted would be held inalienably.

Where are the forces of postnational Europe in this Treaty-making? Where is the influence of the transnational political parties, social partners or non-governmental organisations? Are there not new forces — in the media, universities and churches, or even the heads of state, royal or republican — that should be taken to task for being absent from the European stage?

The Amsterdam IGC saw a degree of pluralisation of the constituent process of the European Union. Many NGOs took part in public hearings, organised by the European Parliament. Two MEPs were appointed non-voting members on sufferance of the Conference itself. It was a start, but a modest one.

Those who are left dissatisfied by the Treaty of Amsterdam should not merely grumble about the inadequacy of its authors but galvanise themselves and fellow European citizens to claim their fair share and more direct participation in the governance of the Union. The imminent introduction of the euro as sovereign currency in much of Europe may shock the citizen out of complacency about how the Union is governed. In that case, the Amsterdam Intergovernmental Conference will have been the last of its kind.

---

[1] For the full text of the Turin mandate to the IGC, see EC Bulletin, No. 3, 1996, pp. 9-11. For a detailed analysis of the issues involved based on the work of the Federal Trust Round Table on the IGC, see Andrew Duff, *Reforming the European Union*, London, Federal Trust, 1997.

POST-NATIONAL EUROPE

INTEGRATION

DEMOCRACY

EFFICIENCY

Text and Commentary on the Treaty of Amsterdam

Section One
Freedom, Security and Justice

FUNDAMENTAL RIGHTS AND NON-DISCRIMINATION

GENERAL PRINCIPLES UNDERLYING THE UNION

AMENDED ARTICLE F OF THE TREATY ON EUROPEAN UNION

1. The Union is founded on the principles of liberty, democracy, respect for human rights and fundamental freedoms, and the rule of law, principles which are common to the Member States.

2. The Union shall respect fundamental rights, as guaranteed by the European Convention for the Protection of Human Rights and Fundamental Freedoms signed in Rome on 4 November 1950 and as they result from the constitutional traditions common to the Member States, as general principles of Community law.

3. The Union shall respect the national identities of its Member States.

4. The Union shall provide itself with the means necessary to attain its objectives and carry through its policies.

A NEW RECITAL INSERTED IN THE PREAMBLE TO THE TREATY ON EUROPEAN UNION

CONFIRMING their attachment to fundamental social rights as defined in the European Social Charter signed at Turin on 18 October 1961 and in the 1989 Community Charter of the Fundamental Social Rights of Workers.

ACTION IN THE EVENT OF A BREACH BY A MEMBER STATE OF THE PRINCIPLES ON WHICH THE UNION IS FOUNDED

NEW ARTICLE F.1 IN THE TREATY ON EUROPEAN UNION

1. The Council, meeting in the composition of the Heads of State or Government and acting by unanimity on a proposal by one third of the Member States or by the Commission and after obtaining the assent of

3

the European Parliament, may determine the existence of a serious and persistent breach by a Member State of principles mentioned in Article F(1), after inviting the government of the Member State concerned to submit its observations.

2. Where such a determination has been made, the Council, acting by a qualified majority, may decide to suspend certain of the rights deriving from the application of this Treaty to the State in question, including the voting rights of the representative of the Government of that Member State in the Council. In doing so, the Council shall take into account the possible consequences of such a suspension on the rights and obligations of natural and legal persons.

The obligations of the Member State concerned under this Treaty shall in any case continue to be binding on that State.

3. The Council, acting by a qualified majority, may decide subsequently to vary or revoke measures taken under paragraph 2 in response to changes in the situation which led to their being imposed.

4. For the purposes of this Article, the Council shall act without taking into account the vote of the representative of the Member State concerned. Abstentions by members present in person or represented shall not prevent the adoption of decisions referred to in paragraph 1. A qualified majority shall be defined as the same proportion of the weighted votes of the members of the Council concerned as laid down in Article 148(2) of the Treaty establishing the European Community.

The provisions of this paragraph shall also apply in the event of voting rights being suspended pursuant to paragraph 2.

5. For the purposes of this Article, the European Parliament shall act by a two thirds majority of the votes cast, representing a majority of its members.

NEW ARTICLE 236 IN THE TREATY ESTABLISHING THE EUROPEAN COMMUNITY

1. Where a decision has been taken to suspend voting rights of a Member State in accordance with Article F.1(2) of the Treaty on European Union, these voting rights shall also be suspended with regard to this Treaty.

2. Moreover, and where the existence of a serious and persistent breach by a Member State of the principles mentioned in Article F(1) has been determined in accordance with Article F.1(1) of the Treaty on European Union, the Council, acting by a qualified majority, may decide to suspend certain of the rights deriving from the application of this Treaty to the State in question. In doing so, the Council shall take into account the possible consequences of such a suspension on the rights and obligations of natural and legal persons.

The obligations of the Member State concerned under this Treaty shall in any case continue to be binding on that State.

3. The Council, acting by a qualified majority, may decide subsequently to vary or revoke measures taken in accordance with paragraph 2 in response to changes in the situation which led to their being imposed.

4. When taking decisions referred to in paragraphs 2 and 3, the Council shall act without taking into account the votes of the representative of the Member State concerned. By way of derogation from Article 148(2) a qualified majority shall be defined as the same proportion of the weighted votes of the members of the Council concerned as laid down in Article 148(2).

The provisions of this paragraph shall also apply in the event of voting rights being suspended in accordance with paragraph 1. In such cases, a decision requiring unanimity shall be taken without the vote of the representative of the Member State concerned.

RESPECT BY ANY STATE APPLYING TO JOIN THE UNION FOR THE FUNDAMENTAL PRINCIPLES ON WHICH IT IS FOUNDED

AMENDED FIRST PARAGRAPH OF ARTICLE O OF THE TREATY ON EUROPEAN UNION

Any European State which respects the principles set out in Article F(1) may apply to become a member of the Union. It shall address its application to the Council, which shall act unanimously after consulting the Commission and after receiving the assent of the European Parliament, which shall act by an absolute majority of its component members.

STATUS OF CHURCHES

DECLARATION ON THE STATUS OF CHURCHES AND NON-CONFESSIONAL ORGANISATIONS

The European Union will respect and does not prejudice the status under national law of churches and religious associations or communities in the Member States.

The European Union will equally respect the status of philosophical and non-confessional organisations.

ABOLITION OF THE DEATH PENALTY

DECLARATION ON THE ABOLITION OF THE DEATH PENALTY

With reference to Article F(2) of the Treaty on European Union, the Conference recalls that Protocol No. 6 to the European Convention for the Protection of Human Rights and Fundamental Freedoms signed in Rome on 4 November 1950, and which has been signed and ratified by a large majority of Member States, provides for the abolition of the death penalty.

In this context, the Conference notes the fact that since the signature of the above-mentioned Protocol on 28 April 1983, the death penalty has been abolished in most of the Member States of the Union and has not been applied in any of them.

NON-DISCRIMINATION

AMENDED ARTICLE 6, SECOND PARAGRAPH, IN THE TREATY ESTABLISHING THE EUROPEAN COMMUNITY

The Council, acting in accordance with the procedure referred to in Article 189b, may adopt rules designed to prohibit such discrimination.

NEW ARTICLE 6A

Without prejudice to the other provisions of this Treaty and within the limits of the powers conferred by it upon the Community, the Council, acting unanimously on a proposal from the Commission and after consulting the European Parliament, may take appropriate action to combat discrimination based on sex, racial or ethnic origin, religion or belief, disability, age or sexual orientation.

DECLARATION REGARDING PERSONS WITH A DISABILITY

The Conference agrees that, in drawing up measures under Article 100a of the Treaty establishing the European Community, the institutions of the Community shall take account of the needs of persons with a disability.

EQUALITY OF MEN AND WOMEN

AMENDED ARTICLE 2 OF THE TREATY ESTABLISHING THE EUROPEAN COMMUNITY

The Community shall ... promote throughout the Community a harmonious, balanced and sustainable development of economic activities, a high level of employment and of social protection, equality between men and women, sustainable and non-inflationary growth, a high degree of competitiveness and convergence of economic performance, a high level of protection and improvement of the quality of the environment, the raising of the standard of living and quality of life, and economic and social cohesion and solidarity among Member States.

NEW PARAGRAPH TO ARTICLE 3

2. In all the activities referred to in this Article, the Community shall aim to eliminate inequalities, and to promote equality, between men and women.

PROTECTION OF INDIVIDUALS WITH REGARD TO THE PROCESSING AND FREE MOVEMENT OF PERSONAL DATA

NEW ARTICLE 213B

1. From 1 January 1999, Community acts on the protection of individuals with regard to the processing of personal data and the free movement of such data shall apply to the institutions and bodies set up by, or on the basis of, this Treaty.

2. Before the date referred to in paragraph 1, the Council, acting in accordance with the procedure referred to in Article 189b, shall establish an independent supervisory body responsible for monitoring the application of such Community acts to Community institutions and bodies and shall adopt any other relevant provisions as appropriate.

Commentary
Freedom, security and justice

The biggest innovation of the Treaty of Amsterdam was to substantiate the competences of the European Union in the field of civil liberties. In this it was shaped by four factors:

- a sense of failure about the third pillar, concerning cooperation in the field of justice and home affairs, of the Treaty on European Union, and the continuing impediments to the free movement of peoples within the single market;

- the impending enlargement to formerly communist countries of Central and Eastern Europe, where civil society was, and probably still is, fragile;

- a growing alarm in many member states about organised, international criminality (notably in Ireland, which had the presidency of the IGC during the last half of 1996);

- similar consternation about a rising tide of illegal immigration (notably in Germany).

The IGC focused on two problems: how to drive forward the implementation of Article 7a of the Treaty which seeks to create an area without internal frontiers for persons as well as for goods, services and capital, and how to deal with the problematical Schengen Agreement between certain member states. Between the time of Maastricht and Amsterdam the question of the rights of citizens, residents and aliens of the European Union emerged as a driving force of European integration. The Dutch government brought to the presidency their existing lively concerns about the efficacy of Schengen. [1] The changes made at Amsterdam to the Maastricht settlement were in the event dramatic:

- visa, asylum and immigration were transplanted from the third pillar into the first (the old European Community);

- the Schengen Agreement was brought within the purview of the European Union;

- major strides were taken in social policy and in modern anti-discrimination provisions;

- respect for human rights was made an explicit criterion for membership of the Union.

In the Common Provisions of the Treaty (Title I) Article F was heavily revised. Instead of the first sub-clause referring to the national identities of the member states, it now speaks of liberty, democracy, human rights and the rule of law. The language is not quite 'We hold these truths to be self-evident ...' — but the change insofar as it goes is only to be welcomed.

Some member states wanted the European Community or, were it to be given a legal personality of its own, the European Union itself to sign up to the ECHR, but this did not command sufficiently wide support.

The reference to fundamental social rights in the Preamble is a direct consequence of the Labour victory at the recent general election in the United Kingdom. Margaret Thatcher had refused to sign the Social Charter at Strasbourg in December 1989 (having first diluted it) — the first serious example of a British opt-out.

Communitarisation

This fundamental change to the Treaty on European Union has its strong critics among those who take a purist or orthodox view of the supranational integrity of the European Community. The 'communitarisation' of Schengen and immigration policy is indeed untidy, even clumsy. The transplant process was accomplished without consulting the European Parliament or the Court of Justice, although they are both affected by it directly. The true purpose behind the changes is not laid down in the Treaty, and the division within the field of justice and home affairs has not been removed as much as shifted.

Nevertheless, new common instruments are created, the European Commission has the expectation of increased authority and the jurisprudence of the Court is widened.

Breach of obligation

Rather confusingly, Article F.1 is a new European Union provision designed to protect the strengthened character of Article F(1). New Article 236 prescribes equivalent action within the European Community.

The Irish presidency had intended that the right to propose the suspension of a member state be given to the European Parliament; under the final version, however, MEPs may only confirm the action of the Council.

The measure is a delicate one, not least because it would be necessary to protect the legal rights under EC law of firms, non-governmental organisations and citizens within the errant member state despite a flagrant breach of Treaty obligations by its government.

Although it stops short of a revocation of membership, the measure is also a severe one, and reinforces the federal discipline of the Union.

Slovakia, Cyprus and, no doubt, Turkey were in the collective mind of the IGC when it bore on this subject; and the addition to Article O serves to heighten the threshold for accession. This approach had been presaged by the European Council at Copenhagen in June 1993.

Religious discrimination

The Treaty of Amsterdam is littered with cryptic declarations that reflect the special interest or idée fixe of only one or two member states.

The Declaration on the status of the church was generated by the German government which had come under pressure from its conservative church elements (both Catholic and Protestant) to maintain the enhanced status of Christianity in particular against the American importation of the Church of Scientology. Italy and Austria were sympathetic. Greece has a special problem with regard to the all-male autonomous Orthodox republic of Mount Athos, a place to which the values of freedom of movement and non-discrimination are alien.

This Declaration is a bizarre Treaty provision, made only slightly more palatable by the inclusion at the Amsterdam European Council itself of the second sentence. Fortunately, being only in the form of a Declaration, its own legal status is ambiguous.

Capital punishment

As the Union moves decisively into the field of civil liberties, matters of ethics are not to be avoided.

Yet this is a curious declaration in the context of the present European Union, where only Greece keeps capital punishment on its statute books for misdemeanours other than treason, and even the Greeks not with conviction.

But the Declaration is one of several insurances against reversion by a yet-to-enter state to barbarism.

Non-discrimination

Some of the most powerful aspects of the Treaty of Rome have been its prohibition of discrimination on the grounds of nationality (Article 6), and on the basis of gender in terms of pay (Article 119). The principle of equal pay has had both economic and social purpose, and has been deemed to have had direct effect since 1976.

The additions to Articles 2 and 3 now allow the Community to take positive action to promote equality between men and women in pursuit of all its objectives.

It was also natural for the Union in its post-modern age to move to extend the principles of non-discrimination to other spheres, and Amsterdam does this here. New Article 6a is a veritable portmanteau of political correctness, and its effect is bound to spread steadily across a whole range of EU policies and law — despite the unprecedented explicit qualification that the Council may only act 'within the limits of the powers conferred by it upon the Community' (when else, indeed?). The initial 'without prejudice' also limits the scope of the intention at least not to interfere in the management of the single market.

The Irish draft Treaty had included 'social origin' as another target for combating discrimination, but this was quietly and no doubt sensibly dropped by the Dutch. The Irish also invited the IGC to introduce gender neutral language into the Treaty, although this made little sense to those who were not conversant in American English.

Article 6a promises to be the basis of much political lobbying, especially from the UK, where age, religion and sexuality currently form no part of its common law regime. The revision to Article 6 allows the co-decision procedure with the European Parliament to apply to the adoption of anti-discrimination measures.

It is certain that none of these changes could have been effected under the UK Conservative government, although the fact that legislation in this area can only be achieved by unanimity lessens the immediate impact of the revision. And as far as non-discrimination is concerned, as there is no Treaty obligation on the Commission to act in terms of schedule or programme, the prime mover is bound to be jurisprudence. The prospect is already opening up of the European Court of Justice and the Court of First Instance being overwhelmed by the litigious aggrieved.

Data protection

The Dutch presidency were particularly keen to protect the citizen from misuse by the EU institutions of personal data records.

This is an important safeguard of civil liberty in the first pillar area — although disconcertingly its ambit does not cover the remaining third pillar (police and judicial cooperation) except insofar as the Commission is involved.

PROGRESSIVE ESTABLISHMENT OF AN AREA OF FREEDOM, SECURITY AND JUSTICE

OVER-ARCHING OBJECTIVES

AMENDED FOURTH INDENT OF ARTICLE B IN THE TREATY ON EUROPEAN UNION

• to maintain and develop the Union as an area of freedom, security and justice, in which the free movement of persons is assured in conjunction with appropriate measures with respect to external borders controls, immigration, asylum and the prevention and combating of crime.

VISAS, ASYLUM, IMMIGRATION AND OTHER POLICIES RELATED TO FREE MOVEMENT OF PERSONS

NEW TITLE IIIA IN THE TREATY ESTABLISHING THE EUROPEAN COMMUNITY

ARTICLE 73I

In order to establish progressively an area of freedom, security and justice, the Council shall adopt:

(a) within a period of five years after the entry into force of the Treaty of Amsterdam, measures aimed at ensuring the free movement of persons in accordance with Article 7a, in conjunction with directly related flanking measures with respect to external borders controls, asylum and immigration, in accordance with the provisions of Article 73j(2) and (3) and Article 73k(1)(a) and (2)(a), and measures to prevent and combat crime in accordance with the provisions of Article K.3(e) of the Treaty on European Union;

(b) other measures in the fields of asylum, immigration and safeguarding the rights of third country nationals, in accordance with the provisions of Article 73k;

(c) measures in the field of judicial cooperation in civil matters as provided for in Article 73m;

(d) appropriate measures to encourage and strengthen administrative cooperation, as provided for in Article 73n;

(e) measures in the field of police and judicial cooperation in criminal matters aimed at a high level of security by preventing and combating crime within the Union in accordance with the provisions of the Treaty on European Union.

DECLARATION ON THE PRESERVATION OF THE LEVEL OF PROTECTION AND SECURITY PROVIDED BY THE SCHENGEN ACQUIS

The Conference agrees that measures to be adopted by the Council, which will have the effect of replacing provisions on the abolition of checks at common borders contained in the 1990 Schengen Convention, should provide at least the same level of protection and security as under the aforementioned provisions of the Schengen Convention.

ARTICLE 73J [2]

The Council, acting in accordance with the procedure referred to in Article 73o, shall, within a period of five years after the entry into force of the Treaty of Amsterdam, adopt:

1. measures with a view to ensuring, in compliance with Article 7a, the absence of any controls on persons, be they citizens of the Union or nationals of third countries, when crossing internal borders.

2. measures on the crossing of the external borders of the Member States which shall establish:

(a) standards and procedures to be followed by Member States in carrying out checks on persons at such borders;

(b) rules on visas for intended stays of no more than three months, including:

(i) the list of third countries whose nationals must be in possession of visas when crossing the external borders and those whose nationals are exempt from that requirement;

(ii) the procedures and conditions for issuing visas by Member States;

(iii) a uniform format for visas;

(iv) rules on a uniform visa.

3. measures setting out the conditions under which the nationals of third countries shall have the freedom to travel within the territory of the Member States during a period of no more than three months.

PROTOCOL ON EXTERNAL RELATIONS OF THE MEMBER STATES WITH REGARD TO THE CROSSING OF EXTERNAL BORDERS

THE HIGH CONTRACTING PARTIES,

TAKING INTO ACCOUNT the need of the Member States to ensure effective controls at their external borders, in cooperation with third countries where appropriate,

HAVE AGREED upon the following provisions, which shall be annexed to the Treaty establishing the European Community:

The provisions on the measures on the crossing of external borders included in Article 73j(2) of Title IIIa shall be without prejudice to the competence of Member States to negotiate or conclude agreements with third countries as long as they respect Community law and other relevant international agreements.

DECLARATION ON ARTICLE 73J(2)(B)

The Conference agrees that foreign policy considerations of the Union and the Member States shall be taken into account in the application of Article 73j(2)(b) of the Treaty establishing the European Community.

ARTICLE 73K

The Council, acting in accordance with the procedure referred to in Article 73o, shall, within a period of five years after the entry into force of the Treaty of Amsterdam, adopt:

1. measures on asylum, in accordance with the Convention of 28 July 1951, the Protocol of 31 January 1967 relating to the Status of Refugees and other relevant treaties, within the following areas:

(a) criteria and mechanisms for determining which Member State is responsible for considering an application for asylum submitted by a third country national in one of the Member States;

(b) minimum standards on the reception of asylum seekers in Member States;

(c) minimum standards with respect to the qualification of third country nationals as refugees;

(d) minimum standards on procedures in Member States for granting or withdrawing refugee status.

2. measures on refugees and displaced persons within the following areas:

(a) minimum standards for giving temporary protection to displaced persons from third countries who cannot return to their country of origin and for persons who otherwise need international protection;

(b) promoting a balance of effort between Member States in receiving and bearing the consequences of receiving refugees and displaced persons.

3. measures on immigration policy within the following areas:

(a) conditions of entry and residence, and standards on procedures for the issue by Member States of long term visas and residence permits, including those for the purpose of family reunion;

(b) illegal immigration and illegal residence, including repatriation of illegal residents.

4. measures defining the rights and conditions under which nationals of third countries who are legally resident in a Member State may reside in other Member States.

5. Measures adopted by the Council pursuant to points 3 and 4 shall not prevent any Member State from maintaining or introducing in the areas concerned national provisions which are compatible with this Treaty and with international agreements.

Measures to be adopted pursuant to paragraphs 2(b), 3(a) and 4 shall not be subject to the five year period referred to above.

DECLARATION ON ARTICLE 73K

Consultations shall be established with the United Nations High Commissioner for Refugees and other relevant international organisations on matters relating to asylum policy.

DECLARATION ON ARTICLE 73K(3)(A)

The Conference agrees that Member States may negotiate and conclude agreements with third countries in the domains covered by Article 73k(3)(a) of the Treaty establishing the European Community as long as such agreements respect Community law.

ARTICLE 73L

1. This Title shall not affect the exercise of the responsibilities incumbent upon Member States with regard to the maintenance of law and order and the safeguarding of internal security.

2. In the event of one or more Member States being confronted with an emergency situation characterised by a sudden inflow of nationals from a third country and without prejudice to paragraph 1, the Council may, acting by qualified majority on a proposal from the Commission, adopt

provisional measures of a duration not exceeding six months for the benefit of the Member States concerned.

DECLARATION ON THE RESPONSIBILITIES OF MEMBER STATES UNDER ARTICLE 73L(1)

The Conference agrees that Member States may take into account foreign policy considerations when exercising their responsibilities under Article 73l(1) of the Treaty establishing the European Community.

ARTICLE 73M

Measures in the field of judicial cooperation in civil matters having cross-border implications, to be taken in accordance with Article 73o and insofar as necessary for the proper functioning of the internal market, shall include:

(a) improving and simplifying:

• the system for cross-border service of judicial and extra-judicial documents;

• cooperation in the taking of evidence;

• the recognition and enforcement of decisions in civil and commercial cases, including extra-judicial cases;

(b) promoting the compatibility of the rules applicable in the Member States concerning the conflict of laws and of jurisdiction;

(c) eliminating obstacles to the good functioning of civil proceedings, if necessary by promoting the compatibility of the rules on civil procedure applicable in the Member States.

DECLARATION ON ARTICLE 73M

Measures adopted pursuant to Article 73m shall not prevent any Member State from applying its constitutional rules relating to freedom of the press and freedom of expression in other media.

ARTICLE 73N

The Council, acting in accordance with the procedure referred to in Article 73o, shall take measures to ensure cooperation between the relevant departments of the administrations of the Member States in the areas covered by this Title, as well as between those departments and the Commission.

ARTICLE 73O

1. During a transitional period of five years following the entry into force of the Treaty of Amsterdam, the Council shall act unanimously on a proposal from the Commission or on an initiative of a Member State and after consulting the European Parliament.

2. After this period of five years:

• the Council shall act on proposals from the Commission; the Commission shall examine any request made by a Member State that it submit a proposal to the Council;

• the Council, acting unanimously after consulting the European Parliament, shall take a decision with a view to making all or parts of the areas covered by this Title governed by the procedure referred to in Article 189b and adapting the provisions relating to the powers of the Court of Justice.

3. By derogation from the provisions of paragraphs 1 and 2:

• measures referred to in Article 73j(2)(b) (i) and (iii) shall, from the entry into force of this Treaty, be adopted by the Council acting by a qualified majority on a proposal from the Commission and after consulting the European Parliament;

• measures referred to in Article 73j(2)(b) (ii) and (iv) shall, after a period of five years following the entry into force of this Treaty, be adopted by the Council acting in accordance with the procedure referred to in Article 189b.

DECLARATION ON ARTICLE 73O

The Conference agrees that the Council will examine the elements of the decision referred to in Article 73o(2), second indent, of the Treaty establishing the European Community before the end of the five year period referred to in Article 73o with a view to taking and applying this decision immediately after the end of that period.

ARTICLE 73P

1. The provisions of Article 177 shall apply to this Title under the following circumstances and conditions: where a question on the interpretation of this Title or on the validity or interpretation of acts of the institutions of the Community based on this Title is raised in a case pending before a court or a tribunal of a Member State against whose decisions there is no judicial remedy under national law, that court or tribunal shall, if it considers that a decision on the question is necessary to enable it to give judgement, request the Court of Justice to give a ruling thereon.

2. In any event, the Court of Justice shall not have jurisdiction to rule on any measure or decision taken pursuant to Article 73j(1) relating to the maintenance of law and order and the safeguarding of internal security.

3. The Council, the Commission or a Member State may request the Court of Justice to give a ruling on a question of interpretation of this Title or of acts of the institutions of the Community based on this Title. The ruling given by the Court of Justice in response to such a request shall not apply to judgements of courts or tribunals of the Member States which have become *res judicata*.

Commentary
Bridging the pillars

Part of the Maastricht bequest was that the 1996 IGC should look again at the three pillar structure. Initially there was considerable anxiety about re-opening the matter of the architecture of the Treaty, especially because John Major boasted of it as one of his few achievements. But the short-comings especially of the third pillar became ever more obvious (except to the British Conservatives), and, led by Germany, a determination grew to shift common immigration policy from the third pillar to the first. Because the UK, under a Tory or Labour government, was due to be unmoveable on these matters, it had to be by-passed. The concept of differentiation or flexibility emerged as one of the obsessions of the IGC.

A majority of member states were agreed that the Maastricht third pillar had four major deficiencies: a lack of objectives, weak definition, a paucity of appropriate instruments and no driving force. One of the worst features was that its diplomatic conventions could only come into effect once ratified by all member states. No third pillar convention (see below) is yet in force. The transfer of asylum and immigration to the European Community overcomes the obstacle of national ratification procedures. Although Maastricht had a *passerelle* (old Article K.9) across which certain matters could cross to the first pillar, it was in practice unusable because any one national veto could lock the gate.

THIRD PILLAR CONVENTIONS

Dublin Convention 1990 on determining responsibility for examining asylum applications

Control of External Frontiers Convention (still unsigned)

Europol Convention 1995

Protection of the Financial Interests of the Communities Convention 1995

Customs Information System Convention 1995

Simplified Extradition Procedure Convention 1995

Improving Extradition Convention 1996

It must be admitted that the retention of unanimity in the Council (apart from new Articles 73j(2)(b)(i) and (iii)) implies that progress towards forging common policies will still be slow. But the agreement in Article 73o(3) about the phased extension of QMV in visa policy is hopeful.

The immediate gain is that the transfer of asylum and immigration to the European Community brings such matters within the jurisdiction of the European Court of Justice. In the Maastricht and pre-Maastricht Conventions the Court had a negligible role; now at least the Court can hope to ensure a uniform interpretation of texts in asylum and immigration.

The reform also removes the danger that progress under the first pillar could run up against the immovable object of the third. The presidency was however disappointed that the revised Article 73j did not contain a combined work programme and deadlines for the institutions and member states' authorities across both the first pillar and the residuary third.

Gradual free movement

Article 73j, of course, is a compromise between the timid and the impatient. It allows for the progressive establishment of free movement of persons after a five year period in which, one hopes, a sufficient degree of trust has been built up between member states' ministries of the interior and customs authorities.

This provision effectively re-unites all aspects of visa policy that had been split by Maastricht between the first and the third pillars — albeit under different decision-making procedures during the five-year transitional period (Article 73o).

The duration of the transitional period fluctuated during the latter stages of the IGC. The Dublin draft in December 1996 had one year.

The Protocols and Declarations spawned by this and subsequent Articles seek to ensure external and internal cohesion of the Union's eventual common immigration policy.

How to treat refugees and asylum-seekers

Towards the late stages of the IGC the member states became more cautious in their proposed treatment of refugees. The emphasis shifted in Article 73k from developing common rules to setting minimum standards, and the transitional period stretched from two or three years to five.

It is to be noted that the five year pause does not apply to the sharing of the refugee 'balance of effort' between member states, to the settling of general conditions of entry and residence or to defining the rights of third country nationals in other member states. But unanimity in the Council will apply.

Article 73l provides for an emergency influx of refugees — with the Albanian flight to Italy uppermost in the mind of the European Council.

Civil proceedings

A curiosity crept into the final wording of Article 73m, namely the reference to the 'proper functioning of the internal market'. This would seem to restrict unnecessarily the scope of collaboration between civil courts. Would it, for example, exclude divorce settlements?

The motivation of the Irish presidency was more drugs-orientated and, in Article 73n, focused on customs authorities. And an earlier emphasis on the simplification of judicial proceedings and improving access to justice was also lost.

Making the change

The European Commission argued that in the field of freedom of movement of persons and the internal security of the Union, unanimity meant either paralysis in the Council or decisions reduced to the lowest common denominator. It proposed that QMV should be the general rule, that the Parliament should be more closely involved, and that the Commission itself should have the power of initiative.

Reform postponed

The Commission and its ally the presidency made a strong effort to make the end of the five-year period of unanimity automatic. In the end, however, in Article 73o, the lifting of the tyranny of the national veto was itself made subject to a national veto — the very self-defeating double lock that had disfigured the third pillar of Maastricht. Chancellor Kohl was again the main culprit here. However, the shift to QMV if it comes will not require another IGC, which is heartening.

At least the Commission acquires the exclusive right of initiative after the five year interim period.

Judicial review

The European Court of Justice fared better. The IGC was impressed by the number of requests for preliminary rulings in asylum and immigration cases that were likely to come before the Court. It considered making changes to the working practices of the Court to enable it to cope with the expected heavy workload. In the end, in Article 73p, it agreed to permit references (Article 177) from national courts when there was no other remedy at member state level. But it restricted the scope of the European Court's jurisdiction by excluding all matters that may affect domestic law and order or security. And it did not allow direct access to the Court by the citizen (Article 173).

Article 73p(3) allows a member state government, the Council or the Commission (but not the Parliament) to seek interpretative rulings.

IRELAND AND THE UNITED KINGDOM

ARTICLE 73Q

The application of this Title shall be subject to the provisions of the Protocol on the position of the United Kingdom and Ireland and to the Protocol on the position of Denmark, without prejudice to the Protocol on the application of certain aspects of Article 7a to the United Kingdom and to Ireland.

PROTOCOL ON THE POSITION OF THE UNITED KINGDOM AND IRELAND

THE HIGH CONTRACTING PARTIES,

DESIRING to settle certain questions relating to the United Kingdom and Ireland,

HAVING REGARD to the Protocol on the application of certain aspects of Article 7a of the Treaty establishing the European Community to the United Kingdom and to Ireland,

HAVE AGREED upon the following provisions which shall be annexed to the Treaty establishing the European Community and the Treaty on European Union,

ARTICLE 1

Subject to Article 3, the United Kingdom and Ireland shall not take part in the adoption by the Council of proposed measures pursuant to Title IIIa of the Treaty establishing the European Community. By way of derogation from Article 148(2) of the Treaty establishing the European Community, a qualified majority shall be defined as the same proportion of the weighted votes of the members of the Council concerned as laid down in Article 148(2). The unanimity of the members of the Council, with the exception of the representative of the governments of the United Kingdom and Ireland, shall be necessary for decisions of the Council which must be adopted unanimously.

ARTICLE 2

In consequence of Article 1 and subject to Articles 3, 4 and 6, none of the provisions of Title IIIa of the Treaty establishing the European Community, no measure adopted pursuant to that Title, no provision of any international agreement concluded by the Community pursuant to that Title, and no decision of the Court of Justice interpreting any such provision or measure shall be binding upon or applicable in the United Kingdom or Ireland; and no such provision, measure or decision shall in any way affect the competences, rights and obligations of those States; and no such provision, measure or decision shall in any way affect the acquis communautaire nor form part of Community law as they apply to the United Kingdom or Ireland.

ARTICLE 3

1. The United Kingdom or Ireland may notify the President of the Council in writing, within three months after a proposal or initiative has been presented to the Council pursuant to Title IIIa of the Treaty establishing the European Community, that it wishes to take part in the adoption and application of any such proposed measure, whereupon that State shall be entitled to do so. By way of derogation from Article 148(2) of the Treaty establishing the European Community, a qualified majority shall be defined as the same proportion of the weighted votes of the members of the Council concerned as laid down in Article 148(2).

The unanimity of the members of the Council, with the exception of a member which has not made such a notification, shall be necessary for decisions of the Council which must be adopted unanimously. A measure adopted under this paragraph shall be binding upon all Member States which took part in its adoption.

2. If after a reasonable period of time a measure referred to in paragraph 1 cannot be adopted with the United Kingdom or Ireland taking part, the Council may adopt such measure in accordance with Article 1 without the participation of the United Kingdom or Ireland. In that case Article 2 applies.

ARTICLE 4

The United Kingdom or Ireland may at any time after the adoption of a measure by the Council pursuant to Title IIIa of the Treaty establishing the European Community notify its intention to the Council and to the Commission that it wishes to accept such measure. In that case, the procedure provided for in Article 5a(3) of the Treaty establishing the European Community shall apply mutatis mutandis.

ARTICLE 5

A Member State which is not bound by a measure adopted pursuant to Title IIIa of the Treaty establishing the European Community shall bear no financial consequences of that measure other than administrative costs entailed for the institutions.

ARTICLE 6

Where, in cases referred to in this Protocol, the United Kingdom or Ireland is bound by a measure adopted by the Council pursuant to Title IIIa of the Treaty establishing the European Community, the relevant provisions of that Treaty, including Article 73p, shall apply to that State in relation to that measure.

ARTICLE 7

Articles 3 and 4 shall be without prejudice to the Protocol integrating the Schengen acquis into the framework of the European Union.

ARTICLE 8

Ireland may notify the President of the Council in writing that it no longer wishes to be covered by the terms of this Protocol. In that case, the normal Treaty provisions will apply to Ireland.

PROTOCOL ON THE APPLICATION OF CERTAIN ASPECTS OF ARTICLE 7A OF THE TREATY ESTABLISHING THE EUROPEAN COMMUNITY TO THE UNITED KINGDOM AND TO IRELAND

THE HIGH CONTRACTING PARTIES

DESIRING to settle certain questions relating to the United Kingdom and Ireland,

HAVING REGARD to the existence for many years of special travel arrangements between the UK and Ireland,

HAVE AGREED upon the following provisions, which shall be annexed to the Treaty establishing the European Community and to the Treaty on European Union:

ARTICLE 1

The United Kingdom shall be entitled, notwithstanding Article 7a of the Treaty establishing the European Community, any other provision of this Treaty or of the Treaty on European Union, any measure adopted under these Treaties, or any international agreement concluded by the Community or by the Community and its Member States with one or more third States, to exercise at its frontiers with other Member States such controls on persons seeking to enter the United Kingdom as it may consider necessary for the purpose:

(a) of verifying the right to enter the United Kingdom of citizens of States which are Contracting Parties to the Agreement on the European Economic Area and of their dependants exercising rights conferred by

Community law, as well as citizens of other States on whom such rights have been conferred by an agreement to which the UK is bound; and

(b) of determining whether or not to grant other persons permission to enter the United Kingdom.

Nothing in Article 7a of the Treaty establishing the European Community or in any other provision of these Treaties or in any measure adopted under them shall prejudice the right of the United Kingdom to adopt or exercise any such controls. References to the United Kingdom in this Article shall include territories for whose external relations the United Kingdom is responsible.

ARTICLE 2

The United Kingdom and Ireland may continue to make arrangements between themselves relating to the movement of persons between their territories (' the common travel area'), while fully respecting the rights of persons referred to in Article 1(a). Accordingly, as long as they maintain such arrangements, the provisions of Article 1 shall apply to Ireland with the same terms and conditions as for the United Kingdom. Nothing in Article 7a, in any other provision of the Treaties referred to above or in any measure adopted under them, shall affect any such arrangements.

ARTICLE 3

The other Member States shall be entitled to exercise at their frontiers or at any point of entry into their territory such controls on persons seeking to enter their territory from the United Kingdom or any territories whose external relations are under their responsibility for the same purposes stated in Article 1, or from Ireland as long as the provisions of Article 1 apply to Ireland.

Nothing in Article 7a or in any other provision of these treaties or in any measure adopted under them shall prejudice the right of the other Member States to adopt or exercise any such controls.

DECLARATION BY IRELAND ON ARTICLE 3 OF THE PROTOCOL ON THE POSITION OF THE UNITED KINGDOM AND IRELAND

Ireland declares that it intends to exercise its right under Article 3 of the Protocol on the position of the United Kingdom and Ireland to take part in the adoption of measures pursuant to Title IIIa of the Treaty establishing the European Community to the maximum extent compatible with the maintenance of its common travel area with the United Kingdom. Ireland recalls that its participation in the Protocol on the application of certain aspects of Article 7a of the Treaty establishing the European Community reflects its wish to maintain its common travel area with the United Kingdom in order to maximise freedom of movement into and out of Ireland.

Commentary
By-pass for
Britain and Ireland

Neither the United Kingdom nor the Republic of Ireland is to enjoy the new area of freedom, security and justice. In Amsterdam, both Tony Blair and John Bruton were keen to assert that they had neither sought nor got an old Tory-style opt-out, like the notorious Social Protocol of Maastricht, but under examination this claim becomes quite hard to sustain.

What the Treaty says

Under Article 2 of their first Protocol, British and Irish border controls will remain intact and they will not participate in the common policies for asylum, refugees and immigration.

Article 3(1), however, says that the two countries may, within three months of the Commission's publication of any proposal, opt into the debate about and decisions upon any measure they choose. However, the Council will decide whether or not to accept the intrusion of the UK or Ireland by unanimity. In other words, the British and Irish can be black-balled.

Since the European Council, the two abstainers have protested about the second half of Article 3(1), claiming that it had been agreed at Amsterdam that only a qualified majority would be required to accept them into the making of a piece of legislation. Spain, particularly, is insisting on maintaining the veto not least because it may wish to block UK inclusion in a measure that would imply change to the status quo at the Gibraltar frontier.

Article 3(2) means that, in the event of a continuing dispute with the UK or Ireland, the thirteen member states can decide to go ahead on their own in any case.

Article 4 says that the UK or Ireland can join up to an existing measure if the Commission alone were to agree, according to the terms of the famous flexibility clause, Article 5a(3).

Article 8 allows Ireland to resile from this derogation without there having to be an IGC.

The joint Protocol about Article 7a is the first reference in EU law to the Anglo-Irish common travel area, that had previously been subject only to pragmatic arrangements between the UK Home Office and the Irish Department of Justice.

Article 1 of the Protocol establishes that the UK can continue to check people at its borders to verify their European Union or European Economic Area credentials. Article 2 binds Ireland into the UK modalities as long as the common travel area survives. Article 3 gives other member states the right to reciprocate with people arriving from the British Isles. The final Declaration is Ireland's expression of its intent to participate as much in the area of freedom, security and justice as the maintenance of the common travel area with Britain would allow.

What might happen now

Whether the British will always be adamant about preserving their own border controls remains to be seen. The UK government has already signed up to twenty-two Schengen instruments, and the British police are keen to maximise operational collaboration with their mainland counterparts.

It is notable, however, that Mr Blair's otherwise reforming government should follow the Tories so closely in respect of immigration and internal security. One of the main official justifications for Britain's exception is the current relatively calm state of its race relations. Yet already the idea of the British Isles being an impregnable fortress of civility is sentimentality in excess of the facts: the smuggling of drugs, arms and other illicit goods into Ireland or the UK, and exposure to international terrorism, does not appear to be significantly less than in continental Europe.

Eventually, the putting in place of tough external border controls by its mainland European partners would lessen the force of Britain's argument about singularity. Ireland already would take a more positive attitude to the possibility of joining fully within the EU's internal security regime, but finds itself trapped by virtue of its continuing passport union with the UK.

The eventual resolution of the post-Amsterdam argument about Article 3(1) of the first Protocol in favour of Spain and the majority was terribly important. Orthodoxy reigns. Had the Anglo-Irish view triumphed, *l'Europe à la carte* would have arrived. The two countries would virtually have been able to pick and choose what they wanted from a menu of sensitive items closely affecting the citizen. In whose interest such an ad hoc outcome would have been is not entirely clear.

POSITION OF DENMARK

PROTOCOL ON THE POSITION OF DENMARK

THE HIGH CONTRACTING PARTIES,

RECALLING the Decision of the Heads of State or Government, meeting within the European Council at Edinburgh on 12 December 1992, concerning certain problems raised by Denmark on the Treaty on European Union,

HAVING NOTED the position of Denmark with regard to Citizenship, Economic and Monetary Union, Defence Policy and Justice and Home Affairs as laid down in the Edinburgh decision,

BEARING IN MIND Article 3 of the Protocol integrating the Schengen acquis into the framework of the European Union,

HAVE AGREED upon the following provisions, which shall be annexed to the Treaty establishing the European Community and to the Treaty on European Union:

PART I: ARTICLE 1

Denmark shall not take part in the adoption by the Council of proposed measures pursuant to Title IIIa of the Treaty establishing the European Community. By way of derogation from Article 148(2) of the Treaty establishing the European Community, a qualified majority shall be defined as the same proportion of the weighted votes of the members of the Council concerned as laid down in Article 148(2). The unanimity of the members of the Council, with the exception of the representative of the government of Denmark, shall be necessary for the decisions of the Council which must be adopted unanimously.

ARTICLE 2

None of the provisions of Title IIIa of the Treaty establishing the European Community, no measure adopted pursuant to that Title, no provision of any international agreement concluded by the Community pursuant to that Title, and no decision of the Court of Justice interpreting any such provision or measure shall be binding upon or applicable in Denmark; and no such provision, measure or decision shall in any way affect the competences, rights and obligations of Denmark; and no such provision, measure or decision shall in any way affect the acquis communautaire nor form part of Community law as they apply to Denmark.

ARTICLE 3

Denmark shall bear no financial consequences of measures referred to in Article 1, other than administrative costs entailed for the institutions.

ARTICLE 4

Articles 1, 2 and 3 shall not apply to measures determining the third countries whose nationals must be in possession of a visa when crossing the external borders of the Member States, or measures relating to a uniform format for visas.

ARTICLE 5

1. Denmark shall decide within a period of 6 months after the Council has decided on a proposal or initiative to build upon the Schengen acquis under the provisions of Title IIIa of the Treaty establishing the European Community, whether it will implement this decision in its national law. If it decides to do so, this decision will create an obligation under international law between Denmark and the other member States referred to in Article 1 of the Protocol integrating the Schengen acquis into the framework of the European Union as well as with Ireland or the United Kingdom if those Member States take part in the areas of cooperation in question.

2. If Denmark decides not to implement a decision of the Council as referred to in paragraph 1, the Member States referred to in Article 1 of the Protocol integrating the Schengen acquis into the framework of the European Union will consider appropriate measures to be taken.

PART II: ARTICLE 6

With regard to measures adopted by the Council in the field of Articles J.3(1) and J.7 of the Treaty on European Union, Denmark does not participate in the elaboration and the implementation of decisions and actions of the Union which have defence implications, but will not prevent the development of closer cooperation between Member States in this area. Therefore Denmark shall not participate in their adoption. Denmark shall not be obliged to contribute to the financing of operational expenditure arising from such measures.

PART III: ARTICLE 7

At any time Denmark may, in accordance with its constitutional requirements, inform other Member States that it no longer wishes to avail itself of all or part of this Protocol. In that event, Denmark will apply in full all relevant measures then in force taken within the framework of the European Union.

Commentary
The Danish exception

After the loss of its first referendum on the Treaty of Maastricht in June 1992, Denmark had to impose on its European Union partners a set of arrangements designed to persuade the Danish public to change its mind. These arrangements were encapsulated in a decision of the Heads of State or Government meeting within the European Council at Edinburgh in December 1992, declarations by the European Council and unilateral declarations by Denmark of which its partners took cognizance. They consisted of opt-outs *à l'anglaise* to the single currency, common defence arrangements and, crucially, citizenship issues. In theory, these Danish arrangements were to be renegotiated at the 1996 IGC (although the Danish government was less than frank about this at home).

At the European Council in Amsterdam the Danish delegation, alarmed at the prospect of another referendum, fought hard to keep the Maastricht opt-outs. Up to a point the Danes succeeded, although not without obfuscation.

The Danish exceptionalism is particularly problematic over the incorporation of the Schengen Agreement into the Treaty on European Union. After Amsterdam, Denmark appears to remain only politically and not legally attached to Schengen.

The Protocol suggests that Denmark, despite remaining technically a member of Schengen, does not accept the incorporation of the Schengen acquis into the European Union. Denmark will not participate in decisions affecting the area of freedom, security and justice, apart from the former first pillar competences concerning visas, namely the selection of third countries to whom the visas apply and the choice of uniform format (old Article 100c).

On the other hand, Denmark remains a full member of Schengen insofar as its Schengen obligations affect the remaining third pillar on criminal matters.

Article 5 suggests that Denmark may choose to implement on a piecemeal basis the occasional directive made by the thirteen member states concerning the area of freedom, security and justice. Unlike the UK and Ireland, Denmark cannot opt in to the decision-making process, but will have six months to decide whether to accept the completed directive. It may not be prevented from doing so. And if it does, it will create an obligation under international not European Community law. Schengen has the status of international law for Denmark, Iceland and Norway, and of European Community law for the rest.

Quite what the European Court of Justice — or indeed the Danish public — will make of all this is remains to be seen. The Commission's legal service has a heavy duty of disentanglement.

Article 6 maintains Denmark's Maastricht opt-out of defence arrangements in the second pillar.

Article 7 says that Denmark can change its mind unilaterally about its derogations at any time.

PROVISIONS ON POLICE AND JUDICIAL COOPERATION IN CRIMINAL MATTERS

NEW TITLE VI OF THE TREATY ON EUROPEAN UNION

ARTICLE K.1

Without prejudice to the powers of the European Community, the Union's objective shall be to provide citizens with a high level of safety within an area of freedom, security and justice by developing common action among the Member States in the fields of police and judicial cooperation in criminal matters and by preventing and combating racism and xenophobia.

That objective shall be achieved by preventing and combating crime, organised or otherwise, in particular terrorism, trafficking in persons and offences against children, illicit drug trafficking and illicit arms trafficking, corruption and fraud, through:

• closer cooperation between police forces, customs authorities and other competent authorities in the Member States, both directly and, through Europol, in accordance with the provisions of Article K.2 and K.4;

• closer cooperation between judicial and other competent authorities of the Member States in accordance with the provisions of Articles K.3(a) to (d) and K.4;

• approximation, where necessary, of rules on criminal matters in the Member States, in accordance with the provisions of Article K.3(e).

ARTICLE K.2

1. Common action in the field of police cooperation shall include:

(a) operational cooperation between the competent authorities, including the police, customs and other specialised law enforcement services of the Member States in relation to the prevention, detection and investigation of criminal offences;

(b) the collection, storage, processing, analysis and exchange of relevant information, including information held by law enforcement agencies of reports on suspicious financial transactions, in particular through Europol, subject to appropriate provisions on the protection of personal data;

(c) cooperation and joint initiatives in training, the exchange of liaison officers, secondments, the use of equipment, and forensic research;

(d) the common evaluation of particular investigative techniques in relation to the detection of serious forms of organised crime.

2. The Council shall promote cooperation through Europol and shall in particular, within a period of five years after the date of entry into force of the Treaty of Amsterdam:

(a) enable Europol to facilitate and support the preparation, and to encourage the coordination and carrying out of specific investigative actions by the competent authorities of the Member States, including operational actions of joint teams comprising representatives of Europol in a support capacity;

(b) adopt measures allowing Europol to ask the competent authorities of the Member States to conduct and coordinate their investigations in specific cases and to develop specific expertise which may be put at the disposal of Member States to assist them in investigating cases of organised crime;

(c) promote liaison arrangements between prosecuting/investigating officials specialising in the fight against organised crime in close cooperation with Europol;

(d) establish a research, documentation and statistical network on cross-border crime.

DECLARATION ON ARTICLE K.2

Action in the field of police cooperation under Article K.2 of the Treaty on European Union, including activities of Europol, shall be subject to appropriate judicial review by the competent national authorities in accordance with rules applicable in each Member State.

ARTICLE K.3

Common action on judicial cooperation in criminal matters shall include:

(a) facilitating and accelerating cooperation between competent ministries and judicial or equivalent authorities of the Member States in relation to proceedings and the enforcement of decisions;

(b) facilitating extradition between Member States;

(c) ensuring compatibility in rules applicable in the Member States, as may be necessary to improve such cooperation;

(d) preventing conflicts of jurisdiction between Member States;

(e) progressively adopting measures establishing minimum rules relating to the constituent elements of criminal acts and to penalties in the fields of organised crime, terrorism and drug trafficking.

DECLARATION ON ARTICLE K.3(E).

The Conference agrees that the provisions of Article K.3(e) shall not have as a consequence to oblige a Member State whose legal system does not provide for minimum sentences to adopt them.

ARTICLE K.4

The Council shall lay down the conditions and limitations under which the competent authorities referred to in Articles K.2 and K.3 may operate in the territory of another Member State in liaison and in agreement with the authorities of that State.

ARTICLE K.5 (FORMERLY ARTICLE K.2)

This Title shall not affect the exercise of the responsibilities incumbent upon Member States with regard to the maintenance of law and order and the safeguarding of internal security.

ARTICLE K.6 (FORMERLY ARTICLE K.3)

1. In the areas referred to under this Title, Member States shall inform and consult one another within the Council with a view to coordinating their action. To that end, they shall establish collaboration between the relevant departments of their administrations.

2. The Council shall take measures and promote cooperation, using the appropriate form and procedures as set out in this Title, contributing to the pursuit of the objectives of the Union. To that end, acting unanimously on an initiative of any Member State or of the Commission, the Council may:

(a) adopt common positions defining the approach of the Union to a particular matter;

(b) adopt framework decisions for the purpose of approximation of the laws and regulations of the Member States; framework decisions shall be binding upon the Member States as to the result to be achieved but shall leave to the national authorities the choice of form and methods; they shall not entail direct effect;

(c) adopt decisions for any other purpose consistent with the objectives of this Title, excluding any approximation of the laws and regulations of the Member States. These decisions shall be binding and shall not entail direct effect; the Council, acting by a qualified majority, shall adopt measures necessary to implement those decisions at the level of the Union;

(d) establish conventions which it shall recommend to the Member States for adoption in accordance with their respective constitutional requirements. Member States shall begin the procedures applicable within a time limit to be set by the Council.

Unless they provide otherwise, conventions shall, once adopted by at least half of the Member States, enter into force for those Member States. Measures implementing conventions shall be adopted within the Council by a majority of two thirds of the High Contracting Parties.

3. Where the Council is required to act by a qualified majority, the votes of its members shall be weighted as laid down in Article 148(2) of the Treaty establishing the European Community, and for their adoption, acts of the Council shall require at least 62 votes in favour, cast by at least 10 members.

4. For procedural questions, the Council shall act by a majority of its members.

DECLARATION ON ARTICLE K.6(2)

The Conference agrees that initiatives for measures referred to in Article K.6(2) of the Treaty on European Union and acts adopted by the Council thereunder shall be published in the Official Journal of the European Communities, in accordance with the relevant rules of procedure of the Council and the Commission.

ARTICLE K.7

1. The Court of Justice of the European Communities shall have jurisdiction, subject to the conditions laid down in this Article, to give preliminary rulings on the validity and interpretation of framework decisions and decisions, on the interpretation of conventions established under this Title and on the validity and interpretation of the measures implementing them.

2. By a declaration made at the time of the signing of this Treaty or any time thereafter, any Member State shall be able to accept a jurisdiction of the Court of Justice to give preliminary rulings as specified in paragraph 1.

3. A Member State making a declaration pursuant to paragraph 2 shall specify that either:

(a) any court or tribunal of that State against whose decisions there is no judicial remedy under national law may request the Court of

Justice to give a preliminary ruling on a question raised in a case pending before it and concerning the validity or interpretation of an act referred to in paragraph 1 if that court or tribunal considers that a decision on the question is necessary to enable it to give judgement, or

(b) any court or tribunal of that State may request the Court of Justice to give a preliminary ruling on a question raised in a case pending before it and concerning the interpretation or validity of an act referred to in paragraph 1 if that court or tribunal considers that a decision on the question is necessary to enable it to give judgement.

4. Any Member State, whether or not it has made a declaration pursuant to paragraph 2, shall be entitled to submit statements of case or written observations to the Court in cases which arise under paragraph 3.

5. The Court of Justice shall have no jurisdiction to review the validity or proportionality of operations carried out by the police or other law enforcement agencies of a Member State or the exercise of the responsibilities incumbent upon Member States with regard to the maintenance of law and order and the safeguarding of internal security.

6. The Court of Justice shall have jurisdiction to review the legality of framework decisions and decisions in actions brought by a Member State or the Commission on grounds of lack of competence, infringement of an essential procedural requirement, infringement of this Treaty or of any rule of law relating to its application, or misuse of powers. The proceedings provided for in this paragraph shall be instituted within two months of the publication of the measure.

7. The Court of Justice shall have jurisdiction to rule on any dispute between Member States regarding the interpretation or the application of acts adopted under Article K.6(2) whenever such dispute cannot be settled by the Council within six months of its being referred to the Council by one of its members. Moreover, the Court shall have jurisdiction to rule on any dispute between Member States and the Commission regarding the interpretation or the application of conventions established under Article K.6(2)(d).

DECLARATION RELATING TO ARTICLE K.7

The Conference notes that Member States may, when making a declaration pursuant to Article K.7(2) of the Treaty on European Union, reserve the right to make provisions in the ir national law to the effect that, where a question relating to the validity or interpretation of an act referred to in Article K.7(1) is raised in a case pending before a national court or tribunal against whose decision there is no judicial remedy under national law, that court or tribunal will be required to refer the matter to the Court of Justice.

ARTICLE K.8 (FORMERLY ARTICLE K.4)

1. A Coordinating Committee shall be set up consisting of senior officials. In addition to its coordinating role, it shall be the task of the Committee to:

• give opinions for the attention of the Council, either at the Council's request or on its own initiative;

• contribute, without prejudice to Article 151 of the Treaty establishing the European Community, to the preparation of the Council's discussions in the areas referred to in Article K.1.

2. The Commission shall be fully associated with the work in the areas referred to in this Title.

ARTICLE K.9 (FORMERLY ARTICLE K.5)

Within international organisations and at international conferences in which they take part, Member States shall defend the common positions adopted under the provisions of this Title.

The provisions of Articles J.8 and J.9 shall apply as appropriate to matters falling under this Title.

ARTICLE K.10

Agreements referred to in Article J.14 may cover matters falling under this Title.

DECLARATION RELATING TO ARTICLE J.14 AND K.10

The provisions of Article J.14 and K.10 of the Treaty on European Union and any agreements resulting form them shall not imply any transfer of competence from the Member States to the Union.

ARTICLE K.11 (FORMERLY ARTICLE K.6)

1. The Council shall consult the European Parliament before adopting any measure referred to in Article K.6 (2)(b), (c) and (d). The European Parliament shall deliver its opinion within a time-limit which the Council may lay down, which shall not be less than three months. In the absence of an opinion within that time-limit, the Council may act.

2. The Presidency of the Council and the Commission shall regularly inform the European Parliament of discussions in the areas covered by this Title.

3. The European Parliament may ask questions of the Council or make recommendations to it. Each year, it shall hold a debate on the progress made in the areas referred to in this Title.

ARTICLE K.12 (FORMERLY ARTICLE K.7)

1. Member States which intend to establish closer cooperation between themselves may be authorised, subject to Articles K.15 and K.16 to make use of the institutions, procedures and mechanisms laid down by the Treaties provided that the cooperation proposed:

(a) respects the powers of the European Community, and the objectives laid down by this Title;

(b) has the aim of enabling the Union to develop more rapidly into an area of freedom, security and justice.

2. The authorisation referred to in paragraph 1 shall be granted by the Council, acting by a qualified majority at the request of the Member States concerned and after inviting the Commission to present its opinion; the request shall also be forwarded to the European Parliament.

If a member of the Council declares that, for important and stated reasons of national policy, it intends to oppose the granting of an authorisation by qualified majority, a vote shall not be taken. The Council may, acting by a qualified majority, request that the matter be referred to the European Council for decision by unanimity.

The votes of the members of the Council shall be weighted in accordance with article 148(2) of the Treaty establishing the European Community. For their adoption, decisions shall require at least 62 votes in favour, cast by at least 10 members.

3. Any Member State which wishes to become a party to cooperation set up in accordance with this Article shall notify its intention to the Council and to the Commission, which shall give an opinion to the Council within three months of receipt of that notification, possibly accompanied by a recommendation for specific arrangements as it may deem necessary for that Member State to become a party to the cooperation in question. Within four months of the date of that notification, the Council shall decide on the request and on possible specific arrangements as it may deem necessary. The decision shall be deemed to be taken unless the Council, acting by a qualified majority, decides to hold it in abeyance; in this case, the Council shall state the reasons for its decision and set a deadline for re-examining it. For the purposes of this paragraph, the Council shall act under the conditions set out in Article K.16.

4. The provisions of Articles K.1 to K.13 shall apply to the closer cooperation provided for by this Article, save as otherwise provided for in this Article and in Articles K.15 and K.16.

The provisions of the Treaty establishing the European Community concerning the powers of the Court of Justice of the European Communities and the exercise of those powers shall apply to paragraphs 1, 2 and 3.

5. This Article is without prejudice to the provisions of the Protocol integrating the Schengen acquis into the framework of the Union.

ARTICLE K.13 (FORMERLY ARTICLE K.8)

1. The provisions referred to in Articles 137, 138, 138e, 139 to 142, 146, 147, 148(3), 150 to 153, 157 to 163, 191a and 217 of the Treaty establishing the European Community shall apply to the provisions relating to the areas referred to in this Title.

2. Administrative expenditure which the provisions relating to the areas referred to in this Title entail for the institutions shall be charged to the budget of the European Communities.

3. Operational expenditure to which the implementation of those provisions gives rise shall also be charged to the budget of the European Communities, except where the Council acting unanimously decides otherwise. In cases where expenditure is not charged to the budget of the European Communities it shall be charged to the Member States in accordance with the GNP scale, unless the Council acting unanimously decides otherwise.

4. The budgetary procedure laid down in the Treaty establishing the European Community shall apply to the expenditure charged to the budget of the European Communities.

ARTICLE K.14 (FORMERLY ARTICLE K.9)

The Council, acting unanimously on the initiative of the Commission or a Member State, and after consulting the European Parliament, may decide that action in areas referred to in Article K.1 shall fall under Title IIIa of the Treaty establishing the European Community, and at the same time determine the relevant voting conditions relating to it. It shall recommend the Member States to adopt that decision in accordance with their respective constitutional requirements.

DECLARATION BY DENMARK RELATING TO ARTICLE K.14

Article K.14 of the Treaty on European Union requires that unanimity of all members of the Council of the European Union, i.e. all Member States, for the adoption of any decision to apply the provisions in the new Title IIIa in the Treaty establishing the European Community on visas, asylum, immigration and other policies related to free movement of persons to action in areas referred to in Article K.1. Moreover, any unanimous decision of the Council, before coming into force, will have to be adopted in each Member State, in accordance with its constitutional requirements. In Denmark, such adoption will, in the case of a transfer of sovereignty, as defined in the Danish constitution, require either a majority of five sixths of members of the Folketing or both a majority of the members of the Folketing and a majority of voters in a referendum.

Commentary
The remaining third pillar

The old third pillar was called 'cooperation in the fields of justice and home affairs'; the new, less appositely, is called 'police and judicial cooperation in criminal matters'.

Title VI of the Treaty, stripped of asylum and immigration policy, is reformed. The new Article K.1 contains the substance only of old Articles K.1(7), (8) and (9) — judicial cooperation in criminal matters, and cooperation between police and customs authorities.

The reference to paedophilia is a novelty.

Article K.2 sets out the details of police cooperation under the yet-to-be-ratified Europol convention. It is a help from a civil liberties point of view to have the specifics of common police action spelled out in Treaty form. Particularly sensitive was the debate on K.2(b), concerning personal data. The German Länder, too, have important powers over police matters, and were anxious to protect them.

For all the difficulties, what emerges is a picture, in five years time, of an extensive and sophisticated web of police coordination throughout the European Union. Europol will not quite be Europe's Federal Bureau of Investigation, but its services should be capable of acting as a major support capacity for national police forces.

At an earlier stage of the IGC there had been more emphasis on the approximation of laws in criminal matters, including reference to facilitating access to justice, but the UK in particular had opposed an explicit extension of Treaty powers in this field. Article K.3 remains.

Article K.4, importantly, enjoins the Council to lay down rules to govern how police and judicial authorities should comport themselves in member states other than their own.

Streamlining conventions

Article K.6 deals with the decision-making procedures of the third pillar.

The new Article attempts a modest classification of three types of legislative acts. It creates the precedent of the 'framework decision' for the approximation of national laws without direct effect.

Second tier decisions, to replace the previous, ill-defined 'joint action', shall be binding and may be implemented by a type of dual QMV (62 votes in favour cast by two-thirds of the member states).

Thirdly, conventions shall continue to need ratification in member states but they may come into force once adopted by only half the member states within those member states concerned. Moreover, implementing measures must be adopted in Council by only two-thirds of the member states.

This is a significant lightening of the decision process, and will certainly bring conventions on-stream once the new Treaty comes into force.

The other important advance is that the European Commission now has right of co-initiative throughout the third pillar, whereas before it was restricted to policy initiatives in those sectors now transferred by Amsterdam into the new first pillar area of freedom, security and justice. The European Parliament, however, remains excluded from the scrutiny of third pillar conventions.

Judicial review

The intention of Article K.7 is to extend the jurisdiction of the European Court of Justice to the whole of the third pillar. This would be a very substantial advance in that, under Maastricht, member states had to agree to opt into Court jurisdiction on a case by case basis. Usually, they chose not to do so.

Under Article K.7(6) the European Court may rule on on the validity of any framework decision (Article K.6(2)(b)) or decision (Article K.6(2)(c)) of the Council.

Under Maastricht, the Council was responsible for interpreting its own conventions. Under Article K.7(7) of Amsterdam, the European Court shall adjudicate in disputes between member states, or between member states and the Commission, regarding conventions (Article K.6(2)(d)). This reform is critical, as there is every likelihood of heavy litigation about whether or not Europol or other agencies have exceeded their powers.

Member states may use their discretion as to whether or not they will allow references from national courts to the European Court for preliminary rulings (Article K.7(2)).

While it is true that the extension of the competence of the European Court of Justice in the third pillar is a substantial enhancement of the rule of law in the European Union, access to the Court is restricted to member state courts and governments and the Commission: both the Parliament and the citizen are barred.

There is also a restriction on the Court of Justice's jurisdiction concerning domestic law and order or security matters, as within the area of freedom, security and justice.

Managing the third pillar

Third pillar matters are now to be prepared by the 'K.8 Committee' (formerly K.4).

Member states are constrained under the third pillar in their international actions. They shall be represented by the Council presidency, and are required to uphold common positions in international forums (Article K.9).

International negotiations shall be conducted by the presidency, with the assistance of the Commission, under a mandate given by the Council acting by unanimity (Article K.10).

The coy Declaration recalls that member states retain sovereignty in these matters.

Democratic deficit

Article K.11 signifies a slight reinforcement of the powers of the European Parliament to intervene in third pillar matters. Under Maastricht, MEPs were to be consulted only on 'principal aspects of activities', and otherwise kept informed. After Amsterdam, they have to be consulted on legislative measures, including conventions — although not on the orientation of Union policy towards the reaching of common positions, which presages a ministerial preference for common positions.

That the European Parliament did not acquire the right to give its assent to conventions is a shame. National parliaments are not generally efficient in their scrutiny of diplomatic conventions, as the long drawn out story of Schengen affirms. In the UK, the Europol convention was the subject of a (post-ratification) report by the House of Lords Select Committee, but swung through the House of Commons without debate as a statutory instrument. So much for those MPs who lay claim to an enhanced role in European affairs.

Flexibility

The general conditions for the introduction of differentiation between one group of member states and another are set out in Article K.15 (see below). Article K.12 concerns the detailed arrangements for the third pillar. It replaces Article K.7 of Maastricht which allowed for the 'establishment or development of closer cooperation between two or more member states'.

Amsterdam itself incorporates the Schengen Agreement within the Treaty on European Union and uses this clause (and Article 5a of the Treaty establishing the European Community) to do so via the Schengen

Protocol. Specialised institutional arrangements are also made for the specific derogations for Denmark, Ireland and the UK.

It is difficult to see how Article K.12 could be used otherwise to allow a core group to go forward under the third pillar but outside Schengen without jeopardising the political solidarity of the Union.

Article K.12 also means that there is an effective unilateral national veto in the Council on any such adventure (Article K.12(2)).

The Court of Justice has powers of judicial review (Article K.12(4)).

Ties with the first pillar

Article K.13 strengthens the ties that bind the remaining third pillar to the first.

Significantly, the powers of the Ombudsman are extended to these important areas that affect the citizen (Article 138e). And new Article 191a laying down rules about the transparency of the work of the EU institutions, including public access to documents, will apply also.

With regard to operational expenditure, Amsterdam has shifted the imperative. Under Maastricht the Council could choose whether to use the EC budget or to make a special levy on member states. Article K.13(3) implies that the normal rule will be to use the EC budget unless the Council, acting unanimously, decides otherwise. This increases by inference the power of the European Parliament, the second arm of the budgetary authority, over third pillar matters.

At the early stages of the IGC it was assumed that old Article K.9, which built the (unused) bridge from the third pillar to the first, would be abolished. But in the end it survived intact, as Article K.14, offering a scenario in which, one day, even cooperation in police and criminal matters might pass fully within the democratic disciplines of the European Community without the need for Treaty amendments.

Hope springs eternal.

THE SCHENGEN AGREEMENT

PROTOCOL INTEGRATING THE SCHENGEN ACQUIS INTO THE FRAMEWORK OF THE EUROPEAN UNION

THE HIGH CONTRACTING PARTIES TO THE TREATY OF AMSTERDAM

NOTING that the Agreements on the gradual abolition of checks at common borders signed by some Member States of the European Union in Schengen on 14 June 1985 and on 19 June 1990, as well as related agreements and the rules adopted on the basis of these agreements, are aimed at enhancing European integration and, in particular, at enabling the European Union to develop more rapidly into an area of freedom, security and justice,

DESIRING to incorporate the above mentioned agreements and rules into the framework of the European Union,

CONFIRMING that the provisions of the Schengen acquis are applicable only if and as far as they are compatible with the Union and Community law,

TAKING INTO ACCOUNT the special position of Denmark,

TAKING INTO ACCOUNT the fact that Ireland and the United Kingdom of Great Britain and Northern Ireland are not parties to and have not signed the above-mentioned agreements; that provision should, however, be made to allow those Member States to accept some or all of the provisions thereof,

RECOGNISING that, as a consequence, it is necessary to make use of the provisions of the Treaty on European Union and of the Treaty establishing the European Community concerning closer cooperation between some Member States and that those provisions should only be used as a last resort,

TAKING INTO ACCOUNT the need to maintain a special relationship with the Republic of Iceland and the Kingdom of Norway, both States which have confirmed their intention to become bound by the provisions mentioned above, on the basis of the Agreement signed in Luxembourg on 19th December 1996,

HAVE AGREED upon the following provisions, which shall be annexed to the Treaty of Amsterdam,

ARTICLE 1

The Kingdom of Belgium, the Kingdom of Denmark, the Federal Republic of Germany, the Hellenic Republic, the Kingdom of Spain, the French Republic, the Italian Republic, the Grand Duchy of

Luxembourg, the Kingdom of the Netherlands, the Republic of Austria, the Portuguese Republic, the Republic of Finland and the Kingdom of Sweden, signatories to the Schengen Agreements, are authorised to establish closer cooperation among themselves within the scope of those agreements and related provisions, as they are listed in the annex to this Protocol, hereinafter referred to as the 'Schengen acquis'. This cooperation shall be conducted within the institutional and legal framework of the European Union and with respect for the relevant provisions of the Treaty on European Union and of the Treaty establishing the European Community.

ARTICLE 2

1. From the date of entry into force of this Protocol, the Schengen acquis, including the decisions of the Executive Committee established by the Schengen agreements which have been adopted before this date, shall immediately apply to the thirteen Member States referred to in Article 1, without prejudice to the provisions of paragraph 2. From the same date, the Council will substitute itself for the said Executive Committee.

The Council, acting by the unanimity of its Members referred to in Article 1, shall take any measure necessary for the implementation of this paragraph. The Council, acting unanimously, shall determine, in conformity with the relevant provisions of the Treaties, the legal basis for each of the provisions or decisions which constitute the Schengen acquis.

With regard to such provisions and decisions and in accordance with that determination, the Court of Justice of the European Communities shall exercise the powers conferred upon it by the relevant applicable provisions of the Treaties. In any event, the Court of Justice shall have no jurisdiction on measures or decisions relating to the maintenance of law and order and the safeguarding of internal security.

As long as the measures referred to above have not been taken and without prejudice to Article 5(2), the provisions or decisions which constitute the Schengen acquis shall be regarded as acts based on Title VI of the Treaty on European Union.

2. The provisions of paragraph 1 shall apply to the Member States which have signed accession Protocols to Schengen from the dates decided by the Council, acting with the unanimity of its Members mentioned in Article 1, unless the conditions for the accession of any of those States to the Schengen acquis are met before the date of the entry into force of this Protocol.

DECLARATION ON ARTICLE 2 OF THE PROTOCOL INTEGRATING THE SCHENGEN ACQUIS INTO THE FRAMEWORK OF THE EUROPEAN UNION

The High Contracting Parties agree that the Council shall adopt all the necessary measures referred to in Article 2 of the Protocol integrating the Schengen acquis into the framework of the European Union upon the date of entry into force of this Treaty. To that end, the necessary preparatory work shall be undertaken in due time in order to be completed prior to that date.

ARTICLE 3

Following the determination referred to in Article 2(1), second subparagraph, Denmark shall maintain the same rights and obligations in relation to the other signatories to the Schengen agreements, as before the said determination with regard to those parts of the Schengen acquis that are determined to have a legal basis in Title IIIa of the Treaty establishing the European Community.

With regard to those parts of the Schengen acquis that are determined to have legal base in Title VI of the Treaty on European Union, Denmark shall continue to have the same rights and obligations as the other signatories to the Schengen agreements.

ARTICLE 4

Ireland and the United Kingdom of Great Britain and Northern Ireland, which are not bound by the Schengen acquis, may at any time request to take part in some or all of the provisions of this acquis.

The Council shall decide on the request with the unanimity if its members referred to in Article 1 and of the representative of the Government of the State concerned.

DECLARATION ON ARTICLE 4 OF THE PROTOCOL INTEGRATING THE SCHENGEN ACQUIS INTO THE FRAMEWORK OF THE EUROPEAN UNION

The High Contracting Parties undertake to make all efforts in order to make action among all Member States possible in the domains of the Schengen acquis, in particular whenever Ireland and the United Kingdom of Great Britain and Northern Ireland have accepted some or all of the provisions of that acquis in accordance with Article 4 of the Protocol integrating the Schengen acquis into the framework of the European Union.

ARTICLE 5

1. Proposals and initiatives to build upon the Schengen acquis shall be subject to the relevant provisions of the Treaties.

In this context, where either Ireland or the United Kingdom or both have not notified the President of the Council in writing within a reasonable period that they wish to take part, the authorisation referred to in Article 5a of the Treaty establishing the European Community or Article K.12 of the Treaty on European Union shall be deemed to have been granted to the Member States referred to in Article 1 and to Ireland or the United Kingdom where either of them wishes to take part in the areas of cooperation in question.

2. The relevant provisions of the Treaties referred to in the first subparagraph of paragraph 1 shall apply even if the Council has not adopted the measures referred to in Article 2(1), second subparagraph.

DECLARATION ON ARTICLE 5 OF THE PROTOCOL INTEGRATING THE SCHENGEN ACQUIS INTO THE FRAMEWORK OF THE EUROPEAN UNION

The High Contracting Parties agree to make all efforts in order to make action among all Member States possible in the domains of the Schengen acquis, in particular whenever Ireland and the United Kingdom of Great Britain and Northern Ireland have accepted some or all of the provisions of that acquis in accordance with Article 4 of the Protocol integrating the Schengen acquis into the framework of the European Union.

ARTICLE 6

The Republic of Iceland and the Kingdom of Norway shall be associated with the implementation of the Schengen acquis and its further development on the basis of the Agreement signed in Luxembourg on 19 December 1996. Appropriate procedures shall be agreed to that effect in an Agreement to be concluded with those States by the Council, acting by the unanimity of its Members mentioned in Article 1. Such Agreement shall include provisions on the contribution of Iceland and Norway to any financial consequences resulting from the implementation of this Protocol.

A separate Agreement shall be concluded with the above-mentioned countries by the Council, acting unanimously, for the establishment of rights and obligations between Ireland and the United Kingdom of Great Britain and Northern Ireland on the one hand, and Iceland and Norway on the other, in domains of the Schengen acquis which apply to these States.

DECLARATION ON ARTICLE 6 OF THE PROTOCOL INTEGRATING THE SCHENGEN ACQUIS INTO THE FRAMEWORK OF THE EUROPEAN UNION

The High Contracting Parties agree to take all necessary steps so that the Agreements referred to in Article 5 of the Protocol integrating the Schengen acquis into the framework of the European Union may enter into force on the same date as the date of entry into force of the said Protocol.

ARTICLE 7

The Council shall, acting by a qualified majority, adopt the modalities for the integration of the Schengen Secretariat into the General Secretariat of the Council.

ARTICLE 8

For the purposes of the negotiations for the admission of new Member States into the European Union, the Schengen acquis and further measures taken by the institutions within its scope shall be regarded as an acquis which must be accepted in full by all States candidates for admission.

ANNEX

SCHENGEN ACQUIS

1. The Agreement, signed in Schengen on 14 June 1985, between the Governments of the States of the Benelux Economic Union, the Federal Republic of Germany and the French Republic on the gradual abolition of checks at their common borders.

2. The Convention, signed in Schengen on 19 June 1990, between the Kingdom of Belgium, the Federal Republic of Germany, the French Republic, the Grand Duchy of Luxembourg and the Kingdom of Netherlands, implementing the Agreement on the gradual abolition of checks at their common borders, signed in Schengen on 14 June 1985, with related Final Act and common declarations.

3. The Accession Protocols and Agreements to the 1985 Agreement and the 1990 Implementation Convention with Italy (signed in Paris on 27 November 1990), Spain and Portugal (both signed in Bonn on 25 June 1991), Greece (signed in Madrid on 6 November 1992), Austria (signed in Brussels on 28 April 1995) and Denmark, Finland and Sweden (all signed in Luxembourg on 19 December 1996), with related Final Acts and declarations.

4. Decisions and declarations adopted by the Executive Committee established by the 1990 Implementation Convention, as well as acts adopted for the implementation of the Convention by the organs upon which the Executive Committee has conferred decision making powers.

Commentary
Introducing Schengen

The Schengen Agreement is an unsatisfactory compromise, and only partially operational. It was conceived out of frustration with Britain about the abolition of internal frontier controls, and envisaged as a pathfinder to an EU-wide frontier free zone. In effect, the Schengen Agreement duplicates the objectives of the EU Treaty (Article 7a) with respect to the removal of the internal borders of the EU.

The Schengen Treaty was signed in 1985 between Germany, France and Benelux, but it took until 1990 before its practical implications were agreed. Even today they are only rarely understood. The 'Schengen acquis' comprises some 3000 uncollated pages of secondary legislation and technical arrangements generated by its signatory states. It attempts to develop a portfolio of flanking measures to enable the internal borders to be virtually expunged. The measures comprise:

- rules for the removal of all controls on individuals at internal borders, including the definition of internal borders at airports, and an attack on officiousness;

- controls and entry conditions for the crossing of external frontiers;

- visa policy for short-term visits (list of non-member countries, standard model visa, conditions and procedures for issue);

- transit visa policy for long-term visits;

- conditions governing the movement of third-country nationals inside the Union and their residence papers;

- responsibility of member states for processing asylum requests;

- police cooperation (cross-frontier observation and pursuit; exchange of information);

- improved judicial assistance in criminal matters (letters rogatory, transmission of procedural papers);

- closer cooperation on extradition.

- transfer of execution of criminal judgments;

- drugs (cooperation to prevent and combat illegal trafficking, controlled delivery, medical certification);

- alignment of provisions on firearms and ammunition;

- establishment of the Schengen Information System (SIS);

- transport and movement of goods (baggage controls);

- protection of personal data (to ensure at least the same level of protection as under the Council of Europe Convention of 28 January 1981).

The implementation of Schengen has been tortuous. There are four reasons for this: first, problems with the SIS computer system required for data exchange; second, the lack of enthusiasm for the Agreement among those like the Dutch most concerned with transparency and democratic accountability; third, the bureaucratic weaknesses of the southern member states; and fourth, rising panic in France about immigration and drugs. Austria, Italy and Greece are anticipating full, operational membership by October 1997, but widespread concern about Italy's ramshackle administration, and the suspected presence of one million illegal immigrants on Italian soil, give cause for doubt.

What Amsterdam did

It was expected that, as a transitory measure, the IGC would transpose Schengen into the third pillar in order that a reformed version could be later transposed into the first. What happened at Amsterdam, however, was that Schengen was glued in an ungainly manner on to both the first and third pillars. The citizen will not find this straightforward.

The original Schengen Agreement was run by an executive committee. Under the terms of Article B of the Treaty of Amsterdam's Schengen Protocol, this committee will transmogrify into the Council of the European Union *à treize*. The UK and Ireland can apply to join in, but the Council will decide on their application by unanimity. Article D of the Protocol refers to the flexibility clauses (Article 5a, first pillar, and Article K.12, third).

The Council, probably excluding the UK and Ireland, will need to make separate arrangements with Iceland and Norway (Article E). And the Schengen secretariat will move en bloc into the Council secretariat (Article F).

Article G, in the circumstances, is rather startling. It insists that the applicant countries on Europe's porous Eastern frontier must accept Schengen and all its works in full as part of the Union acquis. In theory, this builds up the threshold for accession. In practice, it hardly promises to be functional.

The annex to the Protocol is a very succinct summary of the Schengen acquis — a corpus of literature which is nowhere published in full.

ASYLUM

PROTOCOL TO THE TREATY ESTABLISHING THE EUROPEAN COMMUNITY ON ASYLUM FOR NATIONALS OF EU MEMBER STATES

THE HIGH CONTRACTING PARTIES

WHEREAS pursuant to the provisions of Article F(2) of the Treaty on European Union 'the Union shall respect fundamental rights as guaranteed by the European Convention for the Protection of Human Rights and Fundamental Freedoms signed in Rome on November 4 1950';

WHEREAS the Court of Justice of the European Communities has jurisdiction to ensure that in the interpretation and application of Article F(2) of the Treaty on European Union the law is observed by the European Community;

WHEREAS pursuant to Article O of the Treaty on European Union any European State, when applying to become a Member of the Union, must respect the principles set out in Article F(1) of the Treaty on European Union;

BEARING IN MIND that Article 236 of the Treaty establishing the European Community establishes a mechanism for the suspension of certain rights in the event of a serious and persistent breach by a Member State of those principles;

RECALLING that each national of a Member State, as a citizen of the Union, enjoys a special status and protection which shall be guaranteed by the Member States in accordance with the provisions of Part Two of the Treaty establishing the European Community;

BEARING IN MIND that the Treaty establishing the European Community establishes an area without internal frontiers and grants every citizen of the Union the right to move and reside freely within the territory of the Member States;

RECALLING that the question of extradition of nationals of Member States of the Union is addressed in the European Convention on Extradition of 13 December 1957 and the Convention of 27 September 1996 based on Article K.3 of the Treaty on European Union concerning extradition between the Member States of the European Union;

WISHING to prevent that the institution of asylum is resorted to for purposes alien to those for which it is intended;

WHEREAS this Protocol respects the finality and the objectives of the Convention relating to the Status of Refugees of 28 July 1951;

HAVE AGREED upon the following provisions which shall be annexed to the Treaty establishing the European Community:

Given the level of protection of fundamental rights and freedoms by the Member States of the European Union, Member States shall be regarded as constituting safe countries of origin in respect of each other for all legal and practical purposes in relation to asylum matters. Accordingly, any application for asylum made by a national of a Member State may be taken into consideration or declared admissible for processing by another Member State only in the following cases:

(a) if the Member State of which the applicant is a national proceeds after the entry into force of this Treaty, availing itself of the provisions of Article 15 of the Convention for the Protection of Human Rights and Fundamental Freedoms, to take measures derogating in its territory from its obligations under that Convention;

(b) if the procedure referred to Article F.1(1) of the Treaty on European Union, has been initiated and until the Council takes a decision in respect thereof;

(c) if the Council, acting on the basis of Article F.1(1) of the Treaty on European Union, has determined, in respect of the Member State of which the applicant is a national, the existence of a serious and persistent breach by that Member State of principles mentioned in Article F(1);

(d) if a Member State should so decide unilaterally in respect of the application of a national of another Member State; in that case the Council shall be immediately informed; the application shall be dealt with on the basis of the presumption that it is manifestly unfounded without affecting in any way, whatever the cases may be, the decision-making power of the Member State.

DECLARATION ON THE CONVENTION RELATING TO THE STATUS OF REFUGEES OF 28 JULY 1951

The Protocol on asylum for nationals of Member States of the European Union does not prejudice the right of each Member State to take the organisational measures it deems necessary to fulfil its obligations under the Geneva Convention relating to the status of refugees of 28 July 1951.

DECLARATION BY BELGIUM ON THE PROTOCOL ON ASYLUM FOR NATIONALS OF MEMBER STATES OF THE EUROPEAN UNION

In approving this Protocol, Belgium declares that in accordance with its obligations under the 1951 Geneva Convention and the 1967 New York Protocol, it shall, in accordance with the provision set out in point (d) of the sole Article of that Protocol, carry out an individual examination of any asylum request made by a national of another Member State.

DECLARATION RELATING TO SUBPARAGRAPH (D) OF THE SOLE ARTICLE OF THE PROTOCOL ON ASYLUM FOR NATIONALS OF MEMBER STATES OF THE EUROPEAN UNION

The Conference declares that, while recognising the importance of the Resolution of the Ministers of the Member States of the European Communities responsible for immigration of 30 November/1 December 1992 on manifestly unfounded applications for asylum and of the Resolution of the Council of 9/10 March 1995 on minimum guarantees for asylum procedures, the question of abuse of asylum procedures and appropriate rapid procedures to dispense with manifestly unfounded applications for asylum should be further examined with a view to introducing new improvements in order to accelerate these procedures.

Commentary
Asylum policy

The final Protocol of the third pillar springs from a row between Belgium and Spain about the treatment of Basques suspected of terrorism who sought political asylum in Brussels.

The Protocol seeks to curb the rights of asylum-seekers under international law, notably the 1951 Geneva Convention, within the context of the European Union. Its intention is to limit the freedom of one member state to decide on an asylum application from a national of another.

Although Belgium is hardly justified in making its declaration on the protocol, asylum for the EU citizen-terrorist within the EU cannot be afforded without making a nonsense of the area of freedom, security and justice. At any rate, the Belgian Protocol is certainly unsatisfactory law, and has attracted no less than three qualifying Declarations to the sole article of the Protocol. It is a good candidate for reconsideration when the third pillar and Schengen settlement, which is inherently unstable, next falls prey to re-negotiation.

---

[1]   See the Presidency Note of 19 February 1997, CONF/3823/97.

[2]   As a result of this provision, Articles 100c and 100d of the Treaty establishing the European Community will be repealed.

Section Two

The Union and the Citizen

EMPLOYMENT

AMENDED FIRST INDENT OF ARTICLE B OF THE TREATY ON EUROPEAN UNION

The Union shall set itself the following objectives:

- to promote economic and social progress and a high level of employment and to achieve balanced and sustainable development, in particular through the creation of an area without internal frontiers, through the strengthening of economic and social cohesion and through the establishment of economic and monetary union, ultimately including a single currency in accordance with the provisions of this Treaty;

AMENDED ARTICLE 2 OF THE TREATY ESTABLISHING THE EUROPEAN COMMUNITY

The Community shall ... promote throughout the Community a harmonious, balanced and sustainable development of economic activities, a high level of employment and of social protection, equality between men and women, sustainable and non-inflationary growth, a high degree of competitiveness and convergence of economic performance, a high level of protection and improvement of the quality of the environment, the raising of the standard of living and quality of life, and economic and social cohesion and solidarity among Member States.

NEW FIRST SUB-PARAGRAPH OF ARTICLE 3

- the promotion of coordination between employment policies of the Member States with a view to enhancing their effectiveness by developing a coordinated strategy for employment.

NEW TITLE VIA ON EMPLOYMENT

ARTICLE 109N

Member States and the Community shall, in accordance with this Title, work towards developing a coordinated strategy for employment and particularly for promoting a skilled, trained and adaptable workforce and labour markets responsive to economic change with a view to achieving the objectives defined in Article B of the Treaty on European Union and in Article 2 of this Treaty.

ARTICLE 109o

1. Member States, through their employment policies, shall contribute to the achievement of the objectives referred to in Article 109n in a way consistent with the broad guidelines of the economic policies of the Member States and of the Community adopted pursuant to Article 103(2).

2. Member States, having regard to the national practices related to the responsibilities of management and labour, shall regard promoting employment as a matter of common concern and shall coordinate their action in this respect within the Council, in accordance with the provisions of Article 109q.

ARTICLE 109p

1. The Community shall contribute to a high level of employment by encouraging cooperation between Member States and by supporting and, if necessary, complementing their action. In doing so, the competences of the Member States shall be respected.

2. The objective of a high level of employment shall be taken into consideration in the formulation and implementation of Community policies and activities.

ARTICLE 109q

1. The European Council shall each year consider the employment situation in the Community and adopt conclusions thereon, on the basis of a joint annual report by the Council and the Commission.

2. On the basis of the conclusions of the European Council, the Council, acting by a qualified majority on a proposal from the Commission and after consulting the European Parliament, the Economic and Social Committee, the Committee of the Regions and the Employment Committee referred to in Article 109s, shall each year draw up guidelines which the Member States shall take into account in their employment policies. These guidelines shall be consistent with the broad guidelines adopted pursuant to Article 103(2).

3. Each Member State shall provide the Council and the Commission with an annual report on the principal measures taken to implement its employment policy in the light of the guidelines for employment as referred to in paragraph 2.

4. The Council, on the basis of the reports referred to in paragraph 3 and having received the views of the Employment Committee shall each year carry out an examination of the implementation of the employment policies of the Member States in the light of the guidelines for employment. The Council, acting by a qualified majority on a recommendation from the Commission, may, if it considers it appropriate in the light of that examination, make recommendations to Member States.

5. On the basis of the results of that examination, the Council and the Commission shall make a joint annual report to the European Council on the employment situation in the Community and on the implementation of the guidelines for employment.

ARTICLE 109R

The Council, acting in accordance with the procedure referred to in Article 189b and after consulting the Economic and Social Committee and the Committee of the Regions, may adopt incentive measures designed to encourage cooperation between Member States and to support their action in the field of employment through initiatives aimed at developing exchanges of information and best practices, providing comparative analysis and advice as well as promoting innovative approaches and evaluating experiences, in particular by recourse to pilot projects.

Those measures shall not include harmonisation of the laws and regulations of the Member States.

DECLARATION ON INCENTIVE MEASURES REFERRED TO IN ARTICLE 109R

The Conference agrees that the incentive measures referred to in Article 109r of the Treaty establishing the European Community should always specify the following:

- *the grounds for taking them based on an objective assessment of their need and the existence of an added value at Community level;*

- *their duration, which should not exceed five years;*

- *the maximum amount for their financing, which should reflect the incentive nature of such measures.*

DECLARATION ON ARTICLE 109R

It is understood that any expenditure under Article 109r of the Treaty establishing the European Community will fall within Heading 3 of the financial perspectives.

ARTICLE 109S

The Council, after consulting the European Parliament, shall establish an Employment Committee with advisory status to promote coordination between Member States on employment and labour market policies. The tasks of the Committee shall be:

- to monitor the employment situation and employment policies in the Member States and the Community;

- without prejudice to Article 151, to formulate opinions at the request of either the Council or the Commission or on its own initiative, and to contribute to the preparation of the Council proceedings referred to in Article 109q.

In fulfilling its mandate, the Committee shall consult the social partners.

The Member States and the Commission shall each appoint two members of the Committee.

Commentary
Employment

Unemployment peaked at 11% across the European Union in 1996, which meant that over 18 million people were out of work. Italy, Ireland, France, Finland and Spain were at higher than average levels, with Spain the worst at 22.2%. By the time of the Amsterdam European Council, the unemployment trend was falling in the UK, Ireland, the Netherlands and Spain, but rising in Germany, France, Italy and Finland. Overall, Europe's position continued to compare badly to the USA (5.4%) and Japan (3.4%).

A 'high level of employment' was a well-established principle of the European Community (Article 2). The European Commission under Jacques Delors had sought to generate a debate about the relationship between growth, employment and competitiveness, but the debate was in danger of reducing to a row about expenditure from the EU budget on certain trans-European *grands projets*. The Amsterdam IGC served at least to refresh that debate and proved thereby to be something of a learning process for certain member states.

Proposals were made, particularly by the socialist government of Sweden in September 1995, that the revised Treaty should contain a new chapter committing the Union to full employment. The Swedish intention was to balance the pursuit of monetary stability with growth and job creation. But many thought that this implied an historic misreading by the Swedes of the meaning of Economic and Monetary Union.

Nevertheless, the idea that Maastricht had been at fault for somehow not according a sufficient priority to employment took hold, especially under the Irish presidency, and even those who, like the Germans, were at first hostile to the idea conceded that for the EU not to be seen to be doing something about joblessness would be a public relations mistake.

The IGC touched on the key debate about the future of work and welfare in Europe, about labour market mobility and flexibility — or, just as euphemistically, 'employability'. But the IGC had no chance to go deeply into the reform of the European social model. It did not produce a real consensus and reached few conclusions that were not banal.

The Germans, Dutch and British were instrumental within the IGC in insisting that reference to 'employment' was coupled with 'competitiveness' — and that the 'full' employment of the unreconstructed socialists was modified to 'high'.

63

French démarche

The socialist victory in the French elections on 1 June, on a manifesto promising job creation, gave a new twist to the debate. It also provoked the breakdown of the strong Franco-German coordination that had always been an important feature of previous meetings of the European Council. As if he had remembered little from the experience of the first Mitterrand government, Lionel Jospin proposed the creation of macro-economic conditions for sustainable growth; a review of public revenue and spending to pay for new job-intense investment; an examination by the EIB of a European 'growth fund'; the use of surplus ECSC funds to finance industrial research; and much else. The Germans would have none of it.

France continued to resist New Labour advocacy of flexibility, but eventually settled for 'responsive to economic change' (Article 109n). Promoting employment becomes, like monetary stability, a matter of common concern, but remains a national competence. Incentive measures are provided for, but no new funds.

The Treaty amendments

In the revised Article B, the phrase 'and a high level of employment' is a straight addition.

In the revised Article 2 employment and social protection have moved up from fourth place to second; and competitiveness has joined convergence.

The new indent to Article 3 sets up a coordinated employment strategy as an activity of the Community, the elements of which are set out in the ensuing new Title.

The main points of contention concerned the so-called incentive measures (Article 109r) which implied expenditure. Here the more sceptical governments insisted on the inclusion of a Declaration reiterating the principle of subsidiarity in the field of employment policy.

That employment has been accentuated as a feature of the Union's economic policy serves to emphasise the importance of the Council of economic and finance ministers (Ecofin) in guiding the economic policies of the member states under the third stage of EMU (Article 103). Ecofin will be responsible for the multilateral surveillance of the economic performance and measures of the member states, and can, by QMV, make policy recommendations to individual governments. The enhanced status afforded to employment matters increases the likelihood that Ecofin will assume eventually the character of an economic policy-making cabinet.

The new Employment Committee of Amsterdam was conceived by the Swedes and their supporters to be a counter-balance to the Economic and Financial Committee of Maastricht (Article 109c(2)), although they appeared to have few concrete ideas about what it should do. The British and like-minded will be planning to use the new Employment Committee to spread best practice in the area of labour market flexibility.

Many of these changes made to the Treaty, then, are fairly cosmetic. The European Union after Amsterdam can do nothing about unemployment that it was not able to do beforehand. To hold out a false promise would be misleading; and to be genuine in the belief that the EU holds the answer to unemployment implies a more centralised fiscal policy than is envisaged in the EMU programme of Maastricht. The answer to structural unemployment lies mainly in the hands of the member states. However, the EMU project insists that measures are taken at the national level to curb excessive government spending deficits.

Amsterdam marks the substantial shift towards liberal opinion that has taken place since the Essen European Council decisions in December 1994. That the employment chapter speaks of 'adaptable workforce and labour markets responsive to economic change' is a positive thing for Economic and Monetary Union, which remains a vital driving force of European integration.

SOCIAL POLICY

NEW ARTICLE 117

(SEE ARTICLE 1 SOCIAL AGREEMENT)

The Community and the Member States, having in mind fundamental social rights such as those set out in the European Charter signed at Turin on 18 October 1961 and in the 1989 Community Charter of the Fundamental Social Rights of Workers, shall have as their objectives the promotion of employment, improved living and working conditions, so as to make possible their harmonisation while the improvement is being maintained, proper social protection, dialogue between management and labour, the development of human resources with a view to lasting high employment and the combating of exclusion.

To this end the Community and the Member States shall implement measures which take account of the diverse forms of national practices, in particular in the field of contractual relations, and the need to maintain the competitiveness of the Community economy.

They believe that such a development will ensue not only from the functioning of the common market, which will favour the harmonisation of social systems, but also from the procedures provided for in this Treaty and from the approximation of provisions laid down by law, regulation or administrative action.

NEW ARTICLE 118

(SEE ARTICLE 2 SOCIAL AGREEMENT)

1. With a view to achieving the objectives of Article 117, the Community shall support and complement the activities of the Member States in the following fields:

- improvement in particular of the working environment to protect workers' health and safety;

- working conditions;

- the information and consultation of workers;

- the integration of persons excluded from the labour market, without prejudice to Article 127;

- equality between men and women with regard to labour market opportunities and treatment at work.

2. To this end, the Council may adopt, by means of directives, minimum requirements for gradual implementation, having regard to the conditions and technical rules obtaining in each of the Member States. Such directives shall avoid imposing administrative, financial and legal constraints in a way which would hold back the creation and development of small and medium-sized undertakings.

The Council shall act in accordance with the procedure referred to in Article 189b after consulting the Economic and Social Committee.

The Council, acting in accordance with the same procedure, may adopt measures designed to encourage cooperation between Member States through initiatives aimed at improving knowledge, developing exchanges of information and best practices, promoting innovative approaches and evaluating experiences in order to combat social exclusion.

DECLARATION ON ARTICLE 118

It is understood that any expenditure under Article 118 of the Treaty establishing the European Community will fall within Heading 3 of the financial perspectives.

3. However, the Council shall act unanimously on a proposal from the Commission, after consulting the European Parliament and the Economic and Social Committee, in the following areas:

- social security and social protection of workers;

- protection of workers where their employment contract is terminated;

- representation and collective defence of the interests of workers and employers, including co-determination, subject to paragraph 6;

- conditions of employment for third-country nationals legally residing in Community territory;

- financial contributions for promotion of employment and job-creation, without prejudice to the provisions relating to the Social Fund.

4. A Member State may entrust management and labour, at their joint request, with the implementation of directives adopted pursuant to paragraphs 2 and 3.

In this case, it shall ensure that, no later than the date on which a directive must be transposed in accordance with Article 189, management and labour have introduced the necessary measures by agreement, the Member State concerned being required to take any necessary measure enabling it at any time to be in a position to guarantee the results imposed by that directive.

5. The provisions adopted pursuant to this Article shall not prevent any Member State from maintaining or introducing more stringent protective measures compatible with the Treaty.

6. The provisions of this Article shall not apply to pay, the right of association, the right to strike or the right to impose lock-outs.

DECLARATION ON ARTICLE 118(2)

The High Contracting Parties note that in the discussions on Article 118(2) of the Treaty establishing the European Community it was agreed that the Community does not intend, in laying down minimum requirements for the protection of the safety and health of employees, to discriminate in a manner unjustified by the circumstances against employees in small and medium-sized undertakings.

ARTICLE 118A

(SEE ARTICLE 3 SOCIAL AGREEMENT)

1. The Commission shall have the task of promoting the consultation of management and labour at Community level and shall take any relevant measure to facilitate their dialogue by ensuring balanced support for the parties.

2. To this end, before submitting proposals in the social policy field, the Commission shall consult management and labour on the possible direction of Community action.

3. If, after such consultation, the Commission considers Community action advisable, it shall consult management and labour on the content of the envisaged proposal. Management and labour shall forward to the Commission an opinion or, where appropriate, a recommendation.

4. On the occasion of such consultation, management and labour may inform the Commission of their wish to initiate the process provided for in Article 118b. The duration of the procedure shall not exceed nine months, unless the management and labour concerned and the Commission decide jointly to extend it.

ARTICLE 118B

(SEE ARTICLE 4 SOCIAL AGREEMENT)

1. Should management and labour so desire, the dialogue between them at Community level may lead to contractual relations, including agreements.

2. Agreements concluded at Community level shall be implemented either in accordance with the procedures and practices specific to

management and labour and the Member States or, in matters covered by Article 118, at the joint request of the signatory parties, by a Council decision on a proposal from the Commission.

The Council shall act by qualified majority, except where the agreement in question contains one or more provisions relating to one of the areas referred to in Article 118(3), in which case it shall act unanimously.

DECLARATION ON ARTICLE 118B(2)

The High Contracting Parties declare that the first of the arrangements for application of the agreements between management and labour at Community level — referred to in Article 118b(2) of the Treaty establishing the European Community — will consist in developing, by collective bargaining according to the rules of each Member State, the content of the agreements, and that consequently this arrangement implies no obligation on the Member States to apply the agreements directly or to work out rules for their transposition, nor any obligation to amend national legislation in force to facilitate their implementation.

ARTICLE 118C

(SEE ARTICLE 5 SOCIAL AGREEMENT)

With a view to achieving the objectives of Article 117 and without prejudice to the other provisions of this Treaty, the Commission shall encourage cooperation between the Member States and facilitate the coordination of their action in all social policy fields under this chapter, particularly in matters relating to:

- employment;
- labour law and working conditions;
- basic and advanced vocational training;
- social security;
- prevention of occupational accidents and diseases;
- occupational hygiene;
- the rights of association and collective bargaining between employers and workers.

To this end, the Commission shall act in close contact with Member States by making studies, delivering opinions and arranging consultations both on problems arising at national level and on those of concern to international organisations.

Before delivering the opinions provided for in this Article, the Commission shall consult the Economic and Social Committee.

ARTICLE 119

(SEE ARTICLE 6 SOCIAL AGREEMENT)

1. Each Member State shall ensure that the principle of equal pay for male and female workers for equal work or work of equal value is applied.

2. For the purpose of this Article, 'pay' means the ordinary basic or minimum wage or salary and any other consideration, whether in cash or in kind, which the worker receives directly or indirectly, in respect of his employment, from his employer.

Equal pay without discrimination based on sex means:

(a) that pay for the same work at piece rates shall be calculated on the basis of the same unit of measurement;

(b) that pay for work at time rates shall be the same for the same job.

3. The Council, acting in accordance with the procedure referred to in Article 189b, and after consulting the Economic and Social Committee, shall adopt measures to ensure the application of the principle of equal opportunities and equal treatment of men and women in matters of employment and occupation, including the principle of equal pay for equal work or work of equal value.

4. With a view to ensuring full equality in practice between men and women in working life, the principle of equal treatment shall not prevent any Member State from maintaining or adopting measures providing for specific advantages in order to make it easier for the underrepresented sex to pursue a vocational activity or to prevent or compensate for disadvantages in professional careers.

DECLARATION ON ARTICLE 119(4)

When adopting measures referred to in Article 119(4) of the Treaty establishing the European Community, Member States should, in the first instance, aim at improving the situation of women in working life.

ARTICLE 119A

(SEE ARTICLE 120 OF TREATY ESTABLISHING THE EUROPEAN COMMUNITY)

Member States shall endeavour to maintain the existing equivalence between paid holiday schemes.

ARTICLE 120

(SEE ARTICLE 7 SOCIAL AGREEMENT)

The Commission shall draw up a report each year on progress in achieving the objectives of Article 117, including the demographic situation in the Community. It shall forward the report to the European Parliament, the Council and the Economic and Social Committee.

The European Parliament may invite the Commission to draw up reports on particular problems concerning the social situation.

Commentary
Social policy regained

If one of the main objectives of Amsterdam was to resolve some of the worst problems of Maastricht, nowhere was it more successful than in the field of social policy. The change of government in the United Kingdom allowed the full incorporation of the Agreement *à onze* of Maastricht into the main social policy chapter of the Treaty (Title VIII). The notorious Social Protocol of Maastricht is abolished, to the great satisfaction of the institutions and of all member states. The abolition of the Social Protocol had been one of the few concrete issues with a European dimension to emerge in the course of the British general election campaign: John Major's heavy defeat made it inevitable that his most vaunted achievement would be overturned.

However, it would be a mistake to think that agreement on the Treaty amendment signified a deeper consensus about the social dimension of the European Union. The UK Labour government may wish to play a full part in the debates in the Council about whether to adopt more social policy directives; but it is not willing to see a wide extension of the social dimension. While the British now accept that there has to be a common base of social rights for all citizens, and are prepared to allow an enhanced role for the social partners, they will resist over-regulation, and will deploy the principle of subsidiarity to kill draft directives that threaten labour market flexibility.

The Amsterdam European Council committed itself to a special summit meeting on employment in the Autumn of 1997 at which these underlying tensions are certain to emerge.

The Social Protocol so far

Only two pieces of legislation have so far been passed under the social policy Agreement of Maastricht — the Works Council Directive (September 1994) and the Parental Leave Directive (March 1996). The former has not proved to be a conspicuous success, at least as far as Renault is concerned, where the profitable plant at Vilvoorde in Belgium was closed by the French board of directors without regard to the appropriate consultation.

Discussions within the Commission itself reflect the wider debate about the future of the European social model. Sir Leon Brittan is thought to be contesting many of the draft proposals floated by DG V and its Swedish Director-General, which include measures concerning the following:

72

- worker participation within management under European company law

- extension of the working time directive to transport workers and junior doctors

- social security for non-EU migrant workers

- extension of worker consultation rights to small and medium-sized firms

- health and safety for scaffolding and explosive workers

- ILO standards for home working.

The social partners — comprising UNICE, the employers' federation, ETUC, the trade unions and CEEP, public enterprises — are seeking to reach prior agreement (according to new Article 118b) on insisting on the employers' burden of proof in the area of sex discrimination. The Council is also considering consolidation of regulations concerning part-time work.

Amsterdam

In general the Treaty of Amsterdam adopted whole and unchanged the clauses of the Maastricht Agreement on social policy within the main body of the Treaty. In Article 119 concerning equal pay for work of equal value full QMV and co-decision were introduced. Elsewhere, however, Britain refused to allow extension of QMV within the social chapter, despite the willingness of some to contemplate an end to unanimity in matters affecting social security (Article 118(3)). Instead, a new Article 118c gave to the European Commission the task of coordinating member states' policies relating to employment, labour law, social security and collective bargaining — a big new responsibility.

New indent (3) to Article 119 gave impetus to the institutions to make progress in the field of equal treatment of men and women; and Article 119(4) creates opportunities for positive discrimination at the level of the member state. Most member states were resolved not to make rash spending commitments, however, and reference to measures for the elderly and disabled were dropped from Article 118(2).

Overall, the new social chapter reflects the same shift to liberal opinion that was evident in the new employment chapter above.

ENVIRONMENT

Amended seventh recital of the Preamble to the Treaty on European Union

Determined to promote economic and social progress for their peoples, taking into account the principle of sustainable development and within the context of the accomplishment of the internal market and of reinforced cohesion and environmental protection, and to implement policies ensuring that advances in economic integration are accompanied by parallel progress in other fields,

Amend Article B of the Treaty on European Union

The Union shall set itself the following objectives:

• to promote economic and social progress and a high level of employment and to achieve balanced and sustainable development, in particular through the creation of an area without internal frontiers, through the strengthening of economic and social cohesion and through the establishment of economic and monetary union, ultimately including a single currency in accordance with the provisions of this Treaty;

New Article 2 of the Treaty establishing the European Community

The Community shall have as its task, by establishing a common market and an economic and monetary union and by implementing common policies or activities referred to in Articles 3 and 3a, to promote throughout the Community a harmonious, balanced and sustainable development of economic activities, a high level of employment and of social protection, equality between men and women, sustainable and non-inflationary growth, a high degree of competitiveness and convergence of economic performance, a high level of protection and improvement of the quality of the environment, the raising of the standard of living and quality of life, and economic and social cohesion and solidarity among Member States.

INTEGRATION OF ENVIRONMENTAL PROTECTION INTO ALL SECTORAL POLICIES

NEW ARTICLE 3C

Environmental protection requirements must be integrated into the definition and implementation of Community policies and activities referred to in Article 3, in particular with a view to promoting sustainable development.

DECLARATION ON ENVIRONMENTAL IMPACT ASSESSMENTS

The Conference notes that the Commission undertakes to prepare environmental impact assessment studies when making proposals which may have significant environmental implications.

ARTICLE 100A(3), (4) AND (5) SHALL BE REPLACED BY THE FOLLOWING

3. The Commission, in its proposals envisaged in paragraph 1 concerning health, safety, environmental protection and consumer protection, will take as a base a high level of protection, taking account in particular of any new development based on scientific facts. Within their respective powers, the European Parliament and the Council will also seek to achieve this objective.

4. If, after the adoption by the Council or by the Commission of a harmonisation measure, a Member State deems it necessary to maintain national provisions on grounds of major needs referred to in Article 36, or relating to the protection of the environment or the working environment, it shall notify the Commission of these provisions as well as the grounds for maintaining them.

5. Moreover, without prejudice to the previous subparagraph, if, after the adoption by the Council or by the Commission of a harmonisation measure, a Member State deems it necessary to introduce national provisions based on new scientific evidence relating to the protection of the environment or the working environment on grounds of a problem specific to that Member State arising after the adoption of the harmonisation measure, it shall notify the Commission of the envisaged provisions as well as the grounds for introducing them.

6. The Commission shall, within six months of the notifications as referred to in paragraphs 4 and 5, approve or reject the national provisions involved after having verified that they are not a means of arbitrary discrimination or a disguised restriction on trade between Member States and that they shall not constitute an obstacle to the functioning of the internal market.

In the absence of a decision by the Commission within this period the national provisions referred to in paragraphs 4 and 5 shall be deemed to have been approved.

When justified by the complexity of the matter and in the absence of danger for human health, the Commission may notify the Member State concerned that the period referred to in this paragraph may be extended for a further period of up to six months.

7. When, pursuant to paragraph 6, a Member State is authorised to maintain or introduce national provisions derogating from a harmonisation measure, the Commission shall immediately examine whether to propose an adaptation to that measure.

8. When a Member State raises a specific problem on public health in a field which has been the subject of prior harmonisation measures, it shall bring it to the attention of the Commission which shall immediately examine whether to propose appropriate measures to the Council.

9. By way of derogation from the procedure laid down in Articles 169 and 170, the Commission and any Member State may bring the matter directly before the Court of Justice if it considers that another Member State is making improper use of the powers provided for in this Article.

10. The harmonisation measures referred to above shall, in appropriate cases, include a safeguard clause authorising the Member States to take, for one or more of the non-economic reasons referred to in Article 36, provisional measures subject to a Community control procedure.

Commentary
Environment policy

In general, the Treaty of Amsterdam makes the environment more visible to EU policy-makers. The draftsmen of the Maastricht Treaty had settled on the curious phraseology 'sustainable growth respecting the environment', suggesting a less than complete understanding of the concept of sustainable development. The new Article 2 now rectifies that, and 'sustainable development' is inscribed within both the Preamble and Article B.

The key, however, is to integrate the environmental dimension into every aspect of EU policy-making, and to eliminate inconsistencies across policy sectors.

New Article 3c attempts to do this, and is a significant improvement on the previously rather obscure injunction in old Article 130r(2), which is adjusted accordingly.

The accompanying Declaration about environmental impact assessment is an attempt by the Commission to get around the opposition of the UK government and others to a stalled draft directive on the matter.

Although the European Parliament has been granted powers of co-decision over certain objectives of environmental policy (Article 130s(1)), on the insistence of the Germans there was no extension of QMV in the Council; and the Parliament remains on the periphery in matters concerning environmental taxation, planning, the management of water resources and energy supply (Article 130s(2)). MEPs will have to work hard to ensure the greening of the European Union.

The 'environmental guarantee'

The Treaty of Amsterdam also makes it easier for member states to maintain and introduce more stringent measures in the field of the environment than those set by the EU. There is therefore a risk of protectionism, under the guise of environmental policy, damaging the single market.

Article 100a(5) stipulates that unilateral action must be based on new scientific evidence specific to the member state concerned. The Commission, in considering whether to allow the derogation, must also reassess the original EU harmonisation measure (Article 100a(8)). In this way the environmentally more advanced Nordic countries are seeking to upgrade EU policy. The Commission is happy to be the sole gate-keeper.

The strengthening of the environmental guarantee could be significant in affecting Danish public opinion to vote yes to the Amsterdam Treaty. But the tension between the single market purists (to be found in the Commission's DG III and DG XV) and those who take a more pragmatic view of the development of strong EU environmental policies (DG XI) is bound to grow. And the numerous green pressure groups will continue to campaign for a further reinforcement of the environmental guarantee.

The imminence of enlargement to countries with an appalling record of environmental degradation may be the spur that EU environmental policy needs.

PUBLIC HEALTH AND CONSUMER PROTECTION

AMENDED ARTICLE 129

1. A high level of human health protection shall be ensured in the definition and implementation of all Community policies and activities.

Community action, which shall complement national policies, shall be directed towards improving public health, preventing human illness and diseases, and obviating sources of danger to human health. Such action shall cover the fight against the major health scourges, by promoting research into their causes, their transmission and their prevention, as well as health information and education.

The Community shall complement the Member States' action in reducing drugs related health damage, including information and prevention.

2. The Community shall encourage cooperation between the Member States in the areas referred to in this Article and, if necessary, lend support to their action.

Member States shall, in liaison with the Commission, coordinate among themselves their policies and programmes in the areas referred to in paragraph 1. The Commission may, in close contact with the Member States, take any useful initiative to promote such coordination.

3. The Community and the Member States shall foster cooperation with third countries and the competent international organisations in the sphere of public health.

4. The Council, acting in accordance with the procedure referred to in Article 189b, after consulting the Economic and Social Committee and the Committee of the Regions shall contribute to the achievement of the objectives referred to in this Article through adopting:

(a) measures setting high standards of quality and safety of organs and substances of human origin, blood and blood derivatives; these measures shall not prevent any Member State from maintaining or introducing more stringent protective measures;

(b) by way of derogation from Article 43, measures in the veterinary and phytosanitary fields which have as their direct objective the protection of public health;

(c) incentive measures designed to protect and improve human health, excluding any harmonisation of the laws and regulations of the Member States.

The Council, acting by a qualified majority on a proposal from the Commission, may also adopt recommendations for the purposes set out in this Article.

5. Community action in the field of public health shall fully respect the responsibilities of the Member States for the organisation and delivery of health services and medical care. In particular, measures referred to in paragraph 4(a) shall not affect national provisions on the donation or medical use of organs and blood.

AMENDED ARTICLE 129A

1. In order to promote the interests of consumers and to ensure a high level of consumer protection, the Community shall contribute to protecting the health, safety and economic interests of consumers, as well as to promoting their right to information, education and to organise themselves in order to safeguard their interests.

2. Consumer protection requirements shall be taken into account in defining and implementing other Community policies and activities.

3. The Community shall contribute to the attainment of the objectives referred to in paragraph 1 through:

(a) measures adopted pursuant to Article 100a in the context of the completion of the internal market;

(b) measures which support, supplement and monitor the policy pursued by the Member States.

4. The Council, acting in accordance with the procedure referred to in Article 189b and after consulting the Economic and Social Committee, shall adopt the measures referred to in paragraph 3(b).

5. Measures adopted pursuant to paragraph 4 shall not prevent any Member State from maintaining or introducing more stringent protective measures. Such measures must be compatible with this Treaty. The Commission shall be notified of them.

Commentary
The healthy consumer

A relatively anodyne section of the Treaty in which the amendments sharpened the focus of the Maastricht provisions to refer more directly to the intra-EU trade in blood transfusion to combat the spread of HIV/AIDS. The need to protect the public from poisoning by the carcasses of BSE infected cows informed the revision to both Articles.

It is intended that the interests of the consumer will be more prominent in the minds of policy-makers, especially in food production, at all levels. The new legal base in Article 129(4) in veterinary and phytosanitary matters will have direct effect on the standards of public health of the citizen, whereas under Maastricht incentive measures only were anticipated.

SPECIAL INTERESTS

SERVICES OF GENERAL ECONOMIC INTEREST

NEW ARTICLE 7D

Without prejudice to Articles 77, 90 and 92, and given the place occupied by services of general economic interest in the shared values of the Union as well as their role in promoting social and territorial cohesion, the Community and the Member States, each within their respective powers and within the scope of application of this Treaty, shall take care that such services operate on the basis of principles and conditions which enable them to fulfil their missions.

DECLARATION ON ARTICLE 7D

The provisions of Article 7d of the Treaty establishing the European Community on public services shall be implemented with full respect for the jurisprudence of the Court of Justice, inter alia as regards the principles of equality of treatment, quality and continuity of such services.

PUBLIC SERVICE BROADCASTING

PROTOCOL ON THE SYSTEM OF PUBLIC BROADCASTING IN THE MEMBER STATES

THE HIGH CONTRACTING PARTIES

CONSIDERING that the system of public broadcasting in the Member States is directly related to the democratic, social and cultural needs of each society and to the need to preserve media pluralism;

HAVE AGREED upon the following interpretative provisions, which shall be annexed to the Treaty establishing the European Community,

The provisions of this Treaty shall be without prejudice to the competence of Member States to provide for the funding of public service broadcasting in so far as such funding is granted to broadcasting organisations for the fulfilment of the public service remit as conferred, defined and organised by each Member State, and that such funding does not affect trading conditions and competition in the Community to an extent which would be contrary to the common interest, while the realisation of the remit of that public service shall be taken into account.

GERMAN PUBLIC CREDIT INSTITUTIONS

DECLARATION ON PUBLIC CREDIT INSTITUTIONS IN GERMANY

The Conference notes the Commission's opinion to the effect that the Community's existing competition rules allow services of general economic interest provided by public credit institutions existing in Germany and the facilities granted to them to compensate for the costs connected with such services to be taken into account in full. In this context, the way in which Germany enables local authorities to carry out their task of making available in their regions a comprehensive and efficient financial infrastructure is a matter for the organisation of that Member State. Such facilities may not adversely affect the conditions of competition to an extent beyond that required in order to perform these particular tasks and which is contrary to the interests of the Community.

The Conference recalls that the European Council has invited the Commission to examine whether similar cases exist in the other Member States, to apply as appropriate the same standards on similar cases and to inform the ECOFIN Council.

DECLARATION BY AUSTRIA AND LUXEMBOURG ON CREDIT INSTITUTIONS

Austria and Luxembourg consider that the Declaration on public credit institutions in Germany also applies to credit institutions in Austria and Luxembourg with a comparable organisational structure.

Commentary
Vested Interests

This curious clutch of provisions stem from the lively concern of some mainland member states that an all-pervading force of liberalism is about to crush certain important vested interests of mostly state-owned public undertakings. There is no more stark exposure in the Treaty of the division, apparent in the early work of the Group of Reflection, between those who wish to regulate to protect public utilities and those who wish to make them competitive.

Article 90 of the Treaty gives the Commission power to intervene where it fears that member state governments are favouring with 'special or exclusive rights' their own monopolistic public utilities 'entrusted with the operation of services of general economic interest'. Its use is rare and controversial, especially where, as in the field of telecommunications, the Commission is determined to open up universal access for the citizen.

Articles 77 and 92 refer to dispensations in special circumstances to the general prohibition of state aid.

The new Article 7d will be fairly meaningless to those who have not appreciated how the concept of public service is cherished in certain member states, notably France. French and Belgian anxiety about foreign, and especially US, competition in media and broadcasting also inspires the Protocol on the protection of public service broadcasting. There has been an on-going dispute within the Council about the European content of broadcasting.

The Declaration on the protection of public credit institutions is a concession to Chancellor Kohl who was being harried before Amsterdam by the powerful vested interests of the Landesbanks. It is an unworthy addition to the EU Treaty and puts back the cause of liberalisation of banking services throughout the single market. It is difficult to see how the German banking sector emerges from this with its competitiveness enhanced.

Since the Amsterdam conference concluded, the Austrians and Luxembourgers have persuaded their partners that they too should be included. Hence the late addition of the second paragraph to the German Declaration, and their own.

A French proposal to protect state gas and electricity companies was dropped once it was acknowledged that there would be no strengthening of EU competence in the area of the energy supply industries. And another French proposal to rewrite Article 90 entirely to allow for positive discrimination in favour of the public sector was also defeated.

The European Commission will need to work hard to stop the suspension of competition policy to public sector finance throughout the Union. How to treat state-guaranteed banks promises to deliver a new set of problems to the management of the imminent euro regime.

CITIZENSHIP, TRAVEL, REGIONS AND ANIMALS

CITIZENSHIP OF THE UNION

AMENDED ARTICLE 8(1)

1. Citizenship of the Union is hereby established. Every person holding the nationality of a Member State shall be a citizen of the Union. Citizenship of the Union shall complement and not replace national citizenship.

AMENDED ARTICLE 8A(2)

2. The Council may adopt provisions with a view to facilitating the exercise of the rights referred to in paragraph 1; save as otherwise provided in this Treaty, the Council shall act in accordance with the procedure referred to in Article 189b. The Council shall act unanimously throught this procedure.

IN ARTICLE 8D THE FOLLOWING SHALL BE ADDED AS A THIRD PARAGRAPH

Every citizen of the Union may write to any of the institutions or bodies referred to in this Article or in Article 4 in one of the languages mentioned in Article 248 and have an answer in the same language.

CULTURE

AMENDED ARTICLE 128(4)

4. The Community shall take cultural aspects into account in its action under other provisions of this Treaty, in particular in order to respect and to promote the diversity of its cultures.

NEW RECITAL IN THE PREAMBLE TO THE TREATY ESTABLISHING THE EUROPEAN COMMUNITY

DETERMINED to promote the development of the highest possible level of knowledge for their peoples through a wide access to education and its continuous updating.

VOLUNTARY SERVICE

DECLARATION ON VOLUNTARY SERVICE ACTIVITIES

The Conference recognises the important contribution made by voluntary service activities to developing social solidarity.

The Community will encourage the European dimension of voluntary organisations with particular emphasis on the exchange of information and experiences as well as on the participation of the young and the elderly in voluntary work.

SPORT

DECLARATION ON SPORT

The Conference emphasises the social significance of sport, in particular its role in forging identity and bringing people together. The Conference therefore calls on the bodies of the European Union to listen to sports associations when important questions affecting sport are at issue. In this connection, special consideration should be given to the particular characteristics of amateur sport.

ANIMAL WELFARE

PROTOCOL ON IMPROVED PROTECTION AND RESPECT FOR THE WELFARE OF ANIMALS

THE HIGH CONTRACTING PARTIES,

DESIRING to ensure improved protection and respect for the welfare of animals as sentient beings;

HAVE AGREED upon the following provision which shall be annexed to the Treaty establishing the European Community,

In formulating and implementing the Community's agriculture, transport, internal market and research policies, the Community and the Member States shall pay full regard to the welfare requirements of animals, while respecting the legislative or administrative provisions and customs of the Member States relating in particular to religious rites, cultural traditions and regional heritage.

Commentary
How to treat citizens and animals

The amended Article 8 states the obvious — thereby addressing a flaw in the Maastricht Treaty which failed to say that European Union citizenship is a supplement to and not a substitute for national citizenship. This worried, in particular, the Danes.

Co-decision is brought in for freedom of movement measures — although unanimity will still apply in the Council (Article 8a(2)). The same anomalous procedure will apply for social security for migrant workers (Article 51) and the recognition of professional qualifications (Article 57(2)). The German government, in particular, was anxious at Amsterdam to protect its professions.

The addition to Article 8d was at the behest of language-torn Belgium, which was keen to have explicit recognition of the use of the twelve official languages of the EU.

Belgium was also responsible for initiating the amendment to Article 128(4).

The importance of the voluntary sector was highlighted in the run up to Amsterdam by a number of leading federalists. Their proposal was for the establishment of an EU citizens' voluntary service, and was supported especially by the Spanish, who have a high profile on citizenship issues. The resulting Declaration, however, is only a weak reflection of that proposal.

The appearance of ubiquitous sport in the Treaty was fairly inevitable at a time when the leaders showed very little evidence of self-restraint.

Similarly, the Protocol on 'sentient beings', which came from the British, who love animals. It effectively supersedes a similar Declaration of the Maastricht Treaty; but how this implant accords with the UK's vaunted rigour on subsidiarity is not entirely clear.

NETWORKS AND ISLANDS

TRANS-EUROPEAN NETWORKS

AMENDED THIRD INDENT OF ARTICLE 129c(1)

In order to achieve the objectives referred to in Article 129b, the Community:

- may support projects of common interest supported by Member States, which are identified in the framework of guidelines referred to in the first indent, particularly through feasibility studies, loan guarantees or interest rate subsidies; ...

ISLAND REGIONS

AMENDED SECOND PARAGRAPH OF ARTICLE 130a

In particular, the Community shall aim at reducing disparities between the levels of development of the various regions and the backwardness of the least favoured regions or islands, including rural areas.

DECLARATION ON ISLAND REGIONS

The Conference recognises that island regions suffer from structural handicaps linked to their island status, the permanence of which impairs their economic and social development.

The Conference accordingly acknowledges that Community legislation must take account of these handicaps and that specific measures may be taken, where justified, in favour of these regions in order to integrate them better into the internal market on fair conditions.

OUTERMOST REGIONS

AMENDED ARTICLE 227(2)

2. The provisions of the Treaty establishing the European Community shall apply to the French overseas departments, the Azores, Madeira and the Canary Islands.

However, taking account of the structural social and economic situation of the French overseas departments, the Azores, Madeira and the Canary Islands, which is compounded by their remoteness, insularity, small size, difficult topography and climate, economic dependence on a few products, the permanence and combination of which severely restrain their development, the Council, acting by a qualified majority on a proposal from the Commission and after consulting the European

Parliament, shall adopt specific measures aimed, in particular, at laying down the conditions of application of the present Treaty to those regions, including common policies.

The Council shall, when adopting the relevant measures referred to in the previous subparagraph, take into account areas such as customs and trade policies, fiscal policy, free zones, agriculture and fisheries policies, conditions for supply of raw materials and essential consumer goods, State aids and conditions of access to structural funds and to horizontal Community programmes.

The Council shall adopt the measures referred to in the second subparagraph taking into account the special characteristics and constraints of the outermost regions without undermining the integrity and the coherence of the Community legal order, including the internal market and common policies.

OVERSEAS COUNTRIES AND TERRITORIES

DECLARATION ON THE OVERSEAS COUNTRIES AND TERRITORIES

The Conference recognises that the special arrangements for the association of the OCTs under Part Four of the Treaty establishing the European Community were designed for countries and territories that were numerous, covered vast areas and had large populations. The arrangements have changed little since 1957.

The Conference notes that there are today only 20 OCTs and that they are extremely scattered island territories with a total population of approximately 900,000. Moreover, most OCT lag far behind in structural terms, a fact linked to their particularly severe geographical and economic handicaps. In these circumstances, the special arrangements for association as they were conceived in 1957 can no longer deal effectively with the challenges of OCT development.

The Conference solemnly restates that the purpose of association is to promote the economic and social development of the countries and territories and to establish close economic relations between them and the Community as a whole.

The Conference invites the Council, acting in accordance with the provisions of Article 136 of the Treaty establishing the European Community, to review the association arrangements by February 2000, with the fourfold objective of:

• promoting the economic and social development of the OCTs more effectively;

• developing economic relations between the OCTs and the European Union;

• taking greater account of the diversity and specific characteristics of the individual OCTs, including aspects relating to freedom of establishment;

• ensuring that the effectiveness of the financial instrument is improved.

Commentary
Networks and the Periphery

The implementation of the EU's programme of Trans-European Networks has been impaired by the difficulty of creating effective public-private partnerships combining management, entrepreneurship and adequate finance. Jacques Delors, as President of the Commission before 1995, advanced the idea of European Union bonds that would assist the implementation of TENs. The Council of finance ministers has continued to oppose not only an EU bond flotation but also any meaningful expenditure from the EU budget on the TENs projects except by way of the EIB. The European Council at Amsterdam resolved this dispute in favour of the Commission by replacing the original wording of Article 129c(1) — 'may support the financial efforts made by Member States' — with 'may support projects of common interest supported by Member States'. This creates the legal base for more financial innovation at Community level.

The provisions regarding the special status of island regions were proposed by Greece, and will allow the Commission to propose integrated packages for islands.

The amendment to Article 227(2) has the effect of adding the Atlantic archipelagos of Spain and Portugal into the category of the French overseas departments. It effectively supersedes a similar Declaration of the Maastricht Treaty.

The final Declaration commits the Union to a review of the status and condition of its Overseas Countries and Territories.

CUSTOMS, FRAUD AND FIGURES

STRENGTHENING CUSTOMS COOPERATION

NEW TITLE VIIA ON CUSTOMS COOPERATION

ARTICLE 116

Within the scope of application of this Treaty, the Council, acting in accordance with the procedure referred to in Article 189b, shall take measures in order to strengthen customs cooperation between Member States and between the latter and the Commission. These measures shall not concern the application of national criminal law and the national administration of justice.

COUNTERING FRAUD AFFECTING THE FINANCIAL INTERESTS OF THE COMMUNITY

AMENDED ARTICLE 209A

1. The Community and the Member States shall counter fraud and any other illegal activities affecting the financial interests of the Community through measures to be taken in accordance with this Article, which shall act as a deterrent and be such as to afford effective protection in the Member States.

2. Member States shall take the same measures to counter fraud affecting the financial interests of the Community as they take to counter fraud affecting their own financial interests.

3. Without prejudice to other provisions of this Treaty, the Member States shall coordinate their action aimed at protecting the financial interests of the Community against fraud. To this end they shall organise, together with the Commission, close and regular cooperation between the competent authorities.

4. The Council, acting in accordance with the procedure referred to in Article 189b, after consulting the Court of Auditors, shall adopt the necessary measures in the fields of the prevention of and fight against fraud affecting the financial interests of the Community with a view to affording effective and equivalent protection in the Member States. These measures shall not concern the application of national criminal law and the national administration of justice.

5. The Commission, in cooperation with Member States, shall each year submit to the Council and to the European Parliament a report on the measures taken for the implementation of this Article.

STATISTICS

NEW ARTICLE 213A

1. Without prejudice to the provisions of Article 5 of the Protocol on the Statute of the European System of Central Banks and of the European Central Bank, the Council, acting in accordance with Article 189b, shall adopt measures for the production of statistics where necessary for the performance of the activities of the Community.

2. The production of Community statistics shall conform to impartiality, reliability, objectivity, scientific independence, cost-effectiveness and statistical confidentiality; it shall not entail excessive burdens on economic operators.

Commentary
Fraud and Customs

The new Article on customs cooperation aims to stimulate more effective cooperation between relevant government departments of the member states and is consonant with the creation of the area of freedom, security and justice.

Both customs matters and the fight against fraud were previously under the third pillar. Amsterdam has transposed them (except for their criminal law aspects) to the first pillar, and full co-decision will apply. The legal base is consolidated and the focus on embezzlement of EU funds has sharpened. This is significant progress.

Another new legal base is added to the Treaty to allow for the uniform production of statistics. This will benefit proper accountancy of EU activities, and, accordingly, financial control.

These three items all contribute in a modest manner to the deepening of the Union in preparation for its enlargement.

SUBSIDIARITY

The HIGH CONTRACTING PARTIES

DETERMINED to establish the conditions for the application of the principles of subsidiarity and proportionality enshrined in Article 3b of the Treaty establishing the European Community with a view to defining more precisely the criteria for applying them and to ensure their strict observance and consistent implementation by all institutions;

WISHING to ensure that decisions are taken as closely as possible to the citizens of the Union;

TAKING ACCOUNT of the Interinstitutional Agreement of 28 October 1993 between the European Parliament, the Council and the Commission on procedures for implementing the principle of subsidiarity;

HAVE CONFIRMED that the conclusions of the Birmingham European Council on 16 October 1992 and the overall approach to the application of the subsidiarity principle agreed by the European Council meeting in Edinburgh on 11-12 December 1992, will continue to guide the action of the Union's institutions as well as the development of the application of the principle of subsidiarity, and, for this purpose, have agreed on the following provisions which shall be annexed to the Treaty establishing the European Community:

1. In exercising the powers conferred on it, each institution shall ensure that the principle of subsidiarity is complied with. It shall also ensure compliance with the principle of proportionality, according to which any action by the Community shall not go beyond what is necessary to achieve the objectives of the Treaty.

2. The application of the principles of subsidiarity and proportionality shall respect the general provisions and the objectives of the Treaty, particularly as regards the maintaining in full of the acquis communautaire and the institutional balance; it shall not affect the principles developed by the Court of Justice regarding the relationship between national and Community law, and it should take into account Article F(4) of the Treaty on European Union, according to which 'the Union shall provide itself with the means necessary to attain its objectives and carry through its policies'.

3. The principle of subsidiarity does not call into question the powers conferred on the European Community by the Treaty, as interpreted by the Court of Justice. The criteria referred to in the second subparagraph of Article 3b shall relate to areas for which the Community does not have exclusive competence. The principle of subsidiarity provides a

guide as to how those powers are to be exercised at the Community level. Subsidiarity is a dynamic concept and should be applied in the light of the objectives set out in the Treaty. It allows Community action within the limits of its powers to be expanded where circumstances so require, and conversely, to be restricted or discontinued where it is no longer justified.

4. For any proposed Community legislation, the reasons on which it is based shall be stated with a view to justifying that it complies with the principles of subsidiarity and proportionality; the reasons for concluding that a Community objective can be better achieved by the Community must be substantiated by qualitative or, wherever possible, quantitative indicators.

5. For Community action to be justified, both aspects of the subsidiarity principle shall be met: the objectives of the proposed action cannot be sufficiently achieved by Member States' action in the framework of their national constitutional system and can therefore be better achieved by action on the part of the Community.

The following guidelines should be used in examining whether the above mentioned condition is fulfilled:

- the issue under consideration has transnational aspects which cannot be satisfactorily regulated by action by Member States;

- actions by Member States alone or lack of Community action would conflict with the requirements of the Treaty (such as the need to correct distortion of competition or avoid disguised restrictions on trade or strengthen economic and social cohesion) or would otherwise significantly damage Member States' interests;

- action at Community level would produce clear benefits by reason of its scale or effects compared with action at the level of the Member States.

6. The form of Community action shall be as simple as possible, consistent with satisfactory achievement of the objective of the measure and the need for effective enforcement. The Community shall legislate only to the extent necessary. Other things being equal, directives should be preferred to regulations and framework directives to detailed measures. Directives as provided for in Article 189, while binding upon each Member State to which they are addressed as to the result to be achieved, shall leave to the national authorities the choice of form and methods.

7. Regarding the nature and the extent of Community action, Community measures should leave as much scope for national decision as possible, consistent with securing the aim of the measure and observing the requirements of the Treaty. While respecting Community law, care

should be taken to respect well established national arrangements and the organisation and working of Member States legal systems. Where appropriate and subject to the need for proper enforcement, Community measures should provide Member States with alternative ways to achieve the objectives of the measures.

8. Where the application of the principle of subsidiarity leads to no action being taken by the Community, Member States are required in their action to comply with the general rules laid down in Article 5 of the Treaty, by taking all appropriate measures to ensure fulfilment of their obligations under the Treaty and by abstaining from any measure which could jeopardise the attainment of the objectives of the Treaty.

9. Without prejudice to its right of initiative, the Commission should:

- except in cases of particular urgency or confidentiality, consult widely before proposing legislation and, wherever appropriate, publish consultation documents;

- justify the relevance of its proposals with regard to the principle of subsidiarity; whenever necessary, the explanatory memorandum accompanying a proposal will give details in this respect. The financing of Community action in whole or in part from the Community budget shall require an explanation;

- take duly into account the need for any burden, whether financial or administrative, falling upon the Community, national governments, local authorities, economic operators and citizens, to be minimised and proportionate to the objective to be achieved;

- submit an annual report to the European Council, the Council and the European Parliament on the application of Article 3b of the Treaty. This annual report shall also be sent to the Committee of the Regions and to the Economic and Social Committee.

10. The European Council shall take account of the Commission report referred to in the fourth indent of point 9, within the report on the progress achieved by the Union which it is required to submit to the European Parliament in accordance with Article D of the Treaty on European Union.

11. While fully observing the procedures applicable, the European Parliament and the Council shall, as an integral part of the overall examination of Commission proposals, consider their consistency with Article 3b. This concerns the original Commission proposal as well as amendments which the European Parliament and the Council envisage making to the proposal.

12. In the course of the procedures referred to in Articles 189b and 189c, the European Parliament shall be informed of the Council's

position on the application of Article 3b, by way of a statement of the reasons which led the Council to adopt its common position. The Council shall inform the European Parliament of the reasons on the basis of which all or part of a Commission proposal is deemed to be inconsistent with Article 3b of the Treaty.

13. Compliance with the principle of subsidiarity shall be reviewed in accordance with the rules laid down by this Treaty.

DECLARATION RELATING TO THE PROTOCOL ON THE APPLICATION OF THE PRINCIPLES OF SUBSIDIARITY AND PROPORTIONALITY

The High Contracting Parties confirm, on the one hand, Declaration No. 19 annexed to the Treaty establishing the European Community on the implementation of Community law and, on the other, the conclusions of the Essen European Council stating that the administrative implementation of Community law shall in principle be the responsibility of the Member States in accordance with their constitutional arrangements. This shall not affect the supervisory, monitoring and implementing powers of the Community Institutions as provided under Article 145 and 155 of the Treaty establishing the European Community.

DECLARATION BY GERMANY, AUSTRIA AND BELGIUM ON SUBSIDIARITY

It is taken for granted by the German, Austrian and Belgian governments that action by the European Community in accordance with the principle of subsidiarity not only concerns the Member States but also their entities to the extent that they have their own law-making powers conferred on them under national constitutional law.

Commentary
Subsidiarity

This important Protocol is the definitive statement about the principle of subsidiarity, what it is and how it should be applied. In seeking to demonstrate how and when the rule of subsidiarity must be deployed, the Amsterdam Protocol draws on Article 3b of the Treaty of Maastricht, the statements of the two European Councils under the UK presidency in 1992 and the benefit of experience since.

Article 3b says:

'The Community shall act within the limits of the powers conferred upon it by this Treaty and of the objectives assigned to it therein.

'In areas which do not fall within its exclusive competence, the Community shall take action, in accordance with the principle of subsidiarity, only if and in so far as the objectives of the proposed action cannot be sufficiently achieved by the Member States and can therefore, by reason of the scale or effects of the proposed action, be better achieved by the Community.

'Any action by the Community shall not go beyond what is necessary to achieve the objectives of the Treaty'.

The application of Article 3b goes to the heart of the constitutional debate about the future of European Union, and is deserving of a detailed excursion.

Origins of subsidiarity

The origins of subsidiarity lie deep within Catholic social doctrine and federal political thought. The concept first surfaced explicitly in the European Commission's submission to the Tindemans enquiry on the future of the European Community in 1975. It proposed that a new constitution should be drawn up to found 'European Union', and continued:

'... European Union is not to give birth to a centralising super-state. Consequently, and in accordance with the *principe de subsidiarité*, the Union will be given responsibility only for those matters which the Member States are no longer capable of dealing with efficiently ... Hence, the competence of the Union will be limited to what is assigned to it, meaning that its fields of competence will be specified in the Act of Constitution, other matters being left to the Member States... Of course, in deciding on the Union's competence, application of the *principe de subsidiarité* is restricted by the fact that the Union must be given extensive enough competency for its cohesion to be ensured'. [1]

The Commission went on to explain that, as in German Basic Law, there were three types of competence: exclusive, concurrent and potential. With concurrent powers, the Union 'would assert its authority only when it felt the need' — by acting only with regard to certain aspects, or by passing outline legislation with actions specified for the Union and for member state governments, leaving the latter free to act in all unspecified matters. In a telling coda, the Commission asked how consistency was to be assured between Union and member state level action.

> 'The answer is that Union law takes precedence over national law. Clearly, coordination between the two types of action cannot be provided simply by legal texts or by establishing procedures: it must also rest at any given time on the balance of the political forces involved.' [2]

The Tindemans Report suggested that the building of European Union required the adoption of four criteria to determine change: authority, efficiency, legitimacy and coherence. It did not repeat the term subsidiarity; nor did it go as far as the Commission in seeking the exercise of massive new powers at the Union level. But Tindemans still expected that the Union would seize the initiative when it found member states performing ineffectively and inefficiently. [3]

Tindemans was followed by the MacDougall Report on fiscal federalism, which identified three criteria for assessing the involvement of the EC: economies of scale, transnational effect and political, economic and social cohesion (although the term 'cohesion' was not used until the Single European Act). MacDougall favoured transfers of resources between member states and regions, orchestrated where necessary by the Community, rather than the development of a large scale public finance capability at the European level. [4]

The high tide of the federal project, so far, was the European Parliament's Draft Treaty on European Union in 1984, whose chief inspirer was the veteran Italian federalist Altiero Spinelli. It was here that 'subsidiarity' was used for the first time in English. The Preamble said:

> 'Intending to entrust common institutions, in accordance with the principle of subsidiarity, only with those powers required to complete successfully the tasks they may carry out more satisfactorily than the States acting independently'.

This means, effectively, that the powers of the Union are subsidiary to those of the member states. Spinelli, indeed, who had been imprisoned by Mussolini, saw subsidiarity as the way to check over-weening central authority. Articles 11 and 12 of the Draft Treaty sought to define each of the wide competences of the Union as either exclusive, concurrent or potential. Where the Treaty conferred concurrent competence, member states could continue to act until the Union did so; the Union could act only where it could do so 'more effectively', and particularly where the action had cross-border effects; and the Union's first action in a new field would take the form of an organic or framework law under whose auspices member states would then act to carry out Union law. (The term 'virtual competence' is perhaps a more accurate expression in English than 'concurrent'.) [5]

The Single European Act (1986) was a lesser creature than the Parliament had proposed but represented, nevertheless, a qualitative leap forward in the federalisation process. It assigned major new competences to the Community, set the objective of Economic and Monetary Union, and in many cases prescribed decision-taking in the Council by qualified majority vote. Although the term was not used, the growing influence of the principle of subsidiarity was plain to see — notably, in Article 130r.4 on environment policy, which stated that the Community 'shall take action ... to the extent to which the objectives ... can be attained better at Community level than at the level of the individual Member States'.

Concerned about the implications of the single market programme and about the growing diversity of the enlarging Community, President Delors had set up an enquiry under the distinguished federalist Tommaso Padoa-Schioppa. The report applied rigorously the principle of subsidiarity and recommended systemic reforms in the direction of greater decentralisation of Community policies, more selectivity in the choice of Community responsibilities and stronger powers for the Community institutions in some key areas such as monetary policy, competition and budgetary control. [6] Relentless harmonisation should be checked, even in social policy, except where there was clear transnational spillover; EC action should occur only on the basis of a cost/benefit analysis; the Community should frame member states' actions but not replace them.

The Treaty on European Union

The next step, at the instigation of Delors, was to write subsidiarity into the Treaty on European Union (1992), which also created the entity of EU citizenship and a Committee of the Regions to formalise consultation with regional and local authorities. In the run up to Maastricht, Valéry Giscard d'Estaing had produced a report for the European Parliament in which he attempted to spell out the distinction between exclusive and shared competence. He succeeded only in demonstrating the complexity of the European integration process, the rapidly expanding scope of the acquis communautaire and the essential ambiguity of subsidiarity. [7] In the event, the Treaty chose to follow the Commission's more pragmatic approach.

Article 3b contains, as well as the definition of subsidiarity, a reaffirmation of the traditional principle of assigned competence and a fresh definition of proportionality. The implied tendency to decentralisation was reinforced by Article A of the preamble of the Treaty, which said that 'decisions are taken as closely as possible to the citizen'. Article B appeared to seek to spread the application of the 'principle of subsidiarity as defined in Article 3b' to the achievement of all the objectives of the Union. In addition, Article K.3.2(b) provided that the Council may take joint action in the area of justice and interior affairs 'in so far as the objectives of the Union can be attained better by joint action than by Member States acting individually on account of the scale or effects of the action envisaged'.

What is curious is that the second indent of Article 3b appears to apply subsidiarity only to areas of concurrent competence, whereas the principle of proportionality or intensity of action (the third indent) applies also to exclusive competence. The inherent ambiguity of subsidiarity is compounded because, despite the now commonplace nature of the *political* distinction between the two, there is no explicit distinction drawn anywhere in the Treaty of Rome *in legal terms* between exclusive and non-exclusive competence.

Subsidiarity is a useful political expedient, but it makes sense in practical terms only when considered together with competency and proportionality. Article 3b is not about the allocation of competences but about how they should be exercised; and it does not affect the balance between the EU institutions but only between EU and state authorities. And despite much wishful thinking to the contrary, Article 3b refers only to the Union and member state governments, and cannot be applied to regional and local government without further Treaty amendment to that effect.

After the Maastricht Treaty had been signed, and on the basis of a draft from the Commission, the European Council at Edinburgh in December 1992, set out guidelines about how Article 3b should be applied, and also related it to the newly-fashionable concept of 'transparency'. [8] Subsidiarity was then articulated in all the Union's interinstitutional agreements and its application was seen certainly to affect the behaviour of the Commission, where self-restraint in drafting new legislation prevails, and in the Council, where all drafts are put to the subsidiarity test. Some draft measures have even been withdrawn, although there has been no large-scale repatriation of EC law, as many nationalists had hoped.

The 1996 IGC

The inclusion of subsidiarity in the Treaty on European Union was hailed (by the British) as a triumph of Anglo-Saxon diplomacy. The Conservative government brought forward proposals to entrench subsidiarity more firmly within the Treaty — ironically, a gesture that met with warm approval by the federalists to whom John Major's party was so bitterly opposed. But the UK Memorandum to the IGC of August 1996 was biased towards the exercise of powers at the level of the member state and against that of the Union. Its draft protocol said:

'In the exercise of its jurisdiction, the Court of Justice shall always have regard to the principle of subsidiarity. In particular, it shall be presumed that, in the absence of a clear contrary intention, the Community legislator intends to conserve the freedom of the Member States as far as possible. Accordingly, when faced with more than one possible interpretation of provisions of Community law, the Court shall, unless there is a clear contrary intention, prefer the interpretation which least constrains the freedom of the Member States'.

How to interpret, especially in a Europe of differentiated integration, which approach would impact least on each member state government, with their diverse national jurisdictions and legislative forms, was not explained.

The British concept of member state freedom from the regime of the European Union failed to attract supporters, even from those, such as the Austrians, who wanted a simplification of the subsidiarity rules and a greater role for national parliaments. The reaction of the Court of Justice itself is unrecorded.

The Group of Reflection had simply — and rather unhelpfully — defined subsidiarity as 'who does what?' — a question that immediately provoked strongly differing answers. Westendorp and his colleagues, fearing that the IGC would fail to resolve such elementary differences, took refuge in ambiguity: 'It is felt that the principle of subsidiarity should serve as a guide to the proper exercise of the powers shared between the Community and the member states and avoid their misuse either to excess or the contrary'.

Most member states retained a similarly ambivalent attitude to subsidiarity. Italy, for example, in its submission to the IGC, argued that, although 'adequate importance should be given to the principles of subsidiarity, proximity and proportionality, which respond to the double need of respecting national and local decision-making competencies and avoiding the dangers of an excess of regulations at the European level,' an 'excessive importance' attached to subsidiarity might weaken the Commission's right of initiative, break up the single market and threaten the integrity of EC law. [9]

France launched the idea of a 'high parliamentary council' made up of national deputies which 'would be consulted on the subsidiarity aspect and on any third pillar issue'. [10] But the French government sensibly redirected itself as soon as no support for the proposal was realised (other than from certain 'Euro-sceptics' in Britain).

The German and Scandinavian governments, for their part, chose to invoke subsidiarity in support of more 'nearness' or closeness of the EU institutions and procedures to the citizen. They were anxious that a stricter interpretation of subsidiarity would weaken EU competence in the social and environmental fields — an approach shared by the European Parliament, although MEPs also called subsidiarity in aid of their plea for more financial autonomy for the Union and the reform of the system of Community 'own resources'. [11]

The Dutch government trod a middle way between the British and continental approach. It took the view that 'the Union should put its own house in order through deregulation and subsidiarity before enlargement. [12] It complained that in the field of justice and home affairs subsidiarity was not being applied — in other words, that more should be done at the EU level. At the same time the Dutch criticised the Commission for failing to explain why regulations at European level were required, and the other institutions for failing to exercise adequate scrutiny. The Dutch proposed that a member state may be able to request a first reading 'admissibility' debate in Council, where the Commission's justification for the draft legislation and public responses from a fixed consultative period are aired — in public — before the measure is sent to the Council working groups. In case the British were too comforted by this proposal, the Dutch insisted that this procedure should not be used as a covert means of undermining the powers of either the Commission or the Court of Justice, which would continue to be eligible to hear appeals on the grounds of alleged breaches of subsidiarity in the normal way.

Before the British general election, the IGC did not progress very far. With regard to subsidiarity, there was consensus on leaving Article 3b intact. Only Austria and the Netherlands approved of the idea of a list of exclusive competences. Most opposed the British idea of attempting to write into the Treaty an article enforcing deregulation; of introducing 'sunset clauses' to time-limit EU legislation; of providing more Treaty articles that expressly limited EU powers, such as was the case for education, health and cultural affairs; of allowing the Council a preliminary decision on draft legislation on the grounds of subsidiarity; and of setting up a special high-level advisory committee of national parliamentarians to supervise the application of the subsidiarity rule. Most member states also opposed the UK's proposed protocol constraining the Court of Justice.

The Amsterdam Protocol

The new Protocol on Subsidiarity has at least two consequences. First, it confirms that both elements of Article 3b, subsidiarity and proportionality, must be taken together. Second, it makes it potentially more difficult for the Court of Justice to argue that although the interpretation of subsidiarity comes within its jurisidiction it is not in practice justiciable.

The renewed emphasis on the correct use of directives — binding as to results but permissive as to the member states' choice of form and method — is also to be welcomed. The Commission's obligation to use green papers, practised since 1992, is already serving to deepen the consultative element in the Union's law-making processes.

All in all, the Protocol on Subsidiarity is a useful compromise that, if the political will is there to exploit it, will continue to deepen the federal character of the European Union. Doubtless there will be frequent recourse to the text of this Protocol. One of the first areas of likely controversy on the grounds of subsidiarity is that of tax harmonisation.

TRANSPARENCY

AMENDED SECOND PARAGRAPH OF ARTICLE A OF THE TREATY ON EUROPEAN UNION

This Treaty marks a new stage in the process of creating an ever closer Union among the peoples of Europe, in which decisions are taken as openly as possible and as closely as possible to the citizen.

NEW ARTICLE 191A IN THE TREATY ESTABLISHING THE EUROPEAN COMMUNITY

1. Any citizen of the Union, and any natural or legal person residing or having its registered office in a Member State, shall have a right of access to European Parliament, Council and Commission documents, subject to the principles and the conditions to be defined in accordance with paragraphs 2 and 3.

2. General principles and limits on grounds of public or private interest governing this right of access to documents shall be determined by the Council, acting in accordance with the procedure referred to in Article 189b within two years of the entry into force of the Treaty.

3. Each institution referred to above shall elaborate in its own rules of procedure specific provisions regarding access to its documents.

DECLARATION ON ARTICLE 191A(1)

The Conference agrees that the principles and conditions referred to in Article 191a(1) of the Treaty establishing the European Community will allow a Member State to request the Commission or the Council not to communicate to third parties a document originating from that State without its prior agreement.

DECLARATION ON THE QUALITY OF THE DRAFTING OF COMMUNITY LEGISLATION

The Conference notes that the quality of the drafting of Community legislation is crucial if it is to be properly implemented by the competent national authorities and better understood by the public and in business circles. It recalls the conclusions on this subject reached by the Presidency of the European Council in Edinburgh on 11 and 12 December 1992, as well as the Council Resolution on the quality of drafting of Community legislation adopted on 8 June 1993.[13]

The Conference considers that the three institutions involved in the procedure for adopting Community legislation, the European Parliament, the Council and the Commission, should lay down guidelines on the quality of drafting of the said legislation. It also stresses that Community legislation should be made more accessible and welcomes in this regard the adoption and first implementation of an accelerated working method for official codification of legislative texts, established by the Interinstitutional Agreement of 20 December 1994.[14]

Therefore, the Conference declares that the European Parliament, the Council and the Commission ought to:

> • *establish by common accord guidelines for improving the quality of the drafting of Community legislation and follow those guidelines when considering proposals for Community legislation or draft legislation, taking the internal organisational measures they deem necessary to ensure that these guidelines are properly applied;*

> • *make their best efforts to accelerate the codification of legislative texts.*

Commentary
Transparency

The adverse Danish referendum reaction to the Maastricht Treaty and the accession, at the beginning of 1995, of Sweden and Finland increased the pressure on the IGC to make headway in the direction of open government and freedom of public access to official information. A number of well-publicised clashes between the media and the Council about the availability of documents also contributed to the reform movement.

The amended Article A adds the phrase 'as openly as possible and'.

New Article 191a establishes the right of public access to documents and, not unimportantly, that the general rules governing such access shall be formulated according to the co-decision procedure. The measure only refers to the Commission, Council and Parliament — leaving the Court of Justice and the EU's numerous other official bodies unaffected.

Amended Article 151(3) lays down the rules of procedure for the Council, although here it is left up to the Council to decide when it is acting in a legislative capacity. Articles J.18 and K.13 are also relevant here.

A big responsibility now falls to the European Parliament not only to insist on the most liberal possible guidelines but also to improve its own performance with regard to public access.

The Declaration on improving the quality of EU legislation is well-meaning. Earlier attempts had been made by the Council alone; future progress will be the result of inter-institutional agreements.

[1] EC Commission, *Report on European Union*, Bulletin of the European Communities, Supplement 5/1975, pp.10-11.

[2] Ibid., p.11.

[3] EC Commission, *European Union: Report by Mr Leo Tindemans to the European Council*, Bulletin of the European Communities, Supplement 1/1976.

[4] EC Commission, *Report of the Study Group on the Role of Public Finance in European Integration*, (MacDougall Report), 2 vols, Brussels, 1977.

[5] See Francesco Capotorti, Meinhard Hilf, Francis G. Jacobs and Jean-Paul Jacqué, *The European Union Treaty: Commentary on the draft adopted by the European Parliament*, Oxford, Clarendon Press, 1986.

[6] EC Commission, *Efficiency, Stability and Equity: A Strategy for the Evolution of the Economic System of the European Community*, (Padoa-Schioppa Report), Brussels, April 1987.

[7] Committee on Institutional Affairs, *The Principle of Subsidiarity*, (Rapporteur, Valéry Giscard d'Estaing), European Parliament, April 1990, A3-163/90.

[8] See EC Commission, Bulletin of the European Communities, 10/92, 2.2.1 & 12/92.

[9] *Position of the Italian Government on the Intergovernmental Conference for the Revision of the Treaties*, Rome, 18 March 1996, para. III, 1(d).

[10] Michel Barnier, Statement to the National Assembly, Paris, 13 March 1996.

[11] European Parliament's *Opinion on the Convening of the IGC* (Dury/Maij-Weggen Report), Strasbourg, 13 March 1996, para. 3).

[12] *The Netherlands and Europe: The Intergovernmental Conference 1996*, The Hague, Ministry of Foreign Affairs, 1995, p.16.

[13] OJ C 166, 17.6.1993, p. 1.

[14] OJ C 293, 8.11.1995, p. 2.

Section Three

An Effective and Coherent External Policy

THE COMMON FOREIGN AND SECURITY POLICY

AMENDED ARTICLE C, SECOND SUBPARAGRAPH, OF THE TREATY ON EUROPEAN UNION

The Union shall in particular ensure the consistency of its external activities as a whole in the context of its external relations, security, economic and development policies. The Council and the Commission shall be responsible for ensuring such consistency and shall cooperate to this end. They shall ensure the implementation of these policies, each in accordance with its respective powers.

TITLE V

PROVISIONS ON A COMMON FOREIGN AND SECURITY POLICY

ARTICLE J.1

1. The Union shall define and implement a common foreign and security policy covering all areas of foreign and security policy, the objectives of which shall be:

• to safeguard the common values, fundamental interests, independence and integrity of the Union in conformity with the principles of the United Nations Charter;

• to strengthen the security of the Union in all ways;

• to preserve peace and strengthen international security, in accordance with the principles of the United Nations Charter, as well as the principles of the Helsinki Final Act and the objectives of the Paris Charter, including those on external borders;

• to promote international cooperation;

• to develop and consolidate democracy and the rule of law, and respect for human rights and fundamental freedoms.

111

2. The Member States shall support the Union's external and security policy actively and unreservedly in a spirit of loyalty and mutual solidarity.

The Member States shall work together to enhance and develop their mutual political solidarity. They shall refrain from any action which is contrary to the interests of the Union or likely to impair its effectiveness as a cohesive force in international relations.

The Council shall ensure that these principles are complied with.

ARTICLE J.2 (FORMER J.1(3))

The Union shall pursue the objectives set out in Article J.1 by:

• defining the principles of and general guidelines for the common foreign and security policy;

• deciding on common strategies;

• adopting joint actions;

• adopting common positions;

• and strengthening systematic cooperation between Member States in the conduct of policy.

ARTICLE J.3 (FORMER J.8(1) AND (2), FIRST SUBPARAGRAPH)

1. The European Council shall define the principles of and general guidelines for the common foreign and security policy, including for matters with defence implications.

2. The European Council shall decide on common strategies to be implemented by the Union in areas where the Member States have important interests in common.

Common strategies shall set out their objectives, duration and the means to be made available by the Union and the Member States.

3. The Council shall take the decisions necessary for defining and implementing the common foreign and security policy on the basis of the general guidelines defined by the European Council.

The Council shall recommend common strategies to the European Council and shall implement them, in particular by adopting joint actions and common positions.

The Council shall ensure the unity, consistency and effectiveness of action by the Union.

ARTICLE J.4 (FORMER J.3)

1. The Council shall adopt joint actions. Joint actions shall address specific situations where operational action by the Union is deemed to be required. They shall lay down their objectives, scope, the means to be made available to the Union, if necessary their duration, and the conditions for their implementation.

2. If there is a change in circumstances having a substantial effect on a question subject to joint action, the Council shall review the principles and objectives of that action and take the necessary decisions. As long as the Council has not acted, the joint action shall stand.

3. Joint actions shall commit the Member States in the positions they adopt and in the conduct of their activity.

4. The Council may request the Commission to submit to it any appropriate proposals relating to the common foreign and security policy to ensure the implementation of a joint action.

5. Whenever there is any plan to adopt a national position or take national action pursuant to a joint action, information shall be provided in time to allow, if necessary, for prior consultations within the Council. The obligation to provide prior information shall not apply to measures which are merely a national transposition of Council decisions.

6. In cases of imperative need arising from changes in the situation and failing a Council decision, Member States may take the necessary measures as a matter of urgency having regard to the general objectives of the joint action. The Member State concerned shall inform the Council immediately of any such measures.

7. Should there be any major difficulties in implementing a joint action, a Member State shall refer them to the Council which shall discuss them and seek appropriate solutions. Such solutions shall not run counter to the objectives of the joint action or impair its effectiveness.

ARTICLE J.5 (FORMER J.2(2))

The Council shall adopt common positions. Common positions shall define the approach of the Union to a particular matter of a geographical or thematic nature. Member States shall ensure that their national policies conform to the common positions.

ARTICLE J.6 (FORMER J.2(1))

Member States shall inform and consult one another within the Council on any matter of foreign and security policy of general interest in order to ensure that the Union's influence is exerted as effectively as possible by means of concerted and convergent action.

ARTICLE J.7 (FORMER J.4)

1. The common foreign and security policy shall include all questions relating to the security of the Union, including the progressive framing of a common defence policy, in accordance with the second subparagraph, which might lead to a common defence, should the European Council so decide. It shall in that case recommend to the Member States the adoption of such a decision in accordance with their respective constitutional requirements.

The Western European Union (WEU) is an integral part of the development of the Union providing the Union with access to an operational capability notably in the context of paragraph 2. It supports the Union in framing the defence aspects of the common foreign and security policy as set out in this Article. The Union shall accordingly foster closer institutional relations with the WEU with a view to the possibility of the integration of the WEU into the Union, should the European Council so decide. It shall in that case recommend to the Member States the adoption of such a decision in accordance with their respective constitutional requirements.

The policy of the Union in accordance with this Article shall not prejudice the specific character of the security and defence policy of certain Member States and shall respect the obligations of certain Member States, which see their common defence realized in NATO, under the North Atlantic Treaty and be compatible with the common security and defence policy established within that framework.

The progressive framing of a common defence policy will be supported, as Member States consider appropriate, by cooperation between them in the field of armaments.

2. Questions referred to in this Article shall include humanitarian and rescue tasks, peacekeeping tasks and tasks of combat forces in crisis management, including peacemaking.

3. The Union will avail itself of the WEU to elaborate and implement decisions and actions of the Union which have defence implications.

The competence of the European Council to establish guidelines in accordance with Article J.3 shall also obtain in respect of the WEU for those matters for which the Union avails itself of the WEU.

When the Union avails itself of the WEU to elaborate and implement decisions of the Union on the tasks referred to in paragraph 2 all Member States of the Union shall be entitled to participate fully in the tasks in question. The Council, in agreement with the institutions of the WEU, shall adopt the necessary practical arrangements to allow all Member States contributing to the tasks in question to participate fully and on an equal footing in planning and decision-taking in the WEU.

Decisions having defence implications dealt with under this paragraph shall be taken without prejudice to the policies and obligations referred to in paragraph 1, third subparagraph.

4. The provisions of this Article shall not prevent the development of closer cooperation between two or more Member States on a bilateral level, in the framework of the WEU and the Atlantic Alliance, provided such cooperation does not run counter to or impede that provided for in this Title.

5. With a view to furthering the objectives of this Article, the provisions of this Article will be reviewed in accordance with Article N.

PROTOCOL ON ARTICLE J.7 OF THE TREATY ON EUROPEAN UNION

THE HIGH CONTRACTING PARTIES

BEARING IN MIND the need to implement fully the provisions of Article J.7(1), second subparagraph, and (3) of the Treaty on European Union,

BEARING IN MIND that the policy of the Union in accordance with Article J.7 shall not prejudice the specific character of the security and defence policy of certain Member States and shall respect the obligations of certain Member States, which see their common defence realized in NATO, under the North Atlantic Treaty and be compatible with the common security and defence policy established within that framework,

HAVE AGREED upon the following provision, which shall be annexed to the Treaty on European Union,

The European Union shall draw up, together with the Western European Union, arrangements for enhanced cooperation between them, within a year from the entry into force of this Protocol.

DECLARATION ON ENHANCED COOPERATION BETWEEN THE EU AND THE WEU

With a view to enhanced cooperation between the European Union and the Western European Union, the Conference invites the Council to seek the early adoption of appropriate arrangements for the security clearance of the personnel of the General Secretariat of the Council.

ARTICLE J.8 (FORMER J.5)

1. The Presidency shall represent the Union in matters coming within the common foreign and security policy.

2. The Presidency shall be responsible for the implementation of common measures; in that capacity it shall in principle express the position of the Union in international organizations and international conferences.

3. The Presidency shall be assisted by the Secretary-General of the Council who shall exercise the function of High Representative for the common foreign and security policy.

4. The Commission shall be fully associated in the tasks referred to in paragraphs 1 and 2. The Presidency shall be assisted in those tasks if need be by the next Member State to hold the Presidency.

5. The Council may, whenever it deems it necessary, appoint a special representative with a mandate in relation to particular policy issues.

ARTICLE J.9 (FORMER J.2(3) AND J.5(4))

1. Member States shall coordinate their action in international organizations and at international conferences. They shall uphold the common positions in such fora.

In international organizations and at international conferences where not all the Member States participate, those which do take part shall uphold the common positions.

2. Without prejudice to the previous paragraph and Article J.4(3), Member States represented in international organizations or international conferences where not all the Member States participate shall keep the latter informed of any matter of common interest.

Member States which are also members of the United Nations Security Council will concert and keep the other Member States fully informed. Member States which are permanent members of the Security Council will, in the execution of their functions, ensure the defence of the positions and the interests of the Union, without prejudice to their responsibilities under the provisions of the United Nations Charter.

ARTICLE J.10 (FORMER J.6)

The diplomatic and consular missions of the Member States and the Commission Delegations in third countries and international conferences, and their representations to international organizations, shall cooperate in ensuring that the common positions and common measures adopted by the Council are complied with and implemented.

They shall step up cooperation by exchanging information, carrying out joint assessments and contributing to the implementation of the provisions referred to in Article 8c of the Treaty establishing the European Community.

ARTICLE J.11 (FORMER J.7)

The Presidency shall consult the European Parliament on the main aspects and the basic choices of the common foreign and security policy and shall ensure that the views of the European Parliament are duly taken into consideration. The European Parliament shall be kept regularly informed by the Presidency and the Commission of the development of the Union's foreign and security policy.

The European Parliament may ask questions of the Council or make recommendations to it. It shall hold an annual debate on progress in implementing the common foreign and security policy.

ARTICLE J.12 (FORMER J.8(3) AND (4))

1. Any Member State or the Commission may refer to the Council any question relating to the common foreign and security policy and may submit proposals to the Council.

2. In cases requiring a rapid decision, the Presidency, of its own motion, or at the request of the Commission or a Member State, shall convene an extraordinary Council meeting within forty-eight hours or, in an emergency, within a shorter period.

ARTICLE J.13

1. Decisions under this Title shall be taken by the Council acting unanimously. Abstentions by members present in person or represented shall not prevent the adoption of such decisions.

When abstaining in a vote, any member of the Council may qualify its abstention by making a formal declaration under the present subparagraph. In that case, it shall not be obliged to apply the decision, but shall accept that the decision commits the Union. In a spirit of mutual solidarity, the Member State concerned shall refrain from any action likely to conflict with or impede Union action based on that decision and the other Member States shall respect its position. If the members of the Council qualifying their abstention in this way represent more than one third of the votes weighted in accordance with Article 148(2) of the Treaty establishing the European Community, the decision shall not be adopted.

2. By derogation from the provisions of paragraph 1, the Council shall act by qualified majority:

- when adopting joint actions, common positions or taking any other decision on the basis of a common strategy;

- when adopting any decision implementing a joint action or a common position.

If a member of the Council declares that, for important and stated reasons of national policy, it intends to oppose the adoption of a decision to be taken by qualified majority, a vote shall not be taken. The Council may, acting by a qualified majority, request that the matter be referred to the European Council for decision by unanimity.

The votes of the members of the Council shall be weighted in accordance with article 148(2) of the Treaty establishing the European Community. For their adoption, decisions shall require at least 62 votes in favour, cast by at least 10 members.

This paragraph shall not apply to decisions having military or defence implications.

3. For procedural questions, the Council shall act by a majority of its members.

New Article J.14

When it is necessary to conclude an agreement with one or more States or international organizations in implementation of this Title, the Council, acting unanimously, may authorize the Presidency, assisted by the Commission as appropriate, to open negotiations to that effect. Such agreements shall be concluded by the Council acting unanimously on a recommendation from the Presidency. No agreement shall be binding on a Member State whose representative in the Council states that it has to comply with the requirements of its own constitutional procedure; the other members of the Council may agree that the agreement shall apply provisionally to them.

The provisions of this Article shall also apply to matters falling under Title VI.

Declaration relating to Articles J.14 and K.10

The provisions of Articles J.14 and K.10 of the Treaty on European Union and any agreements resulting from them shall not imply any transfer of competence from the Member States to the Union.

Article J.15 (former J.8(5))

Without prejudice to Article 151 of the Treaty establishing the European Community, a Political Committee shall monitor the international situation in the areas covered by common foreign and security policy and contribute to the definition of policies by delivering opinions to the Council at the request of the Council or on its own initiative. It shall also monitor the implementation of agreed policies, without prejudice to the responsibility of the Presidency and the Commission.

Declaration on Article J.15

The Conference agrees that Member States shall ensure that the Political Committee referred to in Article J.15 of the Treaty on European Union is able to meet at any time, in the event of international crises or other urgent matters, at very short notice at Political Director or deputy level.

ARTICLE J.16

The Secretary-General of the Council, High Representative for the common foreign and security policy, shall assist the Council in matters coming within the scope of the common foreign and security policy, in particular through contributing to the formulation, preparation and implementation of policy decisions, and, when appropriate and acting on behalf of the Council at the request of the Presidency, through conducting political dialogue with third parties.

ARTICLE J.17 (FORMER J.9)

The Commission shall be fully associated with the work carried out in the common foreign and security policy field.

ARTICLE J.18 (FORMER J.11)

1. The provisions referred to in Articles 137, 138, 139 to 142, 146, 147, 150 to 153, 157 to 163, 191a and 217 of the Treaty establishing the European Community shall apply to the provisions relating to the areas referred to in this Title.

2. Administrative expenditure which the provisions relating to the areas referred to in this Title entail for the institutions shall be charged to the budget of the European Communities.

3. Operational expenditure to which the implementation of those provisions gives rise shall also be charged to the budget of the European Communities, except for such expenditure arising from operations having military or defence implications, and cases where the Council acting unanimously decides otherwise.

In cases where expenditure is not charged to the budget of the European Communities it shall be charged to the Member States in accordance with the GNP scale, unless the Council acting unanimously decides otherwise. As for expenditure arising from operations having military or defence implications, Member States which have made a formal declaration under Article J.13(1), second subparagraph, shall not be obliged to contribute to the financing thereof.

4. The budgetary procedure laid down in the Treaty establishing the European Community shall apply to the expenditure charged to the budget of the European Communities.

119

INTER-INSTITUTIONAL AGREEMENT BETWEEN THE EUROPEAN PARLIAMENT, THE COUNCIL AND THE EUROPEAN COMMISSION ON PROVISIONS REGARDING FINANCING OF THE COMMON FOREIGN AND SECURITY POLICY

General Provisions

A. CFSP operational expenditure shall be charged to the budget of the European Communities, unless the Council decides otherwise, in accordance with Article J.17 of the treaty.

B. CFSP expenditure shall be treated as expenditure not necessarily resulting from the Treaty. However, the following specific modalities of implementation of the expenditure in question are hereby laid down by common agreement between the European Parliament, the Council and the Commission.

Financial Arrangements

C. On the basis of the preliminary draft budget established by the Commission, the European Parliament and the Council shall annually secure agreement on the amount of the operational CFSP expenditure to be charged to the Communities' budget and on the allocation of this amount among the articles of the CFSP budget chapter (for articles: see suggestions under G).

In the absence of agreement, it is understood that the European Parliament and the Council shall at least agree to enter in the CFSP budget the amount contained in the previous budget, unless the Commission proposes to lower that amount.

D. The total amount of operational CFSP expenditure shall be entirely entered in one (CFSP) budget chapter, under the articles of this chapter (as suggested in G). This amount shall cover the real predictable needs and a reasonable margin for unforeseen actions. No funds will be entered into a reserve. Each article shall cover common strategies or joint actions already adopted, measures which are foreseen but not yet adopted and all future - i.e. unforeseen - actions to be adopted by the Council during the financial year concerned.

E. In conformity with the Financial Regulation, the Commission, on the basis of a Council decision, will have the authority to, autonomously, make credit-transfers between articles within one budget chapter, i.e. the CFSP envelope, the flexibility deemed necessary for a speedy implementation of CFSP actions will be assured.

F. In the event of the amount of the CFSP budget during the financial year being insufficient to cover the necessary expenses, the European Parliament and the Council shall agree to find a solution as a matter of urgency, on a proposal by the Commission.

G. Within the CFSP budget chapter, the articles into which the CFSP actions are to be entered, could read along the following lines:

- observation and organisation of elections/participation in democratic transition processes

- EU-envoys

- Prevention of conflicts/peace and security processes

- Financial assistance to disarmament processes

- Contributions to international conferences

- Urgent actions

The European Parliament, the Council and the Commission agree that the amount for actions entered under the article mentioned in the sixth indent cannot exceed 20 per cent of the global amount of the CFSP budget chapter.

Ad hoc concertation procedure

H. An ad hoc concertation procedure shall be set up, with a view to reaching an agreement between the two arms of the budgetary authority as far as the aforementioned amount of CFSP expenditure and the distribution of this amount over the articles of CFSP budget chapter are concerned.

I. This procedure will be applied at the request of the European Parliament or the Council, notably if either of these institutions intends to depart from the preliminary draft budget of the Commission.

J. The ad hoc concertation procedure has to be concluded before the date set by the Council for establishing its draft budget.

K. Each arm of the budgetary authority shall take whatever steps are required to ensure that the results which will be secured in the ad hoc concertation procedure, are respected throughout the budgetary procedure.

Consultation and information of the European Parliament

L. On a yearly basis the Presidency of the Council shall consult the European Parliament on a document established by the Council on the main aspects and basic choices of the CFSP, including the financial implications for the Communities budget. Furthermore, the Presidency shall on a regular basis inform the European Parliament on the development and implementation of CFSP actions.

M. The Council shall, each time it adopts a decision in the field of CFSP entailing expenses, immediately and in each case communicate to the European Parliament an estimate of the costs envisaged ('fiche financière'), in particular those regarding time-frame, staff employed, use of premises and other infrastructure, transport facilities, training requirements and security arrangements.

N. The Commission shall inform the budgetary authority on the execution of CFSP actions and the financial forecasts for the remaining period of the year on a quarterly basis.

DECLARATION ON THE ESTABLISHMENT OF A POLICY PLANNING AND EARLY WARNING UNIT

The Conference agrees that:

1. A policy planning and early warning unit, shall be established in the General Secretariat of the Council under the responsibility of its Secretary-General, High Representative for the CFSP. Appropriate cooperation shall be established with the Commission in order to ensure full coherence with the Union's external economic and development policies.

2. The tasks of the unit shall include the following:

(a) monitoring and analysing developments in areas relevant to the CFSP;

(b) providing assessments of the Union's foreign and security policy interests and identifying areas where the CFSP could focus in future;

(c) providing timely assessments and early warning of events or situations which may have significant repercussions for the Union's foreign and security policy, including potential political crises;

(d) producing, at the request of either the Council or the Presidency or on its own initiative, argued policy options papers to be presented under the responsibility of the Presidency as a contribution to policy formulation in the Council, and which may contain analyses, recommendations and strategies for the CFSP.

3. The unit shall consist of personnel drawn from the General Secretariat, the Member States, the Commission and the WEU.

4. Any Member State or the Commission may make suggestions to the unit for work to be undertaken.

5. Member States and the Commission shall assist the policy planning process by providing, to the fullest extent possible, relevant information, including confidential information.

EXTERNAL ECONOMIC RELATIONS

NEW ARTICLE 113(5) OF THE TREATY ESTABLISHING THE EUROPEAN COMMUNITY

5. The Council, acting unanimously on a proposal from the Commission and after consulting the European Parliament, may extend the application of paragraphs 1 to 4 to international negotiations and agreements on services and intellectual property insofar as they are not covered by these paragraphs.

AMENDED ARTICLE 228(1), SECOND SUBPARAGRAPH

In exercising the powers conferred upon it by this paragraph, the Council shall act by a qualified majority, except in the cases where the first subparagraph of paragraph 2 provides that the Council shall act unanimously.

AMENDED ARTICLE 228(2)

2. Subject to the powers vested in the Commission in this field, the signing, which may be accompanied by a decision on provisional application before entry into force, and the conclusion of the agreements shall be decided on by the Council, acting by a qualified majority on a proposal from the Commission. The Council shall act unanimously when the agreement covers a field for which unanimity is required for the adoption of internal rules and for the agreements referred to in Article 238.

By way of derogation from the rules laid down in paragraph 3, the same procedures shall apply for a decision to suspend the application of an international agreement, and for the purpose of establishing the position to be adopted on behalf of the Community in a body set up by an agreement based on Article 238, when that body is called upon to adopt decisions having legal effects, with the exception of decisions supplementing or amending the institutional framework of the agreement.

The European Parliament shall be immediately and fully informed on any decision under this paragraph concerning the provisional application or the suspension of agreements, or the establishment of the Community position in a body set up by an agreement.

Commentary
Foreign policy —
or trompe l'oeil?

To strengthen the European Union's Common Foreign and Security Policy (CFSP) was one of the fundamental aims of the 1996 IGC. The Treaty on European Union had been extremely tentative in its approach — speaking, in Article B, of asserting the Union's international identity 'in particular through the implementation of a common foreign and security policy including the eventual framing of a common defence policy, which might in time lead to a common defence'. Such timidity was, if anything, exacerbated since Maastricht by the accession of the three 'neutral' countries in 1995. And there had been no obvious foreign policy successes with which the so-called second pillar of Maastricht could be credited in the meanwhile. Rather the contrary: what concerted progress was made in the Balkans, for example, was the product of ad hoc arrangements under the Nato umbrella, principally by Britain and France.

In its preparatory stages, the IGC had spent too much of its time worrying about how to articulate a distinct European Union identity in international affairs, and too little on the content of what it was the European Union might have to say. The effort to focus more sharply on the purpose of a European Union common foreign policy was frustrated. In the amended Article J.1 only one new goal was inscribed, namely, to safeguard the territorial integrity of the Union — in itself, not a bad ambition but hardly a lively issue even in the perspective of enlargement.

The idea that a strong and coherent European Union could play a leading part in reforming the world's international organisations, or in fighting the environmental degradation of the planet, or in alleviating world hunger and disease was somehow lost sight of. The result was less than transparent, more a crafty illusion.

One conclusion that could be drawn is that without any obvious external challenge, the IGC's efforts to sharpen up its CFSP were driven by domestic rather than international pressures. The Maastricht IGC had had the Gulf War to stimulate it; Amsterdam had nothing comparable.

Byzantine procedures

If the political outcome was disappointing, the procedural negotiations were byzantine. The new Article J.2 purports to see substantive

124

differences between defining principles and general guidelines, deciding common strategies and adopting common positions and joint actions. The engaged citizen, however, may wonder whether any of this is much of an advance on the old system of 'European Political Cooperation' that preceded Maastricht. Certainly the heavy and ornate decision-making procedures — unanimity in the European Council with QMV hedged about in the Council of ministers — suggest the imperatives of ambivalence and compromise. And the real possibility of conflict arises between those whose 'common strategy' (decided by unanimity) is another's 'joint action' (decided by QMV).

A perhaps more significant change to the procedure for a joint action, in new Article J.4(4), is that the European Commission may now be invited to intervene. Similarly, in the revised Article C at the beginning of the Treaty, the Council is enjoined to cooperate with the Commission. But if the Commission cannot broker a deal, the tendency will be to push awkward decisions up to the level of the heads of state or government for arbitration — or for indecision and facile rhetoric.

Constructive abstention has always been a rather discreet feature of EU foreign policy, intended to facilitate decisions. As a result of the attention given by the IGC to the whole issue of flexibility or enhanced cooperation (see Section Five), Amsterdam witnessed the apotheosis of abstentionism. In future, constructive abstention is going to be not only very public but also extended to a wider range of possibilities.

Article J.13 is effectively the second pillar's flexibility clause. It offers a recalcitrant member state every opportunity to opt out of a majority decision and a group of states commanding a third of the votes in the Council the chance to bring any common policy initiative grinding to a halt. A derogation by one, preferably small, member state from a joint action is perfectly feasible; but the possibility, which Amsterdam admits, of there being also constructive abstention from a supposedly 'common position' is rather mind-boggling.

The European Union's joint actions will remain hampered by uncertain funding arrangements which will defy financial planning and evade democratic accountability. The sensible option, much canvassed at the IGC, was to put spending on joint actions under the Petersberg Tasks within the EU budget; yet the decision taken at Amsterdam was to attempt to raise ad hoc levies from participating member states. The unhappy experience of the United Nations Organisation had much to teach the EU in this respect — in vain.

That having been said, the agreement at Amsterdam between the institutions (also reproduced here) on the financing of CFSP is encouraging: the fear had been that money allotted for the Community's external relations was to be purloined to keep the second pillar afloat.

In the event, the European Parliament's scrutiny of expenditure on CFSP is much augmented.

What next for WEU?

In security and defence matters, the IGC suffered from a major disagreement among the partners about whether and, if so, how far and how fast it was wise to incorporate WEU within the EU. In the end, honour was fairly satisfied: the UK had the EU commitment to Nato reaffirmed, the Petersberg Tasks were written into the EU Treaty on terms acceptable to the Swedes, Austrians, Finns and Irish; and France and Germany were gratified that an eventual merger of the two organisations was far from precluded (Article J.7(1)).

What the reform means for WEU is less clear. Already its cogency is being stretched to accommodate the observing non-member states of the EU to say nothing of its associates from Central and Eastern Europe. This dilution coupled with the basic lack of agreement between the British and French about its long-term role may prevent WEU from being anything other than a fairly useful conduit between Nato and the EU. Certainly, its claims, in the immediate aftermath of Amsterdam, to be the operational 'European politico-military body' seem rather fanciful.

Cometh the hour

The long-running debate about the personalisation of the Union's common foreign and security policy reached its conclusion in the decision to give the Secretary-General of the Council bigger responsibilities in this field. This is not the autonomous 'Monsieur ou Madame PESC' who trailed his or her coat before the IGC. It provides as much of a headache for the Council secretariat as it offers an opportunity for the new vice-president of the Commission who is to be charged with taking hold of all that body's external portfolios (Article J.8(4)). The key to the success of the international representation of the Union will be the relationship between those two and the Council president-in-office — and that relationship may well supersede the tröika of past, present and future presidencies in both status and efficiency.

Equally important is the well-rehearsed decision to establish a policy planning and early warning unit, and the Commission's participation and shared right of initiation in this exercise is also vital. As its political intelligence will be drawn from member state governments, one might not anticipate any immediate shocks. But the fact that the Commission will be involved in the early planning of any element of CFSP is a considerable advance for that body, and the long-term benefits of the change, especially in some forward-thinking about the Union's common interest, may be striking.

One notable example of where such a capability has been lacking concerns enlargement, where different decisions have a habit of being taken by much the same partners within Nato and the European Union — with the interests of the latter most comprehensively ignored by the Americans. One obvious purpose of a CFSP is to ensure that Nato will never again be able to sign a treaty that simply ignores the EU.[1] The necessity of tying together the widening (and deepening) of those two organisations has never been more strong. The Treaty of Amsterdam may have provided at least some of the tools for this effort in coordinated strategy.

Who speaks for Europe?

The question of the European Union's legal personality has not been settled at Amsterdam, for the mandate given to the Council presidency to conclude an international agreement on behalf of the Union is not watertight (new Article J.14 and the qualifying declaration). Here again, constitutional let-outs have been written into the procedure. And the fear must be that the member states will prefer to use this ambiguous mandatory procedure to the more clear-cut arrangements pertaining to the first pillar.

In this latter respect, the revision to Article 113 was a setback for the ambitions of the European Commission, which had badly wanted to acquire the authority to negotiate within the World Trade Organisation on issues of services and intellectual property. None of the alternative texts circulating before Amsterdam was acceptable to the Commission, and Santer could declare himself quite satisfied that the final result, leaving open the possibility of future change (without another IGC), was not disastrous. The check was a classic case of member states' envy of the supranational trade policy powers of the Commission, and does not bode well. Possibly only the introduction of the single currency will force member states to act as one in world trade and finance.

The Article 113 and Article 228 decisions do not promise to be anything more long-lasting than the unstable arrangement with regard to the Union's legal personality. A further disappointment for the Commission lay in the failure to open up Europe's defence procurement industry to the disciplines of the single market. Clearly the climate was not right for this at Amsterdam. In this light, the decision, in Article J.7(5), to carry second pillar matters forward to the next IGC, looks eminently sensible.

Pressure for further reform will also be felt from the European Parliament, which got almost nothing out of Amsterdam in the field of external relations. MEPs demanded, quite reasonably, that the Parliament should be granted the power of assent over all those international agreements whose substance required the use of the co-decision procedure internally. In the field of Article 113 this would include anti-dumping rules. In the revised Article 228(2), concerning the provisional application of international agreements, the suspension of such agreements and the establishment of the Community's position in bodies set up by those agreements, the Parliament is still entirely excluded from the formation of policy.

The European Council will be primarily responsible for making a success of the modest set of arrangements in the field of foreign and security policy. It is a diverting thought that they who are responsible for the Treaty of Amsterdam will now have to make it work.

---

[1] See, for example, the Founding Act on Mutual Relations, Cooperation and Security between the Russian Federation and Nato, Paris, 27 May 1997.

Section Four

The Union's Institutions

PROTOCOL ON THE INSTITUTIONS WITH THE PROSPECT OF ENLARGEMENT OF THE EUROPEAN UNION

THE HIGH CONTRACTING PARTIES,

HAVE AGREED upon the following provisions, which shall be annexed to the Treaty on European Union and to the Treaties establishing the European Communities,

ARTICLE 1

At the date of entry into force of the first enlargement of the Union, notwithstanding Article 157(1) of the Treaty establishing the European Communities, Article 9(1) of the Treaty establishing the European Coal and Steel Community and Article 126(1) of the Treaty establishing the European Atomic Energy Community, the Commission shall comprise one national of each of the Member States, provided that, by that date, the weighting of the votes in the Council has been modified, whether by reweighting of the votes or by dual majority, in a manner acceptable to all Member States, taking into account all relevant elements, notably compensating those Member States which give up the possibility of nominating a second member of the Commission.

ARTICLE 2

At least one year before the membership of the European Union exceeds twenty, a conference of representatives of the governments of Member States shall be convened in order to carry out a comprehensive review of the provisions of the Treaties on the composition and functioning of the institutions.

DECLARATION RELATING TO THE PROTOCOL ON THE INSTITUTIONS WITH THE PROSPECT OF ENLARGEMENT OF THE EUROPEAN UNION

Until the entry into force of the first enlargement it is agreed that the decision of the Council of 29 March 1994 ('the Ioannina Compromise') will be extended and, by that date, a solution for the special case of Spain will be found.

ARTICLE N(2) SHALL BE REPEALED.

Commentary
Disappointment on enlargement — and another IGC to come

This Protocol is a low point of the Amsterdam Treaty. It is an admission of failure on two counts — to reduce the size of the Commission and to reweight the votes on the Council. But it also marks a reduction in ambition of the European Union with regard to enlargement.

But the failure leads to a promise of another IGC to finish the job.

Background

The original agenda of the 1996 IGC, set at Maastricht, was soon to be embellished by the imperative of enlargement. In June 1993 the European Council at Copenhagen agreed that:

'the associated countries in central and eastern Europe that so desire shall become members of the European Union. Accession will take place as soon as an associated country is able to assume the obligations of membership by satisfying the economic and political conditions required.'

These conditions were:

• stability of institutions guaranteeing democracy, the rule of law, human rights and respect for and the protection of minorities;

• the existence of a functioning market economy as well as the capacity to cope with competitive pressure and market forces within the Union;

• ability to take on the obligations of membership including adherence to the aims of political, economic and monetary union.

Enlargement was a second thought, but a sound one. For a time, enlargement was thought to have a crucial influence on the outcome of the IGC. Much was said about the impossibility of running a Union of 25 or 30 member states with the existing institutional set up. The Corfu European Council in June 1994 instructed the Group of Reflection to consider not only those items laid down by Maastricht but also 'any other measure deemed necessary to facilitate the work of the institutions and guarantee their effective operation in the perspective of enlargement'. In addition, in March 1995 the Union promised Cyprus and Malta that accession negotiations would open six months after the end of the IGC.

The Reflection Group put great emphasis on the need to reform the institutions to cope with enlargement. The Commission's Opinion said that the IGC 'is probably the last and only opportunity all 15 Member States will have to reflect together about how the Union is to function in a wider framework'.[1]

However, the Group of Reflection also exposed the complexity of reaching agreement *à quinze* on the mundane agenda of the IGC and, by 1996, the transition of the Central and East European states to democracy and the market economy had begun to seem much more problematical. In many of the existing member states the sense of urgency about enlargement receded. Malta dropped out of the race of its own accord. The worsening internal division of Cyprus was thought by many to preclude its accession.

At the insistence of the Americans, NATO enlargement by 1999 took priority. By the time the leaders met in Amsterdam, expectations had dropped to anticipation of the accession of Poland, the Czech Republic, Hungary and possibly Slovenia — making nineteen member states in all — within a decade. The big preoccupation was EMU. The pressure for radical institutional reform of the Union itself was off.

The Turin mandate

The mandate for the IGC had been established at the Turin European Council in March 1996. The quest was for 'greater efficiency, coherence and legitimacy'. As far as institutions were concerned, the Conference was charged to examine:

- the most effective means of simplifying legislative procedures and making them clearer and more transparent ;

- the possibility of widening the scope of co-decision in truly legislative matters;

- the question of the role of the European Parliament besides its legislative powers, as well as its composition and the uniform procedure for its election;

- how and to what extent national parliaments could better contribute to the Union's tasks;

- the questions of the extent of majority voting in the Council, the weighting of votes and the threshold for qualified majority decisions;

- how the Commission can fulfil its functions with greater efficiency, having regard to its composition and representative capability;

- whether and how to improve the role and functioning of the European Court of Justice and Court of Auditors;

- how to achieve greater quality of legislation and how to fight more effectively against fraud;

- whether and how to introduce rules either of a general nature or in specific areas in order to enable a certain number of member states to proceed faster and further in developing European integration.

The size of the Commission

The European Union of fifteen member states enjoys a Commission of twenty. It is widely suspected that some Commissioners have too little to do and that the college itself is unwieldy. Enlargement just to the favoured four applicant states would result in a Commission of twenty-five (Poland, like Spain, would have two members).

At the IGC, the French, especially, took the technocratic view, and wished to reduce the size of the Commission to ten to twelve, having regard only to regional balance. The Germans were inconsistent in their response to this proposal, but they did seem prepared, as did the British, to sacrifice their second Commissioner. However, all three were concerned to be compensated for their reduction on the Commission by an increase in voting weight in the Council. The prospect of enlargement appeared to threaten a situation whereby a coalition of small and medium-sized member states could out-vote the large.

Thus an obstacle was thrown up to the obvious solution, which was to allow each member state one Commissioner. A second, and strong, argument against this simple course of action was that the Commission would then become merely a pale reflection of Coreper, with national interests predominating at the expense of the common good. The Commission itself was more concerned with the efficacy and independence of the college than with its size.

Spain suggested that the larger states (among which it numbered itself) should always have one Commissioner, while the others would rotate.

All the smaller states appear to have combined to block the French option. Some, like the Irish, were determined to keep their own Commissioner as their way of buying into the Community system. Others, like Belgium, were prepared initially to be flexible but hardened their attitude once the extent of the German retreat on QMV became clear. Dehaene announced that the re-weighting of Council votes was hardly necessary if QMV was not to be extended.

The weighting of votes in the Council

It was unfortunate that the four issues of size of Commission, QMV, the weighting of votes and enlargement became so inextricably linked — the more so because the leaders appeared to be ill-prepared in arithmetical terms for the negotiation on votes.

Successive presidencies had laboured to arrive at a credible compromise.[2] Among the options explored were:

- a reweighting of votes in direct proportion to population size;

- a more arbitrary reallocation of votes according to bands;

- the introduction of a dual majority of QMV plus a certain proportion of population of the Union;

- a dual majority comprising both a certain population and a certain majority of member states.

At the special European Council at Noordwijk on 23 May, the Germans suggested that the status quo on this issue and that of the size of the Commission would be preferable to an open quarrel.

At Amsterdam, the Dutch tabled a draft protocol, setting out new voting weights, which would only have come into effect on enlargement. That the presidential formula gave the Dutch more clout than the Belgians blew the Benelux consensus apart. France opposed the whole idea of a dual majority. Spain then complained that a deal had been struck at the time of its accession that it would have two Commissioners in exchange for fewer Council votes (8) than the four large countries (10 each). Spain now sought compensation in terms of Council votes for the anticipated change to the size of the Commission.

The impasse was now complete. Kohl's proposal to postpone the whole issue was quickly accepted.

At Spanish insistence the notorious Ioannina Compromise, forced on the Union by the UK in 1994, will continue in force. (The UK had tried to raise the threshold for the formation of a qualified majority from 71% to 78%; although this bid failed, it was agreed that the Council would use its best endeavours to avoid falling below the higher figure.)[3] The failure at Amsterdam to agree more significant reform means that the present system as in Article 148(2) will continue to apply for the foreseeable future. A qualified majority is formed by 62 votes. In special cases (as in old Articles J.3.2 and K.4.3), eight member states are also required.

Another IGC

The IGC expended much time and energy on the issue of the size of the Commission. Many of the Commission's internal problems, however, stem not from its size but from poor internal management; and some of these could be solved by having an inner and outer tier of Commissioners. The issue of the re-weighting of Council votes will only be really important once there are a large number of new member states. But the blockage at Amsterdam on these issues is still significant in that it illustrates how intense a cleavage has opened up within the Union between its large and smaller member states. Unless a reasonable solution can be found to these two issues, this cleavage is bound to grow.

The real significance of this Enlargement Protocol is that the EU is now committed to holding a successor IGC. Avoiding the precedent of Maastricht, which, in Article N set the date of 1996, the commitment is only to convene the next IGC at least one year before what will be effectively the second phase of further enlargement.

Prospects for enlargement

The Protocol says, rather mysteriously, that another IGC shall be held 'at least one year before the membership of the European Union exceeds twenty'. Since Amsterdam, on 16 July 1997, the Commission published its *Agenda 2000* containing its Opinions on each applicant state. It recommended that negotiations should open with six states: Poland, Estonia, the Czech Republic, Hungary, Slovenia and Cyprus — making conveniently the magic figure of a potential twenty-one member states. The Commission's proposal has to be confirmed by the Luxembourg European Council in December 1997.

The Commission also recommends a strengthening of the pre-accession strategy and the establishment of a new standing conference in which all the applicant countries and the EU could discuss second and third pillar issues.

The enlargement negotiations plus ratification procedures will last at least three years. In about 2000, towards the end of the negotiations a short IGC will in any case be needed in order to formalise the accession treaties of the new member states. Some of the outstanding issues could certainly be dealt with as part of the accession package, although the failure of Amsterdam means that the applicant states will have to open their membership negotiations without knowing how they are to be represented in the Commission and Council. The implication for the Union is a row postponed. Those who wish the European Union well could be forgiven for not wholly welcoming such a result, despite the prospect of a future IGC.

134

As the deficiency of the Protocol as a basis for future integration becomes more exposed, efforts are underway to improve the situation. At the time of writing, Belgian prime minister Jean-Luc Dehaene yet seeks to insert an additional declaration to the Treaty that would stipulate that before any further enlargement of the Union were to take place the issues of the size of the Commission, weighting in the Council and the extension of QMV will have had to be settled. This initiative is supported by a big majority in the European Parliament and by the Commission in its *Agenda 2000*.

THE EUROPEAN PARLIAMENT

ASSENT PROCEDURE

The assent procedure will apply to the following provisions:

NEW TREATY PROVISIONS

ARTICLE F.1

Sanctions in the event of a serious and persistent breach of
fundamental rights by a Member State

EXISTING TREATY PROVISIONS

ARTICLE O

Accession procedure

ARTICLE 130D

Structural and cohesion funds

ARTICLE 138(4)

Proposals by the European Parliament for a uniform electoral
procedure

ARTICLE 228(3), SECOND SUBPARAGRAPH

Conclusion of certain international agreements

CO-DECISION PROCEDURE

The co-decision procedure will apply to the following provisions.

NEW TREATY PROVISIONS

ARTICLE 109R

Employment incentive measures

ARTICLE 118(2)

Social exclusion measures

ARTICLE 119

Social policy - Equal opportunities and treatment

ARTICLE 129

Public health (former basis Article 43 - consultation)

• minimum requirements regarding quality and safety of organs

• veterinary and phytosanitary measures with the direct objective the protection of public health

ARTICLE 191A

General principles for transparency

ARTICLE 209A

Countering fraud affecting the financial interests of the Community

ARTICLE 116

Customs cooperation

ARTICLE 213A

Statistics

ARTICLE 213B

Establishment of independent advisory authority on data protection

EXISTING TREATY PROVISIONS [4]

ARTICLE 6

Rules to prohibit discrimination on grounds of nationality (cooperation)

ARTICLE 8A(2) [5]

Provisions for facilitating the exercise of citizens' right to move and reside freely within the territory of the Member States (assent)

ARTICLE 51

Internal market (consultation)

• rules on social security for Community immigrant workers

ARTICLE 56(2) [6]

Coordination of provisions laid down by law, regulation or administrative action for special treatment for foreign nationals (right of establishment)

ARTICLE 57(2) [7]

Coordination of the provisions laid down by law, regulation or administrative action in Member States concerning the taking up and pursuit of activities as self-employed persons (consultation). Amendment of existing principles laid down by law governing the professions with respect to training and conditions of access for natural persons (consultation).

ARTICLE 75(1)

Transport policy (cooperation)

• common rules applicable to international transport to or from the territory of a Member State or passing across the territory of one or more Member States;

• the conditions under which non-resident carriers may operate transport services within a Member State;

• measures to improve transport safety.

ARTICLE 84

Transport policy (cooperation)

• sea and air transport

ARTICLE 118(2)

Social policy

• conditions of labour

ARTICLE 125

Implementing decisions relating to the European Social Fund (cooperation)

ARTICLE 127(4)

Vocational training (cooperation)

• Measures to contribute to the achievement of the objectives of Article 127 (excluding harmonisation)

Article 129d 3rd paragraph

Other measures (TENs) (cooperation)

Article 130e

ERDF implementing decisions (cooperation)

Article 130o 2nd paragraph

Adoption of measures referred in Articles 130j, 130k and 130l - research (cooperation)

Article 130s(1)

Environment (cooperation)

• Action by the Community in order to achieve the objectives of Article 130r

Article 130w

Development cooperation (cooperation).

SIMPLIFICATION OF THE CO-DECISION PROCEDURE

Amended Article 189b

1. Where reference is made in this Treaty to this Article for the adoption of an act, the following procedure shall apply.

2. The Commission shall submit a proposal to the European Parliament and the Council.

The Council, acting by a qualified majority after obtaining the opinion of the European Parliament,

• if it approves all the amendments contained in the European Parliament's opinion, may adopt the proposed act thus amended;

• if the European Parliament does not propose any amendments, may adopt the proposed act;

• shall otherwise adopt a common position and communicate it to the European Parliament. The Council shall inform the European Parliament fully of the reasons which led it to adopt its common position. The Commission shall inform the European Parliament fully of its position.

If, within three months of such communication, the European Parliament:

(a) approves the common position or has not taken a decision, the act in question, shall be deemed to have been adopted in accordance with that common position;

(b) rejects, by an absolute majority of its component members, the common position, the proposed act shall be deemed not to have been adopted;

(c) proposes amendments to the common position by an absolute majority of its component members, the amended text shall be forwarded to the Council and to the Commission, which shall deliver an opinion on those amendments.

3. If, within three months of the matter being referred to it, the Council, acting by a qualified majority, approves all the amendments of the European Parliament, the act in question shall be deemed to have been adopted in the form of the common position thus amended; however, the Council shall act unanimously on the amendments on which the Commission has delivered a negative opinion. If the Council does not approve all the amendments, the President of the Council, in agreement with the President of the European Parliament, shall within six weeks convene a meeting of the Conciliation Committee.

4. The Conciliation Committee, which shall be composed of the members of the Council or their representatives and an equal number of representatives of the European Parliament, shall have the task of reaching agreement on a joint text, by a qualified majority of the members of the Council or their representatives and by a majority of the representatives of the European Parliament. The Commission shall take part in the Conciliation Committee's proceedings and shall take all the necessary initiatives with a view to reconciling the positions of the European Parliament and the Council. In fulfilling this task, the Conciliation Committee shall address the common position on the basis of the amendments proposed by the European Parliament.

5. If, within six weeks of its being convened, the Conciliation Committee approves a joint text, the European Parliament, acting by an absolute majority of the votes cast, and the Council, acting by a qualified majority, shall each have a period of six weeks from that approval in which to adopt the act in question in accordance with the joint text. If either of the two institutions fails to approve the proposed act within that period, it shall be deemed not to have been adopted.

6. Where the Conciliation Committee does not approve a joint text, the proposed act shall be deemed not to have been adopted.

7. The periods of three months and six weeks referred to in this Article shall be extended by a maximum of one month and two weeks respectively at the initiative of the European Parliament or the Council.

The Conference calls on the European Parliament, the Council and the Commission to make every effort to ensure that the co-decision procedure operates as expeditiously as possible. It recalls the importance of strict respect for the deadlines set out in Article 189b and confirms that recourse, provided for in paragraph 7 of that Article, to extension of the periods in question should be considered only when strictly necessary. In no case should the actual period between the second reading by the European Parliament and the outcome of the Conciliation Committee exceed nine months.

ORGANISATION AND COMPOSITION OF THE EUROPEAN PARLIAMENT

ADD TO ARTICLE 137

The number of Members of the European Parliament shall not exceed seven hundred.

AMENDED ARTICLE 138(3)

The European Parliament shall draw up a proposal for elections by direct universal suffrage in accordance with a uniform procedure in all Member States or in accordance with principles common to all Member States.

ADD NEW ARTICLE 138(4) [8]

The European Parliament shall, after seeking an opinion from the Commission and with the approval of the Council acting by unanimity, lay down the regulations and general conditions governing the performance of the duties of its Members.

Commentary
More Power for the European Parliament

Extension of the assent procedure (and the end of cooperation)

One of the most popular objectives of the IGC was to simplify and clarify the Union's ways of making law. This implied a rationalisation from the great variety and complexity of legislative procedures bequeathed by Maastricht and earlier Treaties.

Amsterdam claimed to have succeeded in reducing the proliferation of procedures to three:

- consultation — where the Parliament's opinion is required;

- assent — where the Parliament's agreement is required;

- co-decision — where the Parliament may negotiate on draft legislation as a full partner with the Council.

The cooperation procedure, introduced by the Single European Act and extended by the Treaty on European Union (old Article 189c) was largely abolished, apart from its use in certain aspects of EMU which was not touched at Amsterdam. The cooperation procedure was complex, long-winded and ultimately frustrating as far as the European Parliament was concerned — although a valuable first step in building its relationship with the Council.

The assent procedure was also introduced by the Single Act and extended by Maastricht. The Council acts by unanimity. Under Articles 138(4) (electoral reform) and O (enlargement), the Parliament must act by an absolute majority of its members. Because the Parliament may not amend the proposal, but merely approve or reject it, the assent procedure is most suitable for international agreements negotiated or concluded by the Commission and Council. It is less appropriate though better than nothing for quasi-constitutional measures of importance. Maastricht lent the assent procedure to other matters, such as the establishment and reform of the structural funds.

Amsterdam failed to extend the assent procedure to cover all international agreements, as the Parliament would have wished — for instance, to trade agreements under the WTO (Article 113).

Amsterdam also failed to extend the Parliament's right of assent in three important directions:

- decisions over the Community's own financial resources (Article 201);

- extension of the authority of the institutions in pursuit of Treaty objectives (Article 235);

- amendment to the Treaty (Article N).

In these three cases, the co-decision procedure would undoubtedly be best of all. The Amsterdam European Council agreed to replace the assent procedure by co-decision with respect to citizens' rights (Article 8a(2)), but retained it for two aspects of EMU: the supervisory tasks of the ECB (Article 105(6) and amending the Protocol of the ESCB (Article 106(5)).

The rise of co-decision

Co-decision is at the heart of the debate about the Union's democratic deficit. The European Council took a bold step to widen the scope of the co-decision procedure (Article 189b). This makes the European Parliament the big winner of Amsterdam. But there is still much more to do.

Article N(2) of the Treaty of Maastricht obliged the 1996 IGC to consider the extension of co-decision. In the event, most of the items formerly dealt with under the cooperation procedure were transferred to co-decision.

The cooperation procedure survives only in the field of EMU, as follows:

ARTICLE 103(5)

EMU multilateral surveillance

ARTICLE 104A(2)

EMU prohibition on privileged access

ARTICLE 104B(2)

EMU prohibition on purchasing debt

ARTICLE 105A(2)

EMU harmonisation of coinage

With regard to co-decision, the European Commission said of Maastricht:

'As matters stand the application of the co-decision procedure is founded neither on a logical structure nor on precise criteria. This situation has arisen as a result of the different ways of involving the European Parliament, the piecemeal allocation of areas to the co-decision procedure and haphazard differentiation of types of instrument in certain areas. The resulting structure is complex and heterogeneous: the Treaty is something of a maze and the exact role of each institution is far from obvious.'[9]

Under the terms of Maastricht, co-decision with the Council acting by QMV applied to the following areas, mostly concerning the single market:

ARTICLE 49

Free movement of workers

ARTICLES 54(2)

Right of establishment

ARTICLE 56(2)

Treatment of foreign nationals

ARTICLE 57(1)

Mutual recognition of diplomas

ARTICLE 57(2)

Treatment of the self-employed

ARTICLE 66

Services

ARTICLES 100A

Internal market harmonisation

ARTICLE 100B

Internal market recognition

ARTICLE 126(4)

Education (incentives)

ARTICLE 129(4)

Health (incentives)

ARTICLE 129A(2)

Consumer protection

ARTICLE 129D

TENs (guidelines)

ARTICLE 130S(3)

Environment (action programme)

Co-decision with the Council acting by unanimity applied to:

ARTICLE 128(5)

Culture (incentives)

ARTICLE 130I

R & D (framework programme)

The conjunction of co-decision with unanimity in the Council was strange and is attributed to John Major.

Amsterdam and beyond

The Treaty of Amsterdam has made the European Parliament a full player in several new fields and has resolved some of the anomalies of Maastricht. It is particularly to be welcomed that new Treaty competences on social exclusion and transparency are to be governed by co-decision.

Co-decision with the Council acting by unanimity now applies to:

ARTICLE 8A(2)

citizens' rights

ARTICLE 51

social security for migrant workers

ARTICLE 57

rights of self-employed

ARTICLE 128(5)

cultural measures

But Article 130i reverts to QMV.

Under Article 73o of the new title on freedom, security and justice, co-decision will be extended automatically in five years time to:

ARTICLE 73J(2)(B)(II)

Visa procedures and conditions

ARTICLE 73J(2)(B)(IV)

Visa uniformity rules

Co-decision may be extended further within this sector by unanimous decision of the Council after consulting the Parliament.

The Parliament itself was looking for an even wider extension of powers. At the next IGC the onus of proof will be on the member states to argue why co-decision with QMV should not be applicable in the following areas where, at the moment, the European Parliament is now merely consulted (and sometimes ignored), as follows:

OLD TREATY PROVISIONS

ARTICLE 8B(1)

Citizenship and municipal elections

ARTICLE 8E

Citizenship other measures

ARTICLE 43

Reform of the common agricultural and fisheries policies

ARTICLE 59

Freedom to provide services to third country nationals

ARTICLE 63

Abolition of restrictions of freedom of establishment and services

ARTICLE 73C

Free movement of capital with third countries

ARTICLE 87

Reform of competition policy

ARTICLE 92(3)(E)

New categories of state aid

ARTICLE 94

Reform of state aids rules

ARTICLE 99

Harmonisation of indirect taxation

ARTICLE 100

Harmonisation of laws

ARTICLE 100C(3)

Adoption of rules for visas

ARTICLE 103(5)

EMU multilateral surveillance

ARTICLE 104A(2)

EMU prohibition on privileged access

ARTICLE 104B(2)

EMU prohibition on purchasing debt

ARTICLE 126

European dimension in education

ARTICLE 129D 1ST SUBPARAGRAPH

TENs policy

ARTICLE 130(3)

Industrial policy

ARTICLES 130B, 130D

Reform of the structural and cohesion funds

ARTICLE 130N

Setting up of joint undertakings

ARTICLE 130J

R & D framework implementation

ARTICLE 201

The Community's own resources

ARTICLE 209

Budgetary regulations

NEW TREATY PROVISIONS

ARTICLE 6A (FREEDOM, SECURITY & JUSTICE)

Combating discrimination

ARTICLE 73O (FREEDOM, SECURITY & JUSTICE)

Common immigration policy

ARTICLE K.11 (POLICE & JUDICIAL COOPERATION)

Cooperation measures

ARTICLE K.12 (POLICE & JUDICIAL COOPERATION)

Authorisation of flexibility

ARTICLE K.14 (POLICE & JUDICIAL COOPERATION)

The *passerelle* to the first pillar

ARTICLE 109Q (EMPLOYMENT)

Employment guidelines

ARTICLE 113(5) (EXTERNAL ECONOMIC RELATIONS)

Scope of trade negotiations

ARTICLE 5A(2) (FLEXIBILITY)

Authorisation of flexibility

If this IGC has effectively folded up the cooperation procedure into co-decision, the next could follow suit with the consultation procedure. Once the single currency has been introduced, the institutional provisions of EMU need not always be sacrosanct and immune from change. Moreover, the euro regime will increase the importance of fiscal policy at European Union level, and it is unthinkable that common fiscal policies or tax approximation could take place without a strengthening of the democratic system.

However, if the principle were ever established that co-decision should be extended to all legislative acts, it would be necessary to define and classify a hierarchy of European Union law, including drawing a better distinction between executive acts and legislation. This task was put off by Maastricht (Declaration No. 16), and avoided again at Amsterdam.

It may be regretted that the modest but respectable extension of the co-decision procedure was not accompanied at Amsterdam by the equivalent wider use of qualified majority voting in the Council. Indeed the mixture of co-decision and unanimity is bizarre and belies the claim that Amsterdam succeeded in reducing the decision-making procedures of the Union to only three. The unanimity version of Article 189b is, in fact, a significant fourth — and creates circumstances in which all efforts at conciliation could be frustrated.

Budgetary procedure

The European Parliament will be disappointed not to have won concessions over tax harmonisation or CAP reform, where consultation only still applies; and the reform of the budgetary procedure, including the abolition of the distinction between 'obligatory' and 'non-obligatory' expenditure, is still wanting. On the other hand, the Parliament's involvement in budgetary matters is much extended, as follows:

- third pillar operational expenditure will now fall to the EU budget unless the Council decides otherwise;

- second pillar operations (except military actions) similarly do so on the completion of an inter-institutional procedure;

- the application of co-decision procedure to the fight against fraud.

Simplifying co-decision

The original co-decision procedure under Article 189b of Maastricht was long-winded and over-complicated. It also disadvantaged the European Parliament in that the Council, acting by QMV, could, in the event of a failure of the Conciliation Committee to reach agreement, press its original common position to a conclusion — unless an absolute majority of the Parliament could be mustered to reject it (old Article 189b(6)). This third reading phase, which advantaged Coreper over the Parliament, has now been abolished. If the Conciliation Committee fails, the draft legislation is dropped.

Just as important, the system is further simplified and truncated by:

- allowing the Council to adopt the measure at first reading if it and the Parliament are agreed, or if the Parliament fails to make amendments;

- dropping the phase of intent to reject, so the Parliament can now go straight to rejection.

The revised Treaty also seeks to make the Conciliation Committee more expeditious and disciplined. It must meet within six weeks (extendible to eight if necessary); the deliberations of the Committee must take no more than nine months; and it must focus on the common position as the Parliament seeks to amend it as its basic text.

All this is progress.

Reforming the European Parliament

The prospect of an enlarged Union presaged a European Parliament of a size similar to the old Soviet Plenum. The restriction to a maximum of 700 is one of the few concrete steps taken at Amsterdam to prepare the institutions for enlargement. It will be triggered even by the first probable phase of enlargement (Poland, Czech Republic, Hungary and Slovenia), to take effect at the elections of 2004. This reform accords with the Parliament's own proposal.

There is a cryptic addition to Article 2 of the 1976 Act introducing direct elections to the European Parliament concerning the fair representation of both more and less populated member states. Under the present system one German MEP represents a notional 818,000 people, while one Luxembourg MEP represents only 66,700. There is an agreement yet to be hatched about how the balance between big and small member states should be struck in a reformed European Parliament. While a reduction for all is inevitable, the importance of the small states having enough MEPs to allow for a fair representation of the major strands of political opinion must not be overlooked.

Proportional representation

For a British audience, the reform to Article 138(3) should have enormous resonance. The injunction to have a uniform electoral procedure dates from the first Treaty of Rome, but little headway has been made by either the Parliament or the Council in fulfilling the Treaty. One of the obstacles has been the definition of uniformity, and the Amsterdam amendment — to add 'or in accordance with principles common to all Member States' — is intended to avoid the obstacle.

Pushed by the Germans, whose Constitutional Court judgment of October 1993 mentioned the lack of a uniform electoral procedure as one of the weaknesses of parliamentary democracy at the European level, this amendment would certainly have been vetoed by John Major. That Tony Blair let it through was a sign at least that he was not opposed to introducing proportional representation (PR) in time for the 1999

European Parliamentary elections. For the only principle not common to all member states is PR, and the only unorthodox place Great Britain.[10]

On 17 July 1997 the British government announced that it would indeed be introducing a regional list system of PR in time for the 1999 elections. Meanwhile, the institutional affairs committee of the European Parliament is making fresh moves towards defining a uniform procedure based on the principles of regionalism and proportionality.

Probity

Amid increasing concern about the legitimacy of Members of the European Parliament, and conscious of press stories about fraud, Article 138(4) of the revised Treaty offers hope, if governments can agree, for a statute setting out the rights and duties of a European parliamentarian. Anomalies between nationalities are rich, however, and progress on this is unlikely to be quick.

Taken as a whole, the Treaty of Amsterdam does represent democratic progress, and the undoubted reinforcement of the powers of the European Parliament should help the Treaty's chances of ratification within the more federalist-minded member states such as Belgium, Germany and Italy.

THE COUNCIL

QUALIFIED MAJORITY VOTING

New Treaty provisions

Article 5(a)(2)

Flexibility arrangements

Article 73l(2)

Emergency immigration measures

Article 109q

Employment guidelines

Article 109r

Employment incentive measures

Article 116

Customs cooperation

Article 118(2)

Social exclusion

Article 119(3)

Equality of opportunity and treatment of men and women

Article 129(4)

Public health

Article 191a

Transparency

Article 209a

Countering fraud

Article 213a

Statistics

152

ARTICLE 213B

Establishment of independent advisory authority on data protection

ARTICLE 227(2)

Outermost regions

ARTICLE 236 (2) & (3)

Fundamental rights sanctions

EXISTING TREATY PROVISIONS

ARTICLE 45(3)

Compensatory aid for imports of raw materials

ARTICLE 56(2)

Coordination of provisions laid down by law, regulation or administrative action for special treatment for foreign nationals

ARTICLE 130I(1)

Adoption of the research framework programme

ARTICLE 130I(2)

Adapting or supplementing the research framework programme

ARTICLE 130O

Setting up of joint undertakings in R&T development

AMENDED ARTICLE 151

1. A committee consisting of the Permanent Representatives of the Member States shall be responsible for preparing the work of the Council and for carrying out the tasks assigned to it by the Council. The Committee may adopt procedural decisions in cases provided for in the Council's Rules of Procedure.

2. The Council shall be assisted by a General Secretariat, under the responsibility of a Secretary-General seconded by a Deputy Secretary-General who shall be responsible for the running of the General Secretariat. The Secretary-General and the Deputy Secretary-General shall be appointed by the Council acting unanimously.

The Council shall decide on the organisation of the General Secretariat.

3. The Council shall adopt its Rules of Procedure.

For the purpose of applying Article 191a(3), the Council shall elaborate in these Rules the conditions under which the public shall have access to Council documents. For the purpose of this paragraph, the Council shall define the cases in which it is to be regarded as acting in its legislative capacity, with a view to allowing greater access to documents in those cases, while at the same time preserving the effectiveness of its decision-making process. In any event, when the Council acts in its legislative capacity, the results of votes and explanations of vote as well as statements in the minutes shall be made public.

Commentary
Reforming the Council

Qualified majority voting is, with co-decision, a key concept of a European federal union. European integration could never have advanced to the level of its present sophistication had the Council remained in thrall to the tyranny of the national veto. Unanimity makes controversial decisions difficult, and progress of legislation inevitably slow. While the threat of the veto can induce consensus, only the wide application of the rules of QMV results in Council decisions that are not reduced to the level of the lowest common denominator. QMV is bound to articulate the common interest of at least most member state governments; we hope that its use — or even its influence via what has been called the shadow of the vote — builds trust between the partners.

Renversement des alliances

The strongest expectation following the Labour party's election victory in the UK was that more qualified majority voting in the Council would be possible. Certainly a Conservative victory at the polls would have provoked a crisis within the IGC of a huge and probably unmanageable scale. The new UK government fulfilled expectations by agreeing to extend QMV in all the flanking policies of the single market, although not to the second and third pillars. However, those extensions were modest when measured against the continuing areas where unanimity is still required. In particular, Mr Blair disappointed the socialist fraternity of EU leaders by rejecting proposals to extend QMV inside the social chapter (to rules on workers' representation and redundancy).

The biggest surprise at Amsterdam was that Helmut Kohl pulled back from traditional German positions on QMV. Led by Bavaria, the Länder governments, which compose the SPD-led Bundesrat, were anxious to protect their prerogatives over areas of domestic legislation, particularly concerning the environment and immigration. The federal ministries in Bonn had engaged in turf battles about European policy, notably between the FDP-led foreign ministry and the CSU-led finance ministry. The Chancellor himself was said to be preoccupied with the single currency project and unable to forge either a coherent or progressive German policy on institutional questions. Lastly, the shock election of a socialist-communist government in France on 1 June scuppered the usual Franco-German joint formulation of positions before meetings of the European Council.

There was no more curious thing at Amsterdam than the conjunction of a British prime minister who was prepared to give more away in terms of QMV than a German chancellor. Although the two agreed about social policy, they disagreed about whether to concede QMV in industrial policy, pensions and the recognition of the professions. The likelihood of German concessions was minimised once the linkage with the re-weighting of Council votes had been established. And the Germans insisted against the wishes of the presidency and the Commission on retaining a veto on the introduction of QMV in the field of immigration and asylum in five years time.

Amsterdam and beyond

Nevertheless, there were some significant advances at Amsterdam for the practice of QMV, the most notable of them in the Treaty establishing the European Communities being:

ARTICLE 119

equal pay for and treatment of men and women

ARTICLE 130I(1)

R & D framework programme

ARTICLE 191A

access to official documents

ARTICLE 209A

combating fraud

NEW ARTICLE 116

customs cooperation

Perverse was the failure to extend QMV to these areas where co-decision applies:

ARTICLE 8A(2)

citizens' freedom to move and reside

ARTICLE 51

portability of social security for migrant workers

ARTICLE 57(2)

recognition of professional qualifications

156

ARTICLE 128(5)

incentive measures in the field of culture

In addition, the list on pages 146-48 of those areas to which co-decision should yet apply is also relevant in this context. Particularly strong candidates for the introduction of QMV at the next IGC are:

ARTICLE 100

Approximation of laws

ARTICLE 130D

Reform of the structural funds

ARTICLE 130S

Environment policy

ARTICLE 209

Budgetary regulation

The presidency invited in vain the IGC also to permit the use of QMV in the appointment of the Secretary-General of the Council, membership of the Court of Auditors, Economic and Social Committee, the Committee of the Regions, and rules of procedure governing the Courts of Justice and of First Instance and the Committee of the Regions (Articles 151(2), 168a(2)(4), 188, 188b, 194, 198a, 198b).[11]

It is sometimes thought erroneously that the European Union has some general criteria for the retention of unanimity, involving constitutional and fiscal matters as well as derogations from the single market, such as capital movements and state aids. In fact the Union has no settled principles to guide it in the choice of decision-making procedure. A categorisation of a hierarchy of acts is badly needed to distinguish between protecting the basic rights of member states from those quasi-constitutional and tax harmonisation matters where continual supervision, sometimes leading to action, is required of the institutions. Although Italy and Belgium in the IGC took a contrary view, a majority of member states feels strongly that the revision of basic Treaty provisions (Article N) and enlargement (Article O) should remain bound by unanimity. But there are other less fundamental matters, for example, budgetary provisions, where a lighter procedure could in time be applied.

The pace of progress will depend on the quality of the trust built up between the governments by the wider practice of QMV for general legislation. The Commission and Parliament and the federally inclined

157

member states will continue to promote QMV as the general rule in other circumstances, not least if the Council of ministers of an enlarged Union is not to be paralysed. Jacques Santer called the results of Amsterdam 'mediocre' in this regard.

Internal machinery

Article 151(2) creates the post of Deputy Secretary-General of the Council. He or she will be responsible for running the general secretariat in the Justus Lipsius building in Brussels and for servicing the 360 or so Council working groups. The Secretary-General personally takes on extra responsibilities in the field of common foreign and security policy.

Article 151(3) applies in the Council's own rules of procedure the new policy of 'transparency' as prescribed in New Article 191a(3). It instructs the Council to attempt to divide its legislative from its executive activities, and insists that at least the voting record of ministers be in the public domain. This is a prosaic but significant blow for freedom, long contested by the more secretive and centralised governments.

The need for further reform of the Council, however, is suggested by the absence of any significant improvements to the presidency, by the ever-increasing bureaucracy and by the overall lack of parliamentary accountability.

THE COMMISSION

APPOINTMENT OF THE MEMBERS OF THE COMMISSION

AMENDED FIRST AND SECOND SUBPARAGRAPHS OF ARTICLE 158(2)

The governments of the Member States shall nominate by common accord the person they intend to appoint as President of the Commission; the nomination shall be approved by the European Parliament.

The governments of the Member States shall, by common accord with the nominee for President, nominate the other persons whom they intend to appoint as Members of the Commission.

COMPOSITION AND ORGANISATION OF THE COMMISSION

NEW FIRST PARAGRAPH IN ARTICLE 163

The Commission shall work under the political guidance of its President.

DECLARATION ON THE ORGANISATION AND FUNCTIONING OF THE COMMISSION

The Conference notes the Commission's intention to prepare a reorganisation of tasks within the college in good time for the Commission which will take up office in 2000, in order to ensure an optimum division between conventional portfolios and specific tasks.

In this context, it considers that the President of the Commission must enjoy broad discretion in the allocation of tasks within the College, as well as in any reshuffling of those tasks during a Commission's term of office.

The Conference also notes the Commission's intention to undertake in parallel a corresponding reorganisation of its departments. It notes in particular the desirability of bringing external relations under the responsibility of a Vice-President.

Commentary
Reforming the Commission

Having failed to reduce the size of the European Commission as common sense demanded, the European Council managed to agree that the role and status of Commission President should be enhanced. Here, at least, the Germans were in the forefront of the debate.

Under the terms of the Treaty of Maastricht, the European Parliament was consulted about the member state governments' one intended nomination for the President of the Commission. In 1994 an unseemly highly public row was provoked by the British about the relative suitability as candidates of Jean-Luc Dehaene and Jacques Santer. The newly-elected Parliament took its revenge in January 1995, insisting on a series of hearings and votes before the Santer Commission was granted a vote of approval (Article 158(3)). The change agreed at Amsterdam gives de jure recognition of the Parliament's de facto power of investiture of the President of the Commission. It also boosts the role of the President-elect in the choice of other members of the Commission: whereas previously he was only consulted, he or she will now have to agree.

A declaration of intent supports the Commission's reformists. But to break through the vested interests both of the national civil services and of the highly variable Brussels bureaucracy in order to create a streamlined, efficient supranational executive authority might yet defy the Union. What is clearly required is the appointment in 2000 of a President who has exceptional political and managerial qualities. Probing committees of inquiry in the European Parliament and a strong candidate for the foreign affairs Vice-Presidency will also help.

Under the pressure of enlargement, it should be possible to energise the European Commission and to enhance its relevance to the citizen. Party political candidates for the presidency promoted during the European Parliamentary elections of 1999 could be a worthwhile innovation.

THE COURT OF JUSTICE

AMENDED ARTICLE L OF THE TREATY ON EUROPEAN UNION

The provisions of the Treaty establishing the European Community, the Treaty establishing the European Coal and Steel Community and the Treaty establishing the European Atomic Energy Community concerning the powers of the Court of Justice of the European Communities and the exercise of those powers shall apply only to the following provisions of this Treaty:

(a) provisions amending the Treaty establishing the European Economic Community with a view to establishing the European Community, the Treaty establishing the European Coal and Steel Community and the Treaty establishing the European Atomic Energy Community;

(b) provisions of Title VI, under the conditions provided for by Articles K.7 and K.12;

(c) Article F(2) with regard to action of the institutions, insofar as the Court has jurisdiction under the Treaties establishing the European Communities and under this Treaty;

(d) Articles L to S.

Commentary
Reforming the Court

This amendment seeks to widen the jurisdiction of the European Court of Justice in the remaining third pillar (Police and Judicial Cooperation). Provision is made for the Court to give preliminary rulings and to review the validity and interpretation of actions under Title VI, and to arbitrate in the settlement of disputes.

However, under the third pillar's Article K.7(2) member states may volunteer whether to agree or not to references by national courts to the Court of Justice. This is an unprecedented provision, and may force the Court into delivering variable jurisprudence within the Union — with obvious attendant dangers for the integrity of the corpus of European Community law. The clause means that the principle of subsidiarity will apply differently from one member state to another. It will lead to the greater confusion of the European citizen.

Nevertheless, in that it allows for a limited extension of the authority of the Court into potentially very sensitive matters, it has to be welcomed. The Treaty of Maastricht (old Article K.3(2)(c) third subparagraph) allowed third pillar conventions to opt for the jurisdiction of the Court, but this had to be agreed unanimously and operate uniformly. UK opposition to any extension of the competence of the Court into the area of criminal jurisdiction has been overcome by the amendment.

Article K.12 concerns judicial review of any decision to embark on closer cooperation by a group of member states.

Human rights

The amended Article L also extends the jurisdiction of the Court to cover the observance by the institutions of the European Union of the provisions of the European Convention on Human Rights (ECHR).

This is a valuable step, although it falls well short of proposals by some member states that the European Community or Union should sign up lock, stock and barrel to the ECHR. A Court of Justice opinion of March 1996 insisted that such a radical step would require a Treaty amendment. No agreement was reached on this, despite much discussion at and on the fringes of the IGC. The Court itself may not have been opposed to such a radical move even though it would have put the Strasbourg judges of the Court of Human Rights in a superior position.

More reform needed

No further changes at Amsterdam were made to the Court's competences, resources or working practices. This is bound to leave many lawyers dissatisfied, particularly in the light of the increased complexity of the Treaty and of the aggravated problems of the Union's institutional development. One of the outstanding issues is the appointment procedure and mandate of the judges, which, in the interests of cogency and independence, the Commission and the Court itself want extended and made non-renewable (Article 167). In addition, the IGC created no right of appeal to the individual citizen and drafted no catalogue of rights.

The minimalist result must be blamed in part on the attitude of the British, who have been habitually hostile to extending the powers of the Court. Other governments may share more of this negative attitude than they are prepared to admit, however: the German Bundesverfassungsgericht has certainly regarded the Court of Justice as a competitor.

OTHER INSTITUTIONAL ISSUES

COURT OF AUDITORS

AMENDED ARTICLE E OF THE TREATY ON EUROPEAN UNION

The European Parliament, the Council, the Commission, the Court of Justice and the Court of Auditors shall exercise their powers under the conditions and for the purposes provided for, on the one hand, by the provisions of the Treaties establishing the European Communities and of subsequent Treaties and Acts modifying and supplementing them and, on the other hand, by the other provisions of this Treaty.

AMENDED THIRD PARAGRAPH OF ARTICLE 173 OF THE TREATY ESTABLISHING THE EUROPEAN COMMUNITIES

The Court shall have jurisdiction under the same conditions in actions brought by the European Parliament, by the Court of Auditors and by the ECB for the purpose of protecting their prerogatives.

AMENDED SECOND SUBPARAGRAPH OF ARTICLE 188C(1)

The Court of Auditors shall provide the European Parliament and the Council with a statement of assurance as to the reliability of the accounts and the legality and regularity of the underlying transactions which shall be published in the Official Journal of the European Communities.

AMENDED FIRST SUBPARAGRAPH OF ARTICLE 188C(2)

2. The Court of Auditors shall examine whether all revenue has been received and all expenditure incurred in a lawful and regular manner and whether the financial management has been sound. In doing so, it shall report in particular on any cases of irregularity.

AMENDED ARTICLE 188C(3)

The audit shall be based on records and, if necessary, performed on the spot in the other institutions of the Community, on the premises of any body which manages revenue or expenditure on behalf of the Community and in the Member States, including on the premises of any natural or legal person in receipt of payments from the budget. In the Member States the audit shall be carried out in liaison with national audit bodies or, if these do not have the necessary powers, with the competent national departments. The Court of Auditors and the national audit bodies of the Member States shall cooperate in a spirit of trust while maintaining their independence. These bodies or departments shall inform the Court of Auditors whether they intend to take part in the audit.

The other institutions of the Community, any bodies managing revenue or expenditure on behalf of the Community, any natural or legal person in receipt of payments from the budget, and the national audit bodies or, if these do not have the necessary powers, the competent national departments, shall forward to the Court of Auditors, at its request, any document or information necessary to carry out its task.

In respect of the European Investment Bank's activity in managing Community expenditure and revenue, the Court's rights of access to information held by the Bank shall be governed by an agreement between the Court, the Bank and the Commission. In the absence of an agreement, the Court shall nevertheless have access to information necessary for the audit of Community expenditure and revenue managed by the Bank.

DECLARATION ON ARTICLE 188C(3)

The Conference invites the Court of Auditors, the European Investment Bank and the Commission to maintain in force the present Tripartite Agreement. If a succeeding or amending text is required by any party, they shall endeavour to reach agreement on such a text having regard to their respective interests.

AMEND ARTICLE 206(1)

The European Parliament, acting on a recommendation from the Council which shall act by a qualified majority, shall give a discharge to the Commission in respect of the implementation of the budget. To this end, the Council and the European Parliament in turn shall examine the accounts and the financial statement referred to in Article 205a, the annual report by the Court of Auditors together with the replies of the institutions under audit to the observations of the Court of Auditors, the statement of assurance referred to in Article 188c(1), second subparagraph and any relevant special reports by the Court of Auditors.

ECONOMIC AND SOCIAL COMMITTEE

The Economic and Social Committee will be consulted in the following new provisions to be included in the Treaty establishing the European Communities.

ARTICLE 109Q

Employment guidelines

ARTICLE 109R

Employment incentive measures

ARTICLES 118(2) AND 118(3)

Legislation on social matters

ARTICLE 119(3)

Application of the principle of equal opportunities and equal treatment

ARTICLE 129(4)

Measures to contribute to the achievement of the objectives of public health policy

ADD A NEW FOURTH SUBPARAGRAPH TO ARTICLE 198

The Economic and Social Committee may be consulted by the European Parliament.

COMMITTEE OF THE REGIONS

PROTOCOL NO. 16 SHALL BE REPEALED.

AMENDED THIRD PARAGRAPH OF ARTICLE 198A

The members of the Committee and an equal number of alternative members shall be appointed for four years by the Council acting unanimously on proposals from the respective Member States. Their term of office shall be renewable. No member of the Committee shall at the same time be a Member of the European Parliament. [12]

AMENDED SECOND PARAGRAPH OF ARTICLE 198B

It shall adopt its Rules of Procedure.

AMENDED FIRST PARAGRAPH OF ARTICLE 198C

The Committee of the Regions shall be consulted by the Council or by the Commission where this Treaty so provides and in all other cases, in particular those which concern cross-border cooperation, in which one of these two institutions considers it appropriate.

ADD A NEW FOURTH PARAGRAPH TO ARTICLE 198C

The Committee of the Regions may be consulted by the European Parliament.

The Committee of the Regions will be consulted under the following provisions in the Treaty establishing the European Communities.

ARTICLE 109Q

Employment guidelines

ARTICLE 109R

Employment incentive measures

ARTICLE 118(2) AND (3)

Legislation on social matters

ARTICLE 129(4)

Measures to contribute to the achievement of the objectives of public health policy

ARTICLE 130s(1)(2)(3)

Environment

ARTICLE 125

Social Fund implementing decisions

ARTICLE 127(4)

Measures to contribute to the achievement of the objectives of vocational training policy

ARTICLE 75

Transport

FINANCIAL PROVISIONS

AMENDED FIRST SUBPARAGRAPH OF ARTICLE 205

The Commission shall implement the budget, in accordance with the provisions of the regulations made pursuant to Article 209, on its own responsibility and within the limits of the appropriations, having regard to the principles of sound financial management. Member States shall cooperate with the Commission to ensure that the budget appropriations are used in accordance with the principles of sound financial management.

CONFERRING OF IMPLEMENTING POWERS ON THE COMMISSION

DECLARATION RELATING TO COUNCIL DECISION OF 13 JULY 1987

The Conference calls on the Commission to submit to the Council by the end of 1998 at the latest a proposal to amend the Council decision of 13 July 1987 laying down the procedures for the exercise of implementing powers conferred on the Commission.

SEATS

PROTOCOL ON THE LOCATION OF THE SEATS OF THE INSTITUTIONS AND OF CERTAIN BODIES AND DEPARTMENTS OF THE EUROPEAN COMMUNITY

THE REPRESENTATIVES OF THE GOVERNMENTS OF THE MEMBER STATES,

Having regard to Article 216 of the Treaty establishing the European Community, Article 77 of the Treaty establishing the European Coal and Steel Community and Article 189 of the Treaty establishing the European Atomic Energy Community,

HAVING REGARD to the Treaty on European Union,

RECALLING AND CONFIRMING the Decision of 8 April 1965, and without prejudice to the decisions concerning the seat of future institutions, bodies and departments,

HAVE AGREED UPON the following provisions, which shall be annexed to the Treaty on European Union and the Treaties establishing the European Communities,

SOLE ARTICLE

(a) The European Parliament shall have its seat in Strasbourg where the 12 periods of monthly plenary sessions, including the budget session, shall be held. The periods of additional plenary sessions shall be held in Brussels. The committees of the European Parliament shall meet in Brussels. The General Secretariat of the European Parliament and its departments shall remain in Luxembourg.

(b) The Council shall have its seat in Brussels. During the months of April, June and October, the Council shall hold its meetings in Luxembourg.

(c) The Commission shall have its seat in Brussels. The departments listed in Articles 7, 8 and 9 of the Decision of 8 April 1965 shall be established in Luxembourg.

(d) The Court of Justice and the Court of First Instance shall have their seats in Luxembourg.

(e) The Court of Auditors shall have its seat in Luxembourg.

(f) The Economic and Social Committee shall have its seat in Brussels.

(g) The Committee of the Regions shall have its seat in Brussels.

(h) The European Investment Bank shall have its seat in Luxembourg.

(i) The European Monetary Institute and the European Central Bank shall have their seat in Frankfurt.

(j) The European Police Office (Europol) shall have its seat in The Hague.

Commentary
Other institutional reforms

Wider powers for the Court of Auditors

Growing concern about financial control within the European Union created a wide basis of support for a strengthening of the powers of the Court of Auditors.

The first amendment (Article E) extends the scope of the Court of Auditors to expenditure from the European Community budget in the administration of both common foreign and security policy and police and judicial cooperation (the second and third pillars).

The amendment to Article 173 extends to the Auditors the power already given to the Parliament and Central Bank to take action against the other institutions before the Court of Justice in protection of its own prerogatives.

The first change to Article 188c allows the Court to publish its statement of assurance on the accounts; and the change to Article 206(1) says that the institutions shall take the statement into consideration in granting the discharge.

The second amendment to Article 188c gives the Court more scope to expose irregularities. The third extends the Court's powers of investigation to include the EU's agencies and consultancies; it also insists on full cooperation between the Court and national audit offices; and seeks to extend the remit of the Auditors specifically to the EIB in respect of EU projects. A new tripartite agreement between the Court, the EIB and the Commission will be negotiated — in favour of the stricter audit of the financial management of the EIB and the Commission.

Proposals to allow the European Parliament a say in the appointment of members of the Court of Auditors were rejected.

Much of the advance achieved by the Court of Auditors at Amsterdam may be credited to both the British Conservative and Labour governments. Indeed, the UK would have gone further in asserting the right of the Court over the national audit authorities: but a proposal to close the option of national authorities to refuse to cooperate with the EU's auditors was not accepted by the IGC (Article 188c(3), first paragraph, last sentence).

More scope for Ecosoc

The new employment chapter of the Treaty offered the IGC the opportunity to enhance the competences of the consultative Economic and Social Committee (Ecosoc), which it took. But the parallel decision to establish a separate Employment Committee (Article 6, New Title) effectively by-passes Ecosoc in the field of employment and labour market policies. There has for years been tension between Ecosoc on the one hand and, on the other, the 'Val-Duchesse' tripartite meetings between the Commission and social partners on employment matters.

Nevertheless, the integration into the Treaty of the Social Agreement from which the UK had previously enjoyed an opt-out, gave further scope to Ecosoc.

The change to Article 198 permits the European Parliament (with the Commission and Council) to consult Ecosoc whenever it so desires; but the possibility of rivalry between the two bodies as they vie for influence has not been eliminated.

The Economic and Social Committee's own requests to the IGC were aimed at increasing its influence within EMU, European citizenship and cultural policy, as well as measures to give the Committee control over its members expenses and an extension of their term of office from four to five years. [13] In all these, and other matters, it was frustrated.

Second chance for the regions

The Committee of the Regions, drawn on a national basis from regional and local authorities within the European Union, was set up under the Treaty of Maastricht. Its consultative powers were constrained but its first years saw sustained activity and heightened ambition. The Committee has been driven especially by the autonomous regional governments of Germany and Spain, and the prospect of growing regional differentiation under EMU gives the Committee a legitimate raison d'être. Amsterdam gave the regions a second chance to enhance their direct influence on the governance of the European Union.

The Amsterdam IGC set the Committee of the Regions free from sharing the administrative resources of the Economic and Social Committee (by abolishing Protocol No. 16 of the Maastricht Treaty). It also protected the Committee from infiltration by Members of the European Parliament (Article 198a). It abolished the Council's veto over its own rules of procedure (Article 198b).

The IGC did not agree, however, to the principle that the membership of the Committee should be drawn exclusively from elected members of regional and local authorities.

The new Treaty specifically refers to cross-border matters as being legitimate areas for the Council and Commission to seek the advice of the regions, and adds to those who may consult them the European Parliament (Article 198c).

The Committee of the Regions was granted the same new extension of competence as the Economic and Social Committee (employment, social policy and public health), and in addition had its own scope extended to mirror that of Ecosoc in transport, environmental matters and vocational training.

All this adds up to a significant if undramatic enhancement of the status of the Committee. Its own proposals went much further, particularly with regard to its possible role in applying the principle of subsidiarity to levels below that of the member state. [14] It also sought to acquire a privileged status with the Court of Justice (Article 173), in effect exalting it above Ecosoc to become a formal institution of the Union. Its relative disappointment about the outcome of the IGC will not deter the Committee of the Regions from exploiting the new opportunities it nevertheless acquired.

Financial discipline of the member states

This amendment stems from a UK initiative designed to strengthen the discipline with which member state governments spend European Union money. The second sentence is an addition.

The British would have gone further, to seek recompense for the misapplication of the EU budget by the member state concerned.

Comitology

This Declaration seeks to renegotiate the agreement reached after the Single European Act on the implementation of EC decisions, but without indicating how. [15] The Maastricht IGC also failed to agree to a change to what is known as 'comitology'.

Article 145 of the Treaty of Rome allows the Council to confer on the Commission powers to implement the acts and policies of the Union. There are different procedures just as there are different forms of legislative or regulatory act, according to the importance or technicality of the subject area. At the risk of over-simplification, three types of executive committee were established in 1987:

- advisory committee — where the Commission has the maximal role;

- management committee — which allows the Council to act by QMV to overturn a Commission decision;

- regulatory committee — which may allow the Council to act by simple majority to overturn a Commission decision.

The European Parliament has inveighed against this system on the grounds that it is officious, obscure and that it excludes itself, as one arm of the legislative authority. MEPs have often challenged the ministers' choice of executive instrument, seeking to leave with the more accountable Commission sufficient delegated power to effect EU acts. The introduction after Maastricht of the co-decision procedure aggravated Parliament's grievance, and comitology became a frequent bone of contention within the conciliation committees. A modus vivendi was worked out in December 1994 whereby the MEPs would be kept informed at all stages of the passage of delegated legislation, but the situation remained so unsatisfactory that the Council agreed to push the issue forward for proper resolution to the 1996 IGC.

The options remaining include designing the hierarchy of acts so that the Commission should be assigned full power of implementation, subject only to the scrutiny of Council and Parliament — as the Commission already enjoys for the budget (Article 209); or rationalising comitology by abolishing (at least) the regulatory committees. Treaty amendment is not required, and the item fell off the agenda of the IGC at an early stage. But a political agreement, urgently required before enlargement, still seems a long way off.

Where to sit

This Protocol appears courtesy of the French government, which has been determined over many years to secure Strasbourg as the main venue for the plenary sessions of the European Parliament.

The Edinburgh European Council in December 1992 had first opined on this matter, much to the vexation of the Parliament, but nothing had been included in the Treaty of Maastricht.

Predictably, the European Parliament was quick to condemn this outcome of Amsterdam, not least because of public disquiet about its costly transportation and duplication of (equally unedifying) facilities in both Strasbourg and Brussels. [16] It is also certain that the removal of the Parliament from the de facto capital city of the European Union will tend to limit its relevance to the citizen, the media and business. And it is certainly undignified for any parliament to have governments tell it where to sit.

On the other hand, Strasbourg has an historic role as the symbol of Franco-German reconciliation and is a bit farther to the East in a Union that is shortly destined to enlarge in that direction.

A subsidiary effect of this Protocol is to confirm the Council decision to site the European Central Bank in Frankfurt.

ROLE OF NATIONAL PARLIAMENTS

PROTOCOL ON THE ROLE OF NATIONAL PARLIAMENTS IN THE EUROPEAN UNION

THE HIGH CONTRACTING PARTIES,

RECALLING that scrutiny by individual national parliaments of their own government in relation to the activities of the Union is a matter for the particular constitutional organisation and practice of each Member State,

DESIRING, however, to encourage greater involvement of national parliaments in the activities of the European Union and to enhance their ability to express their views on matters which may be of particular interest to them,

HAVE AGREED upon the following provisions, which shall be annexed to the Treaty on European Union and the treaties establishing the European Communities,

I. Information for national Parliaments of Member States

1. All Commission consultation documents (green and white papers and communications) shall be promptly forwarded to national parliaments of the Member States.

2. Commission proposals for legislation as defined by the Council in accordance with Article 151 of the Treaty establishing the European Community, shall be made available in good time so that the Government of each Member State may ensure that its own national parliament receives them as appropriate.

3. A six-week period shall elapse between a legislative proposal or a proposal for a measure to be adopted under Title VI of the Treaty on European Union being made available in all languages to the European Parliament and the Council by the Commission and the date when it is placed on a Council agenda for decision either for the adoption of an act or for adoption of a common position pursuant to Article 189b or 189c, subject to exceptions on grounds of urgency, the reasons for which shall be stated in the act or common position.

II. The Conference of European Affairs Committees

4. The Conference of European Affairs Committees, hereinafter referred to as COSAC, established in Paris on 16-17 November 1989, may make any contribution it deems appropriate for the attention of the EU institutions, in particular on the basis of draft legal texts which Representatives of Governments of the Member States may decide by common accord to forward to it, in view of the nature of its subject matter.

5. COSAC may examine any legislative proposal or initiative in relation to the establishment of an area of freedom, security and justice which might have a direct bearing on the rights and freedoms of individuals. The European Parliament, the Council and the Commission shall be informed of any contribution made by COSAC under this paragraph.

6. COSAC may address to the European Parliament, the Council and the Commission any contribution which it deems appropriate on the legislative activities of the Union, notably in relation to the application of the principle of subsidiarity, the area of freedom, security and justice as well as questions regarding fundamental rights.

7. Contributions made by COSAC shall in no way bind national parliaments or prejudge their position.

Commentary
Helping national parliaments

The parliaments of the member states have an important but clearly defined legislative role in the constituent process of the European Union. They ratify Treaty revision, including the accession of new members, according to their own constitutional procedures. They also have reserved powers to give assent to various changes, for example, concerning the system of financial own resources (Article 201), and the extension of rights to be conferred upon the European Union citizen (Article 8e).

What parliaments should and should not do

The main job of national parliaments is to act strategically, responding to issues of magnitude and defining with the government of the day the received national interest. But effective parliamentary scrutiny of the European Union is important, and member state parliaments should also try to follow the behaviour of their own ministers and civil servants in the Council and its working parties, and to hold them to account. However, no national parliament has had more than a semi-detached role in traditional international affairs (except the power of the purse in times of war), and in practice few of them have found the way to operate effectively in European Union matters. They are not helped in their quest by the habitual opacity of Council procedures, which do not lend themselves to detailed scrutiny.

What national parliaments cannot do is to share with the European Parliament in the routine law-making of the European Union. That way lies certain immobility. Where member state parliaments have tried to interfere in detailed day-to-day EU matters, they have tended to be frustrated. The Danish Folketing is the worst example of a jealous national parliament, keeping a fierce grip on Danish ministers in Brussels, and able to do so because of the perennial weakness of Danish coalition governments. The British House of Commons has let its so-called scrutiny procedures be dominated by anti-Europeans, and the results have been more noisy than effective. The French Assemblée Nationale was panicked into action on European affairs by the *petit oui* of the Maastricht referendum in 1992. And it was the French Gaullists who first put up — in vain — proposals to the IGC to establish a second chamber of the European Parliament (a third chamber of the EU legislature) made up of national deputies.

Maastricht

The previous IGC had experimented, in November 1990 in Rome, with a grand 'assizes' made up of national and European parliamentarians. This event had been captured by the MEPs, far more skilled in the business of Euro-politics, for their own purposes, and the experiment was not repeated before Amsterdam despite a Declaration No. 14 of the Maastricht Treaty that allowed for it.

In Declaration No. 13 the Treaty of Maastricht paid lip service to developing the role of national parliaments in the activities of the European Union. In one or two member states, notably France and Greece as well as in the newly joined member states of Austria, Finland and Sweden, a concerted effort was made by national parliaments to assert themselves. In others, like Belgium, MEPs have a more important role in national parliamentary activities. The German Bundestag also reached a decent modus operandi. The European Commission tried to ensure that the Council secretariat sent its proposals in appropriate languages to national parliaments promptly.

Between Maastricht and Amsterdam, COSAC, the joint committee of the heads of national European affairs committees together with a delegation of MEPs, met more conscientiously.[17] In practice, however, very little of substance changed — and national MPs still felt themselves, quite rightly, to be badly informed and only tangentially involved in the development of European integration. Yet no special effort was made by national parliaments, either singly or collectively, to work together with the European Parliament in the areas of the second and third pillars where the democratic deficit was particularly acute.

Amsterdam

The Group of Reflection laboured the issue. It mentioned only to dismiss it the French proposal for a 'High Consultative Council' of thirty MPs to second-guess the institutions, especially on subsidiarity questions. It recommended that Commissioners should be prepared to appear before national parliamentary committees — despite the fact that they already did and had done so for many years. The European Parliament itself remained for obvious reasons politely cynical about the prospect of an enhanced role for national parliaments. The UK Tory government threatened radical new proposals, but never delivered. Proposals to allow national parliaments the same status of privileged litigant as the EU institutions in the jurisdiction of the Court of Justice came to nothing.

What we are left with is not much. On the basis of an Irish draft, the Dutch presidency steered the IGC towards this Protocol.

It seeks to improve the flow of information to national parliaments, and, within the remaining third pillar (Police and Judicial Cooperation) to ensure a six week delay between the deposition of draft legislation by the Commission and its consideration by the Council.

The role of COSAC is recognised in treaty form for the first time. But it is steered firmly towards the area of freedom, security and justice, which may prove to be a constraint on its developing an eclectic approach to liaising between member state parliaments and the EU institutions.

The future

Amsterdam is unlikely to be the last word in the story about the European Union and national parliaments, but it may have put an end to fanciful speculation about new formal institutional arrangements. The solution is surely pragmatic, and has two objectives:

- to force the Council, in its law-making capacity, to act more like a second chamber of a legislature and less like a classic diplomatic negotiation;

- to build up trust between all the member state parliaments, to share best practice and to work together where appropriate to tackle particularly difficult dossiers of either multilateral or bilateral relevance — for example, mad cows or Gibraltar.

The purpose must be not to rival the European Parliament but to complement it, for example in monitoring expenditure from the EU budget within member states.

As far as the Council is concerned, what will make it more accountable in the long run is the practice of open government. National parliaments will then have a viable role to play in holding their ministers to account. Better collaboration between them is bound to expose the tendentious or partial briefing of the media by ministers with an eye to a domestic constituency, and the glaring inconsistencies between different national interpretations of Council negotiations and decisions.

Given the differences between national parliaments, a wholly uniform approach among them is most unlikely to emerge. But they all share a common interest in making the Council more open and in insisting on progress towards agreement on an early future occasion about a hierarchy of acts.

National parliaments would then be better informed both about what goes on in Brussels and about how the positions of other member states are formed. It is not too much to hope that MPs so engaged politically with the EU process could lead public opinion in their own countries towards a fuller understanding of the full scale and scope of European integration.

[1] Commission Opinion, op. cit., p. 7.

[2] See the Non-Paper of 11 February 1997, CONF/3815/97.

[3] The Ioannina Compromise prescribes that if members of the Council representing between 23 and 25 votes wished to assert their opposition to a measure to be decided by a QMV of 62, 'a reasonable time' would be allowed to try to reach an alternative agreement.

[4] The procedure currently applicable is indicated between brackets after the content of each Article.

[5] The Council shall act unanimously.

[6] As simplified (see CONF/4152/97).

[7] The Council shall act unanimously.

[8] A corresponding amendment will be made to the Act concerning the election of representatives of the European Parliament.

[9] European Commission, *Scope of the Co-Decision Procedure*, SEC(96) 1225, Brussels, 3 July 1996.

[10] For more coverage of this important issue, see *Electoral Reform of the European Parliament*, Report by Andrew Duff for the European Movement, London, Federal Trust, 1996; and Raymond Plant and Michael Steed, *PR for Europe: Proposals to change the electoral system of the European Parliament*, Federal Trust Report, London, Federal Trust, 1997.

[11] See the Non-Paper of 11 February 1997, CONF/3814/97.

[12] Article 6 of the Act of 20 September 1976 will be amended accordingly.

[13] Opinion of 22 November 1995 on the 1996 Intergovernmental Conference and the role of the Economic and Social Committee.

[14] Committee of the Regions, Opinion of 20 April 1995 on the Revision of the Treaty on European Union.

[15] OJ L 197, 18 July 1987, p. 33.

[16] In its resolution of 26 June 1997.

[17] COSAC is the Conférence des organes specialisées dans les affaires communautaires.

Section Five

Closer Cooperation
— or 'Flexibility'

*GENERAL CLAUSES TO BE INSERTED AS A NEW TITLE
VIA IN THE COMMON PROVISIONS OF THE TREATY ON
EUROPEAN UNION*

ARTICLE K.15

1. Member States which intend to establish closer cooperation between them may make use of the institutions, procedures and mechanisms laid down by the Treaties provided that the cooperation:

(a) is aimed at furthering the objectives of the Union and at protecting and serving its interests;

(b) respects the principles of the Treaties and the single institutional framework of the Union;

(c) is only used as a last resort, where the objectives of the Treaties could not be attained by applying the relevant procedures laid down therein;

(d) concerns at least a majority of Member States;

(e) does not affect the acquis communautaire and the measures adopted under the other provisions of the Treaties;

(f) does not affect the competences, rights, obligations and interests of those Member States which do not participate therein;

(g) is open to all Member States and allows them to become parties to the cooperation at any time, provided that they comply with the basic decision and with the decisions taken within that framework;

(h) complies with the specific additional criteria laid down in Article 5a of the Treaty establishing the European Community and Article K.12 of this Treaty, depending on the area concerned and is authorised by the Council in accordance with the procedures laid down therein.

2. Member States shall apply, as far as they are concerned, the acts and decisions adopted for the implementation of the cooperation in which

181

they participate. Member States not participating in such cooperation shall not impede the implementation thereof by the participating Member States.

ARTICLE K.16

1. For the purposes of the adoption of the acts and decisions necessary for the implementation of the cooperation referred to in Article K.15, the relevant institutional provisions of the Treaties shall apply. However, while all members of the Council shall be able to take part in the deliberations, only those representing participating Member States shall take part in the adoption of decisions; the qualified majority shall be defined as the same proportion of votes of the Council members concerned weighted in accordance with Article 148(2) of the Treaty establishing the European Community; unanimity shall be constituted by only those Council members concerned.

2. Expenditure resulting from implementation of the cooperation, other than administrative costs entailed for the institutions, shall be borne by the participating Member States, unless the Council, acting unanimously, decides otherwise.

ARTICLE K.17

The Council and the Commission shall regularly inform the European Parliament of the development of closer cooperation established on the basis of this Title.

AMENDED CLAUSE CONCERNING POLICE AND JUDICIAL COOPERATION IN CRIMINAL MATTERS

ARTICLE K.12

1. Member States which intend to establish closer cooperation between themselves may be authorised, subject to Articles K.15 and K.16 to make use of the institutions, procedures and mechanisms laid down by the Treaties provided that the cooperation proposed:

(a) respects the powers of the European Community, and the objectives laid down by this Title;

(b) has the aim of enabling the Union to develop more rapidly into an area of freedom, security and justice.

2. The authorisation referred to in paragraph 1 shall be granted by the Council, acting by a qualified majority at the request of the Member States concerned and after inviting the Commission to present its opinion; the request shall also be forwarded to the European Parliament.

If a member of the Council declares that, for important and stated reasons of national policy, it intends to oppose the granting of an authorisation by qualified majority, a vote shall not be taken. The Council may, acting by a qualified majority, request that the matter be referred to the European Council for decision by unanimity.

The votes of the members of the Council shall be weighted in accordance with article 148(2) of the Treaty establishing the European Community. For their adoption, decisions shall require at least 62 votes in favour, cast by at least 10 members.

3. Any Member State which wishes to become a party to cooperation set up in accordance with this Article shall notify its intention to the Council and to the Commission, which shall give an opinion to the Council within three months of receipt of that notification, possibly accompanied by a recommendation for specific arrangements as it may deem necessary for that Member State to become a party to the cooperation in question. Within four months of the date of that notification, the Council shall decide on the request and on possible specific arrangements as it may deem necessary. The decision shall be deemed to be taken unless the Council, acting by a qualified majority, decides to hold it in abeyance; in this case, the Council shall state the reasons for its decision and set a deadline for re-examining it. For the purposes of this paragraph, the Council shall act under the conditions set out in Article K.16.

4. The provisions of Articles K.1 to K.13 shall apply to the closer cooperation provided for by this Article, save as otherwise provided for in this Article and in Articles K.15 and K.16.

The provisions of the Treaty establishing the European Community concerning the powers of the Court of Justice of the European Communities and the exercise of those powers shall apply to paragraphs 1, 2 and 3.

5. This Article is without prejudice to the provisions of the Protocol integrating the Schengen acquis into the framework of the Union.

NEW CLAUSES TO BE INSERTED IN THE TREATY ESTABLISHING THE EUROPEAN COMMUNITY

ARTICLE 5A

1. Member States which intend to establish closer cooperation between themselves may be authorised, subject to Articles K.15 and K.16 of the Treaty on European Union, to make use of the institutions, procedures and mechanisms laid down by this Treaty, provided that the cooperation proposed:

(a) does not concern areas which fall within the exclusive competence of the Community;

(b) does not affect Community policies, actions or programmes;

(c) does not concern the citizenship of the Union or discriminate between nationals of Member States;

(d) remains within the limits of the powers conferred upon the Community by this Treaty; and

(e) does not constitute a discrimination or a restriction of trade between Member States and does not distort the conditions of competition between the latter.

2. The authorisation referred to in paragraph 1 shall be granted by the Council, acting by a qualified majority on a proposal from the Commission and after consulting the European Parliament.

If a member of the Council declares that, for important and stated reasons of national policy, it intends to oppose the granting of an authorisation by qualified majority, a vote shall not be taken. The Council may, acting by a qualified majority, request that the matter be referred to the Council, meeting in the composition of the Heads of State or Government, for decision by unanimity.

Member States which intend to establish closer cooperation as referred to in paragraph 1 may address a request to the Commission, which may submit a proposal to the Council to that effect. In the event of the Commission not submitting a proposal, it shall inform the Member States concerned of the reasons for not doing so.

3. Any Member State which wishes to become a party to cooperation set up in accordance with this Article shall notify its intention to the Council and to the Commission, which shall give an opinion to the Council within three months of receipt of that notification. Within four months of the date of that notification, the Commission shall decide on it and on possible specific arrangements as it may deem necessary.

4. The acts and decisions necessary for the implementation of cooperation activities shall be subject to all the relevant provisions of this Treaty, save as otherwise provided for in this Article and in Articles K.15 and K.16 of the Treaty on European Union.

5. This Article is without prejudice to the provisions of the Protocol integrating the Schengen acquis in the framework of the European Union.

Commentary
Flexibility

These clauses represent one of the most important theoretical innovations of Amsterdam — although their practical usefulness is doubtful.

Background

The revised Treaty is only the latest stage in a gradual differentiation between member states that has been developing within the process of European integration for several years. Even within the original Six members of the EEC there were important examples of flexibility outside the European Community legal order. Article 233 of the Treaty of Rome would have allowed the Benelux trio to develop a deeper form of integration — the 'completion of regional unions' — should they have wished to do so. There have also been important bilateral arrangements outside the EU Treaties, notably the January 1963 Elysée Treaty between France and Germany.

Differentiation has always been most marked in the field of defence. Only ten of the fifteen member states have joined (in stages) the Western European Union, although all now have observer status. Likewise, only eleven EU member states have joined Nato, although three others are participants in its Partnership for Peace.

The variable reception given to the hopes expressed at the summits of The Hague in 1969 and Paris in 1972 served to highlight the differences in approach between member states. These differences were accentuated during the first oil crisis immediately after UK entry in 1973. Two years later, the Belgian prime minister, Leo Tindemans, drew attention to the fact that some states were prepared to move ahead faster than others. He suggested that the overall concept and principles of European Union had to be agreed by all states; and that those 'which are able to progress have a duty to forge ahead'. As for the other category of member states, the validity of their reasons for delay should be assessed by the Council on a proposal of the Commission, and they would receive help 'to enable them to catch the others up'.[1] Tindemans insisted that he was not opening the door to '*l'Europe à la carte*'.

'Least possible disturbance'

The Tindemans Report saw monetary union as the key dynamic of future integration. The European Monetary System was indeed established in 1979 but with only seven out of nine currencies within the Exchange Rate Mechanism. Differentiation was also regarded as inevitable in the building of the single market. Article 15 of the Single European Act said that the Commission would have to take into account 'differences in development' of the member states, and that any derogation from internal market provisions should only be temporary and 'must cause the least possible disturbance to the functioning of the common market'.

The European Community was developing for functional reasons a systematic approach to differentiation. UK accession had increased diversity and heightened the need for cohesion and solidarity. But at this stage differentiation was only a question of variable pace towards common objectives, and both pace and objectives were agreed by all member states according to the principle of 'least possible disturbance'. The Maastricht Treaty made greater use of this multi-speed approach to European integration; but it also added greatly to the disturbance.

The big innovation of Maastricht was to allow the UK an opt-out from the single currency even if it were to meet the convergence criteria. And the UK was also granted a permanent derogation from EC social policy. These decisions had been anticipated by the signing by only five member states of the Schengen Agreement on the abolition of border controls, and the Treaty of Maastricht (Article K.7) regularised this situation by allowing two or more member states to develop closer cooperation on third pillar issues. All this formal differentiation was compounded by Denmark, which grabbed further opt-outs in the fields of defence, citizenship and EMU.

Maastricht, then, failed to maintain the consensus between member states about the direction of European integration. Goals were no longer all held in common. Some wished not only to go faster than others, but in different directions. The multi-speed European Community was in the process of being replaced by a wider, multi-tier Europe. Institutional differentiation was added to functional differentiation.

By-passing the British problem

In the preparation for the IGC, the majority of member states took the orthodox view that increased solidarity was necessary for an enlarged Union to thrive, and that it would become very much more difficult to manage wider differentiation, 'variable geometry' or 'flexibility' if the powers of the common institutions, particularly of the Commission and the Court of Justice, were to weaken.

During the IGC's preparation it became clear that a majority of member states wanted:

- the UK to abandon its Social Protocol;
- to write a new employment chapter into the Treaty;

- to develop common foreign and security policy including some QMV and to reinforce the links between the Union and WEU;

- to extend the jurisdiction of the Court of Justice;

- to flesh out European citizenship in terms of civil and social rights;

- to make QMV and co-decision the general rule for legislation;

- to transfer competences for immigration and asylum policy from the third pillar to the first;

- to incorporate Schengen within the EU Treaty.

The problem was that the British government opposed each of these reforms, which, it argued correctly, would take the Union in a more federalist direction. It rapidly became difficult to escape the conclusion that the UK was going to stymie the whole reform programme, a view that was confirmed by the British attitude towards EMU. The UK government sought to avoid the ties that were being designed to associate those without the euro-zone with those within. It cast doubt on both the credibility of the project and its timetable; and in doing so it put itself apart, in a third tier, from those governments, such as the Italian, that would participate but could not yet do so.

To compound matters, the UK engaged in three supplementary battles with its partners during 1996. The first concerned mad cow disease, where the UK reacted to the EU ban on the export of British beef by a systematic policy of non-cooperation which broke Treaty obligations and which caused 118 measures to be blocked in the Council, including the IGC, between 21 May and 24 June. The second battle concerned fish quotas, where the UK threatened to veto all progress at the IGC if it did not get its own way. And, third, the UK sought to undermine the 48 Hour Working Week directive by a futile challenge to the Court on the question of legal base. In all cases, the UK government appeared to be taking a calculated risk that indifference to its interests would be succeeded by discrimination against them.

Franco-German initiatives

The other member states, led by France and Germany, were quick to draw their own conclusions. It was clear that a successful conclusion of the IGC depended on the skill with which the fifteen could negotiate a system of differentiated integration, with some member states going further towards unity in various matters than others and the UK effectively by-passed.

In September 1994 Wolfgang Schäuble and Karl Lamers, on behalf of the CDU/CSU parliamentary party, set out a deliberately provocative proposal for a 'hard core' of states to exercise a centripetal or magnetic effect on the whole Union.[2] They advanced five mutually dependent proposals that were designed to:

- develop European federal democracy;

- strengthen the hard core;

- deepen Franco-German integration;

- improve the Union's capacity for action in foreign and security policy;

- expand the Union towards the East.

Schäuble and Lamers argued that a stronger and more democratic Union was required to cope both with EMU and with the strains of enlargement to the East. They even proposed a revision of Article N which requires unanimity to amend the Treaty.

John Major reacted quickly in a speech in Leiden on 7 September 1994. He insisted that 'the way the Union develops must be acceptable to all member states', and that 'no member state should be excluded from an area of policy in which it wants and is qualified to participate'. Major argued against an 'exclusive hard core' of member states as well as 'chaotic non-conformity'. But, he added, 'conformity can never be seen as an automatic principle'.

In an article in *Le Monde* on 30 November 1994, François Mitterrand's last prime minister, Edouard Balladur, contributed a proposal for concentric circles consisting of two tiers of full member states, as well as a third tier of 'partner states', including Russia and Turkey. Alain Juppé, then foreign minister, said that an EU inner core should have 'solidarités renforcées', and that the IGC must not merely be a 'patching-up exercise, but a genuine refounding act for Greater Europe'. Alain Lamassoure, minister for Europe, spoke of a 'new founders' contract'; and Valéry Giscard d'Estaing of a federal core of 'l'Europe-puissance' and an outer tier of 'l'Europe-espace'.

On 6 December 1995 President Chirac and Chancellor Kohl published a famous letter aimed at Britain, in which they wrote that the 'momentary difficulties of one of the partners in following the move forward should not stand in the way of the Union's ability to take action and advance'. They said that they intended to propose to the IGC a new treaty clause that would allow for 'coopération renforcée' among those member states that had the will and capacity to go forward.

Further reflections

The Group of Reflection concluded that flexibility needed to be considered on a case by case basis, observing the following criteria:

- flexibility should serve the Union's objectives, and should only be deployed if all other solutions had been ruled out;

- no one should be excluded from full participation in actions or common policies previously adopted;

- for those who wanted to take part but were temporarily unable to do so, provision should be made for ad hoc measures to assist them;

- maintaining the acquis must remain a priority;

- a single institutional framework had to be respected.

A large majority of the Reflection Group considered that derogations should not be permanent, and that, while derogations in the Community pillar would jeopardise the internal market, there was greater scope for flexibility in the areas of foreign and security policy and justice and home affairs. There was disagreement about whether an expression of political solidarity would also implicate the minority — possibly the 'neutrals' — in some financial responsibility. It was accepted that some vital national interest might still require the back-stop of a formal veto in security policy, although such an interest would need to be defined and accepted in advance of any decision being taken.

From their various submissions to the IGC, it was clear that all member states accepted the prospect of differentiated integration. Belgium believed 'it would be unacceptable for one or more Member States to be allowed to hold up progress on European integration towards an ever closer union among the peoples of Europe'; 'thought must be given to the political and institutional choices that are bound to arise if the results of the IGC negotiations are not unanimously endorsed'. The IGC must deliver arrangements for differentiation, which while not an end in itself is a last resort to protect integration from any veto; it should create a 'traction effect' to allow all member states to catch up with the leaders; the scope of differentiation must be carefully selected; institutional derogations must be confined to the minimum; the efficient operation of the market and the Community's legal order must not be compromised; and the key to differentiation must be placed in the Commission's hands as the guardian of the common interest, with the Council acting by QMV.[3]

This approach was later adopted by all three Benelux countries in a joint memorandum on the IGC.[4] In addition, the Luxembourg government regretted the inclusion of the opt-out clauses for Britain and Denmark in the Maastricht Treaty.[5] The Dutch were characteristically frank about the dilemma posed for the Union by the reluctance of the UK to agree to progress, particularly in the field of internal security. The Schengen approach, it said, was necessary but regrettable; and it was likely in the future that differentiated integration would continue to be necessary to preserve the dynamism of the integration process. [6] For obvious reasons, Denmark was less forthcoming. [7] Sweden seemed more open to the possibilities than Finland. [8] Greece was strongly opposed to the authorisation of a second-class membership of the EU. [9] Ireland was compelled to be ambivalent because of its close links with the UK. Spain and Portugal were aligned to the Benelux approach, but stressed the need to reinforce cohesion and solidarity. [10] Italy argued for the incorporation in the EU of the Schengen Agreement within the framework of a mechanism of 'differentiated solidarity'. [11]

The emerging strategy of the British government was to concede that other member states could go forward without the UK if they wished to do so, but not without British consent. In its controversial White Paper of March 1996, the Conservative government said:

'The Union needs to accept a degree of flexibility or, as it is sometimes described, 'variable geometry', without falling into the trap of a two-tier Europe with a hard core either of countries or of policies. The pillared structure introduced at Maastricht was welcome recognition that structures which work well for the single market are inappropriate for Common Foreign and Security Policy or Justice and Home Affairs issues. Strict disciplines are right and necessary in certain areas ... But conformity should never be sought for its own sake. There may be areas in which it is perfectly healthy for some Member States to integrate more closely or more quickly than others. It is important however that such policies only become Union policies, and draw on the Community's institutions, including the budget, where this is agreed by all'. [12]

The Commission firmly rejected the idea of a 'pick-and-choose Europe' — for example, the Social Protocol, which 'flies in the face of the common European project and the links and bonds which it engenders'. And it insisted that it would have the duty to ensure that the flexibility criteria were respected. [13]

In its formal mandate to the IGC, the Turin European Council, on 29 March 1996, said:

'The Heads of State or Government ask the Conference to examine whether and how to introduce rules either of a general nature or in specific areas in order to enable a certain number of Member States to develop a strengthened cooperation, open to all, compatible with the Union's objectives, while preserving the acquis communautaire, avoiding discrimination and distortions of competition and respecting the single institutional framework'.

The President of the European Parliament, Klaus Hänsch, caused a stir by warning against having resort to 'generalised permanent opt-outs'. He continued:

'The problem of the British government, with its strong Europhobic, not Eurosceptic element, cannot be resolved by imaginative drafting of Treaty clauses, and by fanciful institutional gadgets. It is a basic political problem ... And we should be wary of writing into the Treaty more permanent exemptions and derogations which weaken the Union's capacity to act in order to deal with a problem and, indeed, a government which may prove to be short-lived'. [14]

After further discussions, a joint declaration on *coopération renforcée* was issued by the French and German foreign ministers, Hervé de Charette and Klaus Kinkel, on 17 October 1996. Stung no doubt by the astonishing British tactic of non-cooperation, France and Germany dropped their previous affirmation that differentiation could only be of a temporary nature. The Irish presidency of the Council followed suit, and proposed that a general clause be added to the Treaty to stipulate the conditions under which differentiation might take place, supplemented by three further articles setting out the arrangements for effecting reinforced cooperation in each pillar.

In addition, De Charette and Kinkel proposed that the Commission should have the right to vet a possible differentiation arrangement to ensure that the acquis communautaire be preserved; and the Council would decide by QMV. Under the second and third pillars, the right of initiative would be shared between the Commission and member state governments. In each case a quorum of member states would have to be established. The financing of the administration of reinforced cooperation would be by the EU budget; operational expenditure might be either from the EU budget or from national levies. Flexibility should only be deployed to strengthen and not dilute the acquis communautaire, so there would be no flexibility for new entrants to the EU, who would have to make do, like their predecessors, with pre-accession strategies and transitional periods.

Making differentiation work

The Irish presidency made little progress on reaching agreement on the detailed legal or institutional issues involved, and even the strongest advocates of closer cooperation failed to offer many convincing examples of areas in which it might be made to work. France and Germany claimed that they saw enhanced cooperation as being useful in the context of future enlargement, but this was hardly credible. There was plenty of time to take tough decisions before the next enlargement was likely to take place. And the controversial part of the IGC negotiation had nothing to do with enlargement, but concerned whether or not the UK should be able to veto differentiation: the Franco-German position suggested never; the British always. The UK was suspected of intending to differentiate in order to loosen the ties that bound the member states. A principal target of the British hardliners was the Court of Justice, from which a repatriation of powers would subvert the existing European legal order and breach the principle of 'least possible disturbance'.

The Dutch presidency emphasised therefore that differentiation would need consistent scrutiny and occasional arbitration. Article 164 gave the Court the general power to 'ensure that in the interpretation and application of this Treaty the law is observed'. Far from being a method of weakening the Court's jurisdiction, differentiation strengthened the argument for extending it beyond the first pillar to cover the whole of the European Union. A variegated Europe needed a strong legal order to hold it together. Diversity without a powerful Court could lead to anarchy.

The European Commission is the close partner of the Court in ensuring that EC law and policy are effectively and equitably applied throughout the Union. If it were accepted that member states in the outer tier may at any stage catch up to join those in the inner, the machinery to change gear would have to be carefully engineered in the first place and well-maintained thereafter. The Commission would have to work within the core acquis on behalf of and within all member states, in other key areas, such as monetary policy, with some core states, and in some, such as foreign policy, with others. And the Commission would have to manage the relationship between the core and the periphery.

Defining the core acquis communautaire is an essential pre-requisite for differentiation. The greater the pressure for flexibility, the more vital it is to measure accurately the current scale and scope of European integration.

Usefully, a similar stock-taking exercise is required of the Commission before a fresh round of enlargement negotiations, but the definition of the core acquis can never be wholly unambiguous. That is because the ambivalent nature of subsidiarity, and the uncertain status and definition of the EC's exclusive and shared competence, complicate the debate about the balance of power and obligation between the Union and its member states. Indeed, the application of the subsidiarity rule will itself be complicated further by a spread of variable geometric formulae. Differentiation will necessarily involve the institutionalisation of different interpretations of subsidiarity and proportionality. It follows that, in a system of differentiated integration, subsidiarity will have to be applied variably — with the powers of the Commission and other EU-level agencies adjusted accordingly.

Nevertheless, any rational definition of the core acquis must be based around the formulation and implementation of common policy concerning the freedom of movement of goods, services, money and people. But the single market, involving the customs union and the common commercial and competition policies, is as yet far from complete. In particular, freedom of movement of persons is barely a reality. Consolidation of the core acquis respecting subsidiarity implies an agreed common external borders policy plus the liberalisation of things which matter to the citizen, such as pensions, mortgages and insurance. That is why a common immigration policy is so important — and why the UK is wrong in assuming that a transfer of competence from the third pillar to the first is not both a necessary and a desirable concomitant of flexibility. Moreover, there was (and is) disagreement about the extent to which the single market needs flanking policies in the field of social and environmental policy. Where regulation is needed to sustain the single market it must be enforced; where it is not needed it may become discretionary. Examples cited of where enhanced cooperation might be valuable if it could be made to work include indirect taxation, environmental standards and the health and safety of workers.

The debate on differentiation at least encouraged the IGC to take a clear look at what the EU was doing and why. It was obvious that flexible integration within the first pillar, with a defined common base and optional extras, would not be easy to manage. And as far as the institutions were concerned, the IGC agreed to respect the collegiality of the Commission and Court in order to serve the interests of the whole Union. But there was continuing disagreement about how the Council and the European Parliament would have to work in two guises.

Although the IGC appeared to regard Cooperation in Justice and Home Affairs as the most fruitful area for differentiation, most third pillar matters are of a legislative nature, more akin and closely associated to the work of the European Community than to the executive style decisions of Common Foreign and Security Policy. The fact is that flexibility is easier to conceive of in executive matters, like joint actions, than in the making of law.

The Irish presidency, indeed, from its 'neutral' perspective, drafted a range of complicated options for the combination of unanimity and QMV in this field. [15] It sought in the first place to establish a basic political solidarity, or comity, binding all member states; then additional security guarantees could be binding only on some. A great deal of flexibility would be required were the European Union ever to acquire a defence capability. Article 5 of the WEU Treaty affords a member state under armed attack 'all the military and other aid and assistance' that it is in the power of its partners to give. The IGC discussed the possibility of attaching an Article 5-type Protocol to the EU Treaty to attract the signature of some but not all member states.

The presidency's proposals

During the run up to the European Council in Amsterdam, the negotiations on flexibility became more fraught as these complexities surfaced. [16] The result of the British general election on 1 May had prompted some second thoughts about the wisdom of proceeding with flexibility clauses. With the Tories gone, what was the point in constructing an elaborate system of differentiation, with all its attendant risks for the Union? But the negotiations had by now achieved an impetus of their own, and residuary anxieties about British policy, especially in relation to third pillar matters, impelled them forward. Moreover, the Labour government was sticking to its predecessor's position of insisting on being able to veto whether or not flexibility would ever apply. The argument in the final days turned on this point to the evident exclusion of everything else.

The Dutch presidency eventually discarded the option of listing precisely all those items where flexibility could not be deployed in favour of establishing broader criteria and conditions. It proposed a general clause plus three enabling clauses for each pillar. [17] The general clause followed the thrust of the earlier debate but established in addition that flexibility would only come into play as a matter of last resort; that a quorum of over half the member states would need to be involved; but that there should be no veto permissible from those not willing to go forward.

Within the first pillar, very stringent conditions were proposed before flexibility could be triggered. Closer cooperation could only be considered:

- outside the exclusive competence of the Community;

- where existing Community policies or programmes were not affected;

- where it would not concern EU citizenship or discriminate between nationals of member states;

- within the limits of the powers conferred on the Community;

- where trade and competition would be unimpeded.

The Council would decide by QMV, on the advice of the Commission, on an application from an outer member state to join the inner core. The European Parliament would be consulted.

194

In the second pillar, the Dutch presidency proposed that closer cooperation between certain member states should be permissible as long as the Treaty was respected and the intention was to 'promote the identity of the Union' and not impair its effectiveness in international affairs. Authorisation to proceed would be by unanimous vote of the whole Council on the advice of the Commission. On an application by an outer member state to join in, the applicant would be admitted unless, within four months, the Council had decided by QMV to postpone a decision. The European Parliament would be informed.

As far as the third pillar was concerned, the presidency proposed that closer cooperation would be permissible as long as it aimed at 'enabling the Union to develop more rapidly into an area of freedom, security and justice'. Similar conditions for decision-making were attached as to Common Foreign and Security Policy.

The Treaty of Amsterdam

At the European Council itself, the draft flexibility clauses were discussed for only seven minutes in the early hours of the final morning. The general clauses in the Common Provisions of the Treaty were accepted as proposed.

In the first pillar, however, (Article 5a(2)) a major change was agreed to accommodate the British insistence on veto. It says that any member state may 'for important and stated reasons of national policy' block the QMV vote to trigger closer cooperation. This enshrines in Treaty form for the first time a version of the notorious Luxembourg Compromise of 1966 — although without the imperative that discussions were to continue indefinitely.

Article 5a(1)(d) restricts the application of flexibility to the powers already attributed to the Community. This is highly restrictive in both substantive and procedural terms, and would make it very difficult for a core group to proceed alone towards a greater degree of integration in, say, taxation matters without being vulnerable to a challenge in the Court of Justice.

This raises the question of the role of the Court in arbitrating flexible arrangements. If differentiation is attempted at all, there is very likely to be litigation. But although flexibility falls squarely within the jurisdiction of the Court it is not easily justiciable. Here there are similarities with the familiar debate about subsidiarity. On both issues, the Court will be inclined to fight shy, and insist that the politicians find a solution to a problem of their own creation.

Taken together, it is difficult to avoid the conclusion that there were those at Amsterdam who were determined to prevent the inclusion in the Treaty of a flexibility clause that would work. With the single and given exception of Schengen, it seems hardly possible for a federal core to go forward in the first pillar area.

Another surprising change to the draft, however, works strongly in the federal direction (Article 5a(3)). Under pressure from the smaller states, it will now be the Commission and not the Council that decides whether to let an applicant join the inner core group.

The leaders scrubbed altogether the draft clauses on flexibility in the field of Common and Foreign and Security Policy in favour of a form of constructive abstention, where dissenting member states are to agree to waive their objections and not participate in a common policy. Article J.13(1) lays down that if the constructive abstainers comprise more than one third of the weighted votes the decision will be blocked. Decisions without military implications will be taken by super QMV — that is, 62 votes in favour cast by at least ten member states — unless Mr Blair's new formulation of the Luxembourg Compromise is invoked (Article J.13(2)). In such circumstances, the Council may vote by QMV to pass the matter up to the European Council for decision by unanimity.

The watering-down of the presidency proposals was moved by the UK, Austria, Ireland and Greece — which is rather indicative as to its likely effect on the emergence of a common foreign policy. The contradiction between the first and second pillars in dealing with differentiation does not appear to have worried the European Council. And the question of who would represent a core group in its external relations autonomously from the Union as a whole does not seem to have been broached.

Closer cooperation is, however, allowed for in the third pillar (Article K.12). Authorisation will be decided by the Council acting by super QMV unless Mr Blair's caveat is deployed. In which case, the Council may vote by QMV to pass the matter up to the European Council for decision by unanimity. Here the problem will be to protect the interests of the non-participating states against unduly restrictive measures.

Downstream

The precedent of flexibility was set at Maastricht and continued at Amsterdam. But the ambitious proposal of the Germans and French to establish a sophisticated set of arrangements to allow a federal core to go forward without the British was not realised. Although there are definite elements of derogation for the UK, Ireland and Denmark in the field of immigration, and clauses to permit enhanced cooperation by certain member states in WEU and in Schengen, as well as the Stability Pact, there is very little practical room for manoeuvre in other sectors.

It is questionable whether flexibility could ever be introduced in sub-treaty form by use of the formal clauses discussed in this section.

Some participants, not excluding the Dutch or the Commission, may be entirely sanguine about that. The articles in question are possibly too dangerous to handle. Like Article 144, which allows the Parliament to sack the Commission, these flexibility clauses may never be used.

It would be ironic, however, if the new British government were to continue to wish to block the emergence of a federal core within the European Union. One may hope in due course for a more positive attitude.

---

[1] *Report by Mr Leo Tindemans to the European Council*, EC Bulletin, Supplement 1/76, p. 20.

[2] Wolfgang Schäuble and Karl Lamers, *Reflections on European Policy*, 1 September 1994.

[3] Government policy paper to the Belgian Parliament on the 1996 IGC, 13 October 1995.

[4] Memorandum of Belgium, the Netherlands and Luxembourg for the IGC, 8 March 1996.

[5] Luxembourg Government memorandum of 30 June 1995 on the 1996 Intergovernmental Conference.

[6] The Netherlands and Europe: the Intergovernmental Conference 1996, Ministry of Foreign Affairs, Den Haag, 1996, p. 21.

[7] Agenda for Europe: the 1996 Intergovernmental Conference. Report of the Danish Foreign Ministry, June 1995

[8] See Note of July 1995 on the fundamental interests of Sweden with a view to the 1996 IGC, and Memorandum of the Foreign Ministry of 18 September 1995 on the views of the Finnish Government concerning the 1996 IGC.

[9] Towards a citizens' Europe — democracy and development: memorandum for the 1996 IGC, Greek Government, January 1995.

[10] *Document on the 1996 Intergovernmental Conference: starting points for a discussion*, Madrid, July 1995.

[11] *Position of the Italian Government on the Intergovernmental Conference for the Revision of the Treaties*, Rome, 18 March 1996, para. III, 1(c).

[12] UK Government White Paper on the IGC, *A Partnership of Nations*, London, HMSO, March 1996, para. 8.

[13] Commission Opinion on the IGC, *Reinforcing Political Union and Preparing for Enlargement*, Brussels, February 1996, paras 45-46.

[14] Robert Schuman Lecture, European University Institute, Florence, 5 July 1996

[15] See General Outline for a draft revision of the Treaties (Dublin II), CONF/2500/96.

[16] See the Non-Paper of 11 February, CONF/3813/97.

[17] Draft Treaty of 12 June, CONF/4000/97.

Section Six

Simplification and Consolidation of the Treaties

SIMPLIFICATION

Amendments for simplifying the Treaties form Part Two of the Treaty of Amsterdam (Articles 6 - 8).

CONSOLIDATION

Amendments for consolidation of the Treaties form Part Three of the Treaty of Amsterdam (General and Final Provisions) (Articles 9 - 12).

DECLARATION ON THE CONSOLIDATION OF THE TREATIES

The High Contracting Parties agreed that the technical work begun during the course of this Intergovernmental Conference shall continue as speedily as possible with the aim to draft a consolidation of all the relevant Treaties, including the Treaty on European Union.

They agreed that the final results of this technical work, which shall be made public for illustrative purposes under the responsibility of the Secretary-General of the Council, shall have no legal value.

Commentary
Understanding the Treaty

The process of treaty building in the European Union has been simply to pile one treaty on top of another without care for consolidation. After the Treaty of Paris in 1951 there have been five major new Treaties (EEC, Euratom, Single Act, Maastricht and Amsterdam) as well as five revisions of major consequence (Merger, Direct Elections, Budget (1971 and 1975), EIB) plus four sets of complex accession treaties. Numerous protocols and declarations have been added on: at Amsterdam alone there were thirteen of the former and fifty-seven of the latter. The corpus of treaty provisions now runs to three 'pillars', scores of parts, sections, titles and chapters, thousands of juxtaposed articles and tens of thousands of pages.

Accessible the Treaties are not. Indeed, the defeat of the first Maastricht referendum in Denmark is often attributed to the government's decision to send a copy of the draft Treaty to every household in the country.

One of the items of unfinished business of Maastricht was to revisit the question of the 'hierarchy of acts' — the classification of EC law by its gravity, nature and purpose; it was hoped that such a codification would lead also to a simplification of the Treaties to remove obsolete provisions. Ideally, the several basic treaties would be merged into one in advance of the expiry of the Treaty of Paris in 2001. The Group of Reflection and all the institutions identified the problem, but it soon became apparent that it would be very difficult to rationalise the treaties without re-opening substantive questions of controversy drafted away by those skilled in the craft of compromise, often many years ago.

A decision was taken to separate the simplification exercise from consolidation. A new second part of the new Treaty is created containing all the technical revisions. These are mainly to do with up-dating or deleting articles that have fallen for one reason or another into desuetude.

The consolidation process, meanwhile, will continue after the end of the IGC under the aegis of the Council secretariat, and will be published in due course for illustrative purposes only (thus avoiding the need for ratification). We look forward to that.[1]

---

[1] An attempt at rationalisation has been made by some distinguished jurists for the European Parliament under the auspices of the European University Institute. *A Unified and Simplified Model of the European Communities Treaties and the Treaty on European Union in Just One Treaty*, Florence, September 1996.

Section Seven

Economic Policy

I. Meeting in Madrid in December 1995, the European Council confirmed the crucial importance of securing budgetary discipline in stage three of Economic and Monetary Union (EMU). In Florence, six months later, the European Council reiterated this view and in Dublin, in December 1996, it reached an agreement on the main elements of the Stability and Growth pact. In stage three of EMU, Member States shall avoid excessive general government deficits: this is a clear Treaty obligation. [1]

The European Council underlines the importance of safeguarding sound government finances as a means to strengthening the conditions for price stability and for strong sustainable growth conducive to employment creation. It is also necessary to ensure that national budgetary policies support stability oriented monetary policies. Adherence to the objective of sound budgetary positions close to balance or in surplus will allow all Member States to deal with normal cyclical fluctuations while keeping the government deficit within the 3 percent of GDP reference value.

II. Meeting in Dublin in December 1996, the European Council requested the preparation of a Stability and Growth pact to be achieved in accordance with the principles and procedures of the Treaty. This Stability and Growth pact in no way changes the requirements for participation in stage three of EMU, either in the first group or at a later date. Member States remain responsible for their national budgetary policies, subject to the provisions of the Treaty; they will take the necessary measures in order to meet their responsibilities in accordance with those provisions.

III. The Stability and Growth pact, which provides both for prevention and strengthening of the surveillance of budgetary positions and the surveillance and coordination of economic policies and another on speeding up and clarifying the implementation of the excessive deficit procedure.

IV. The European Council solemnly invites all parties, namely the Member States, the Council and the Commission, to implement the Treaty and the Stability and Growth pact in a strict and timely manner. This resolution provides firm political guidance to the parties who will implement the Stability and Growth Pact. To this end, the European Council has agreed upon the following guidelines:

The Member States:

1. commit themselves to respect the medium-term budgetary objective of close to balance or in surplus set out in their stability or convergence programmes and to take the corrective budgetary action they deem necessary to meet the objectives of their stability or convergence programmes, whenever they have information indicating actual or expected significant divergence from those objectives;

2. are invited to make public, on their own initiative, the Council recommendations made to them in accordance with Article 103(4);

3. commit themselves to take the corrective budgetary action they deem necessary to meet the objectives of their stability or convergence programmes once they receive an early warning in the form of a Council recommendation issued under Article 103(4);

4. will launch the corrective budgetary adjustments they deem necessary without delay on receiving information indicating the risk of an excessive deficit;

5. will correct excessive deficits as quickly as possible after their emergence; this correction should be completed no later than the year following the identification of the excessive deficit, unless there are special circumstances;

6. are invited to make public, on their own initiative, recommendations made in accordance with Article 104c(7);

7. commit themselves not to invoke the benefit of Article 2 paragraph 3 of the Council Regulation on speeding up and clarifying the excessive deficit procedure unless they are in severe recession; in evaluating whether the economic downturn is severe, the Member States will, as a rule, take as a reference point an annual fall in real GDP of at least 0,75%.

The Commission:

1. will exercise its right of initiative under the Treaty in a manner that facilitates the strict, timely and effective functioning of the Stability and Growth pact;

2. will present, without delay, the necessary reports, opinions and recommendations to enable the adoption of Council decisions under Article 103 and Article 104c; this will facilitate the effective

functioning of the early warning system and the rapid launch and strict application of the excessive deficit procedure;

3. commits itself to prepare a report under Article 104c(3) whenever there is the risk of an excessive deficit or whenever the planned or actual government deficit exceeds the 3 per cent of GDP reference value, thereby triggering the procedure under Article 104c(3);

4. commits itself, in the event that the Commission considers that a deficit exceeding 3% of GDP is not excessive and this opinion differs from that of the Economic and Financial Committee, to present in writing to the Council the reasons for its position;

5. commits itself, following a request from the Council under Article 109d, to make, as a rule, a recommendation for a Council decision on whether an excessive deficit exists under Article 104c(6).

The Council:

1. is committed to a rigorous and timely implementation of all elements of the stability and growth pact in its competence; it will take the necessary decisions under Article 103 and Article 104c as quickly as is practicable;

2. is urged to regard the deadlines for the application of the excessive deficit procedure as upper limits; in particular, the Council, acting under article 104c(7), shall recommend that excessive deficits will be corrected as quickly as possible after their emergence, no later than the year following their identification, unless there are special circumstances;

3. is invited always to impose sanctions if a participating Member State fails to take the necessary steps to bring the excessive deficit situation to an end as recommended by the Council;

4. is urged always to require a non-interest bearing deposit, whenever the Council decides to impose sanctions on a participating Member State in accordance with Article 104c(11);

5. is urged always to convert a deposit into a fine after two years of the decision to impose sanctions in accordance with Article 104c(11), unless the excessive deficit has in the view of the Council been corrected;

6. is invited to always state in writing the reasons which justify a decision not to act, if at any stage of the excessive deficit or surveillance of budgetary positions procedures the Council did not act on a Commission recommendation, and, in such a case, to make public the votes cast by each Member State.

[1] Under Article 5 of Protocol No. 11 of the Treaty on European Union, this obligation does not apply to the United Kingdom unless it moves to the third stage; the obligation under Article 109e(4) to endeavour to avoid excessive deficits shall continue to apply to the UK.

Commentary
Towards a common economic policy?

The Intergovernmental Conference had no mandate to revisit the EMU articles (Title VI of the Treaty establishing the European Community) agreed at Maastricht. Indeed, there was a firm and almost universal agreement that to reopen the EMU box would be to court disaster. Even the Swedes, who were disaffected with the impact of the Maastricht convergence criteria, were persuaded to resist the temptation and to concentrate instead on developing employment policy.

The technical development of EMU was continued beyond Maastricht without further Treaty change. Recourse to Article 235, that allows appropriate action to be taken in pursuit of Community objectives even if the Treaty has not provided the necessary powers, was much in evidence. The name of the euro, its conversion with the Ecu and the settlement of contracts were, for example, all accomplished on the basis of Article 235. Nevertheless, the European Council meeting in Amsterdam on 16-17 June 1997 cannot be understood without reference to EMU.

We have noted earlier in this commentary how the surprise election of the new French government on 1 June was thought to jeopardise the consensus on EMU. The days immediately before the official opening of the European Council (on the morning of Monday 16 June) were taken up with intense discussions between officials and, latterly, finance ministers about how to settle the quarrel over the preparations for the single currency. Not to have succeeded would certainly have triggered a loss of confidence in the financial markets about the credibility of the whole EMU package. For steering the French and Germans towards a settlement of their differences, the Dutch presidency deserves much praise.

Fleshing out EMU

During the first stages of the European Council, three resolutions were passed. The first, whose essentials had first been agreed at Dublin in December 1996, lays down the firm commitments of the member states, the Commission and the Council to stabilise economic convergence once the single currency has been introduced. The second attempts to flesh out a common approach to employment policy required by the new employment chapter of the Treaty (see Section Two), and the third concerns the revised exchange rate mechanism. (Neither of the latter two are reproduced here.)

It would be easy to be cynical about what are blatantly political declarations about the management of public finance and budgetary policy in the single currency regime that has yet to happen. But how macro-economic policy is to be managed and what it will be is one of the most vital ingredients for the success of the Economic and Monetary Union. The Maastricht Treaty, having established the monetary policy and institutional framework for EMU, sensibly left the highly political questions about rates of growth and unemployment for future resolution. So the Amsterdam IGC was shadowed throughout its life by the on-going preparation for EMU, some parts of which, in the hands of the Commission and Council, aided by the European Monetary Institute at Frankfurt, were quiet and efficient, but others, such as the terms of the stability pact, were exposed and controversial. In that respect Amsterdam represented a major step forward towards EMU, and stands out from the febrile tone of much of the day-to-day debate.

ERM 2

The Amsterdam European Council agreed to establish a new Exchange Rate Mechanism (ERM 2) to link the currencies of those within and without the euro zone. Stress is put on the need for those without to follow the same financial disciplines as the core in order to prevent exchange rate misalignments and excessive fluctuation. This agreement, which had been contested by the former UK government, puts flesh on the obligation under Article 109m to treat member states' exchange rate policy as a matter of mutual interest.

Although membership of ERM 2 is voluntary, it would be unthinkable for a member state intent on joining the euro one day to abstain. Its primary purpose, after all, is to assist member states who want to converge. The European Central Bank will intervene to support a currency on the margins of the 15% fluctuation against the central rates against the euro. In the case of any deliberately competitive, unilateral devaluation of a currency, the ECB will withdraw support.

Who's in charge of economic policy?

At Amsterdam the member states of the European Union recommitted themselves to achieving medium-term budgetary balance, to strict mutual and public surveillance of each other's economic performance and to tough counteraction to correct excessive deficits. They affirmed their original purpose of more than five years previously to proceed to the third stage of EMU on 1 January 1999, this time with a deeper understanding of what is entailed. The package of measures, including the orientation towards boosting the level of employment, achieves a new level of coordination and convergence of economic policy as called for under Articles 102a and 103.

After Amsterdam, and despite the nervousness caused by the French socialist victory, the financial markets have ceased to question the determination of both the large majority of the member state governments and the European Commission to proceed with the single currency. The likelihood must be that, despite alarums, the euro will begin on time, at least in a formal sense, that it will be broader than anticipated with a large majority of member states on board, but not so soft as to significantly damage initial expectations of sustained convergence.

In such circumstances, it may not be long before new impetus develops behind the efforts to develop a stronger system of economic governance for the European Union. The European Central Bank will be a new and powerful part of the institutional equation. Pressure for a more political counterweight to the federal bank is bound to rise.

PART TWO

Treaty of Amsterdam amending the Treaty on European Union and the Treaty establishing the European Community

DRAFT TREATY OF AMSTERDAM AMENDING THE TREATY ON EUROPEAN UNION, THE TREATIES ESTABLISHING THE EUROPEAN COMMUNITIES AND CERTAIN RELATED ACTS [1]

HIS MAJESTY THE KING OF THE BELGIANS,

HER MAJESTY THE QUEEN OF DENMARK,

THE PRESIDENT OF THE FEDERAL REPUBLIC OF GERMANY,

THE PRESIDENT OF THE HELLENIC REPUBLIC,

HIS MAJESTY THE KING OF SPAIN,

THE PRESIDENT OF THE FRENCH REPUBLIC,

THE PRESIDENT OF IRELAND,

THE PRESIDENT OF THE ITALIAN REPUBLIC,

HIS ROYAL HIGHNESS THE GRAND DUKE OF LUXEMBOURG,

HER MAJESTY THE QUEEN OF THE NETHERLANDS,

THE FEDERAL PRESIDENT OF THE REPUBLIC OF AUSTRIA,

THE PRESIDENT OF THE PORTUGUESE REPUBLIC,

THE PRESIDENT OF THE REPUBLIC OF FINLAND,

THE GOVERNMENT OF THE KINGDOM OF SWEDEN,

HER MAJESTY THE QUEEN OF THE UNITED KINGDOM OF GREAT BRITAIN AND NORTHERN IRELAND,

HAVE RESOLVED to amend the Treaty on European Union, the Treaties establishing the European Communities and certain related acts,

.....

HAVE AGREED AS FOLLOWS:

PART ONE

SUBSTANTIVE AMENDMENTS TO THE TREATY ON EUROPEAN UNION, THE TREATIES ESTABLISHING THE EUROPEAN COMMUNITIES AND CERTAIN RELATED ACTS

ARTICLE 1

The Treaty on European Union shall be amended in accordance with the provisions of this Article.

(1)   After the third recital the following recital shall be inserted:

"CONFIRMING their attachment to fundamental social rights as defined in the European Social Charter signed at Turin on 18 October 1961 and in the 1989 Community Charter of the Fundamental Social Rights of Workers."

(2)   The existing seventh recital shall be replaced by the following:

"DETERMINED to promote economic and social progress for their peoples, taking into account the principle of sustainable development and within the context of the accomplishment of the internal market and of reinforced cohesion and environmental protection, and to implement policies ensuring that advances in economic integration are accompanied by parallel progress in other fields,"

(3)   The existing ninth recital shall be replaced by the following:

"RESOLVED to implement a common foreign and security policy including the progressive framing of a common defence policy, which might lead to a common defence in accordance with the provisions of Article J.7, thereby reinforcing the European identity and its independence in order to promote peace, security and progress in Europe and the world,"

(4)   In Article A the second paragraph shall be replaced by the following:

"This Treaty marks a new stage in the process of creating an ever closer Union among the peoples of Europe, in which decisions are taken as openly as possible and as closely as possible to the citizen."

(5)   Article B shall be replaced by the following:

"Article B

The Union shall set itself the following objectives:

-     to promote economic and social progress and a high level of employment and to achieve balanced and sustainable development, in particular through the creation of an area without internal frontiers, through the strengthening of economic and social cohesion and through the establishment of economic and monetary union, ultimately including a single currency in accordance with the provisions of this Treaty;

- to assert its identity on the international scene, in particular through the implementation of a common foreign and security policy including the progressive framing of a common defence policy, which might lead to a common defence, in accordance with the provisions of Article J.7;

- to strengthen the protection of the rights and interests of the nationals of its Member States through the introduction of a citizenship of the Union;

- to maintain and develop the Union as an area of freedom, security and justice, in which the free movement of persons is assured in conjunction with appropriate measures with respect to external border controls, immigration, asylum and the prevention and combating of crime;

- to maintain in full the acquis communautaire and build on it with a view to considering to what extent the policies and forms of cooperation introduced by this Treaty may need to be revised with the aim of ensuring the effectiveness of the mechanisms and the institutions of the Community.

The objectives of the Union shall be achieved as provided in this Treaty and in accordance with the conditions and the timetable set out therein while respecting the principle of subsidiarity as defined in Article 3b of the Treaty establishing the European Community."

(6)   In Article C, the second paragraph shall be replaced by the following:

"The Union shall in particular ensure the consistency of its external activities as a whole in the context of its external relations, security, economic and development policies. The Council and the Commission shall be responsible for ensuring such consistency and shall cooperate to this end. They shall ensure the implementation of these policies, each in accordance with its respective powers."

(7)   Article E shall be replaced by the following:

"Article E

The European Parliament, the Council, the Commission, the Court of Justice and the Court of Auditors shall exercise their powers under the conditions and for the purposes provided for, on the one hand, by the provisions of the Treaties establishing the European Communities and of the subsequent Treaties and Acts modifying and supplementing them and, on the other hand, by the other provisions of this Treaty."

(8)   Article F shall be amended as follows:

(a) paragraph 1 shall be replaced by the following:

"1. The Union is founded on the principles of liberty, democracy, respect for human rights and fundamental freedoms, and the rule of law, principles which are upheld by the Member States.";

(b) the existing paragraph 3 shall become paragraph 4 and a new paragraph 3 shall be inserted as follows:

"3. The Union shall respect the national identities of its Member States."

(9)   The following Article shall be inserted at the end of Title 1:

"Article F.1

1. The Council, meeting in the composition of the Heads of State or Government and acting by unanimity on a proposal by one third of the Member States or by the Commission and after obtaining the assent of the European Parliament, may determine the existence of a serious and persistent breach by a Member State of the principles mentioned in Article F(1), after inviting the government of the Member State concerned to submit its observations.

2. Where such a determination has been made, the Council, acting by a qualified majority, may decide to suspend certain of the rights deriving from the application of this Treaty to the State in question, including the voting rights of the representative of the Government of that Member State in the Council. In doing so, the Council shall take into account the possible consequences of such a suspension on the rights and obligations of natural and legal persons.

The obligations of the Member State concerned under this Treaty shall in any case continue to be binding on that State.

3. The Council, acting by a qualified majority, may decide subsequently to vary or revoke measures taken under paragraph 2 in response to changes in the situation which led to their being imposed.

4. For the purposes of this Article, the Council shall act without taking into account the vote of the representative of the government of the Member State concerned. Abstentions by members present in person or represented shall not prevent the adoption of decisions referred to in paragraph 1. A qualified majority shall be defined as

the same proportion of the weighted votes of the members of the Council concerned as laid down in Article 148(2) of the Treaty establishing the European Community.

This paragraph shall also apply in the event of voting rights being suspended pursuant to paragraph 2.

5. For the purposes of this Article, the European Parliament shall act by a two thirds majority of the votes cast, representing a majority of its members."

(10)   Title V shall be replaced by the following:

"TITLE V

Provisions on a common foreign and security policy

Article J.1

1. The Union shall define and implement a common foreign and security policy covering all areas of foreign and security policy, the objectives of which shall be:

- to safeguard the common values, fundamental interests, independence and integrity of the Union in conformity with the principles of the United Nations Charter;

- to strengthen the security of the Union in all ways;

- to preserve peace and strengthen international security, in accordance with the principles of the United Nations Charter, as well as the principles of the Helsinki Final Act and the objectives of the Paris Charter, including those on external borders;

- to promote international cooperation;

- to develop and consolidate democracy and the rule of law, and respect for human rights and fundamental freedoms.

2. The Member States shall support the Union's external and security policy actively and unreservedly in a spirit of loyalty and mutual solidarity.

The Member States shall work together to enhance and develop their mutual political solidarity. They shall refrain from any action which is contrary to the interests of the Union or likely to impair its effectiveness as a cohesive force in international relations.

The Council shall ensure that these principles are complied with.

Article J.2

The Union shall pursue the objectives set out in Article J.1 by:

- defining the principles of and general guidelines for the common foreign and security policy;

- deciding on common strategies;

- adopting joint actions;

- adopting common positions;

- and strengthening systematic cooperation between Member States in the conduct of policy.

Article J.3

1. The European Council shall define the principles of and general guidelines for the common foreign and security policy, including for matters with defence implications.

2. The European Council shall decide on common strategies to be implemented by the Union in areas where the Member States have important interests in common.

Common strategies shall set out their objectives, duration and the means to be made available by the Union and the Member States.

3. The Council shall take the decisions necessary for defining and implementing the common foreign and security policy on the basis of the general guidelines defined by the European Council.

The Council shall recommend common strategies to the European Council and shall implement them, in particular by adopting joint actions and common positions.

The Council shall ensure the unity, consistency and effectiveness of action by the Union.

Article J.4

1. The Council shall adopt joint actions. Joint actions shall address specific situations where operational action by the Union is deemed to be required. They shall lay down their objectives, scope, the means to be made available to the Union, if necessary their duration, and the conditions for their implementation.

2. If there is a change in circumstances having a substantial effect on a question subject to joint action, the Council shall review the principles and objectives of that action and take the necessary decisions. As long as the Council has not acted, the joint action shall stand.

3. Joint actions shall commit the Member States in the positions they adopt and in the conduct of their activity.

4. The Council may request the Commission to submit to it any appropriate proposals relating to the common foreign and security policy to ensure the implementation of a joint action.

5. Whenever there is any plan to adopt a national position or take national action pursuant to a joint action, information shall be provided in time to allow, if necessary, for prior consultations within the Council. The obligation to provide prior information shall not apply to measures which are merely a national transposition of Council decisions.

6. In cases of imperative need arising from changes in the situation and failing a Council decision, Member States may take the necessary measures as a matter of urgency having regard to the general objectives of the joint action. The Member State concerned shall inform the Council immediately of any such measures.

7. Should there be any major difficulties in implementing a joint action, a Member State shall refer them to the Council which shall discuss them and seek appropriate solutions. Such solutions shall not run counter to the objectives of the joint action or impair its effectiveness.

Article J.5

The Council shall adopt common positions. Common positions shall define the approach of the Union to a particular matter of a geographical or thematic nature. Member States shall ensure that their national policies conform to the common positions.

Article J.6

Member States shall inform and consult one another within the Council on any matter of foreign and security policy of general interest in order to ensure that the Union's influence is exerted as effectively as possible by means of concerted and convergent action.

Article J.7

1. The common foreign and security policy shall include all questions relating to the security of the Union, including the progressive framing of a common defence policy, in accordance with the second subparagraph, which might lead to a common defence, should the European Council so decide. It shall in that case recommend to the Member States the adoption of such a decision in accordance with their respective constitutional requirements.

The Western European Union (WEU) is an integral part of the development of the Union providing the Union with access to an operational capability notably in the context of paragraph 2. It supports the Union in framing the defence aspects of the common foreign and security policy as set out in this Article. The Union shall accordingly foster closer institutional relations with the WEU with a view to the possibility of the integration of the WEU into the Union, should the European Council so decide. It shall in that case recommend to the Member States the adoption of such a decision in accordance with their respective constitutional requirements.

The policy of the Union in accordance with this Article shall not prejudice the specific character of the security and defence policy of certain Member States and shall respect the obligations of certain Member States, which see their common defence realized in NATO, under the North Atlantic Treaty and be compatible with the common security and defence policy established within that framework.

The progressive framing of a common defence policy will be supported, as Member States consider appropriate, by cooperation between them in the field of armaments.

2. Questions referred to in this Article shall include humanitarian and rescue tasks, peacekeeping tasks and tasks of combat forces in crisis management, including peacemaking.

3. The Union will avail itself of the WEU to elaborate and implement decisions and actions of the Union which have defence implications.

The competence of the European Council to establish guidelines in accordance with Article J.3 shall also obtain in respect of the WEU for those matters for which the Union avails itself of the WEU.

When the Union avails itself of the WEU to elaborate and implement decisions of the Union on the tasks referred to in paragraph 2 all Member States of the Union shall be entitled to participate fully in the tasks in question. The Council, in agreement with the institutions of the WEU, shall adopt the necessary practical arrangements to allow all Member States contributing to the tasks in question to participate fully and on an equal footing in planning and decision-taking in the WEU.

Decisions having defence implications dealt with under this paragraph shall be taken without prejudice to the policies and obligations referred to in paragraph 1, third subparagraph.

4. The provisions of this Article shall not prevent the development of closer cooperation between two or more Member States on a

bilateral level, in the framework of the WEU and the Atlantic Alliance, provided such cooperation does not run counter to or impede that provided for in this Title.

5. With a view to furthering the objectives of this Article, the provisions of this Article will be reviewed in accordance with Article N.

Article J.8

1. The Presidency shall represent the Union in matters coming within the common foreign and security policy.

2. The Presidency shall be responsible for the implementation of decisions taken under this Title; in that capacity it shall in principle express the position of the Union in international organizations and international conferences.

3. The Presidency shall be assisted by the Secretary-General of the Council who shall exercise the function of High Representative for the common foreign and security policy.

4. The Commission shall be fully associated in the tasks referred to in paragraphs 1 and 2. The Presidency shall be assisted in those tasks if need be by the next Member State to hold the Presidency.

5. The Council may, whenever it deems it necessary, appoint a special representative with a mandate in relation to particular policy issues.

Article J.9

1. Member States shall coordinate their action in international organizations and at international conferences. They shall uphold the common positions in such fora.

In international organizations and at international conferences where not all the Member States participate, those which do take part shall uphold the common positions.

2. Without prejudice to paragraph 1 and Article J.4(3), Member States represented in international organizations or international conferences where not all the Member States participate shall keep the latter informed of any matter of common interest.

Member States which are also members of the United Nations Security Council will concert and keep the other Member States fully informed. Member States which are permanent members of the Security Council will, in the execution of their functions, ensure the defence of the positions and the interests of the Union, without prejudice to their responsibilities under the provisions of the United Nations Charter.

Article J.10

The diplomatic and consular missions of the Member States and the Commission Delegations in third countries and international conferences, and their representations to international organizations, shall cooperate in ensuring that the common positions and common measures adopted by the Council are complied with and implemented.

They shall step up cooperation by exchanging information, carrying out joint assessments and contributing to the implementation of the provisions referred to in Article 8c of the Treaty establishing the European Community.

Article J.11

The Presidency shall consult the European Parliament on the main aspects and the basic choices of the common foreign and security policy and shall ensure that the views of the European Parliament are duly taken into consideration. The European Parliament shall be kept regularly informed by the Presidency and the Commission of the development of the Union's foreign and security policy.

The European Parliament may ask questions of the Council or make recommendations to it. It shall hold an annual debate on progress in implementing the common foreign and security policy.

Article J.12

1. Any Member State or the Commission may refer to the Council any question relating to the common foreign and security policy and may submit proposals to the Council.

2. In cases requiring a rapid decision, the Presidency, of its own motion, or at the request of the Commission or a Member State, shall convene an extraordinary Council meeting within forty-eight hours or, in an emergency, within a shorter period.

Article J.13

1. Decisions under this Title shall be taken by the Council acting unanimously. Abstentions by members present in person or represented shall not prevent the adoption of such decisions.

When abstaining in a vote, any member of the Council may qualify its abstention by making a formal declaration under the present subparagraph. In that case, it shall not be obliged to apply the decision, but shall accept that the decision commits the Union. In a spirit of mutual solidarity, the Member State concerned shall refrain from any action likely to conflict with or impede Union action based on that decision and the other Member States shall respect its position. If the members of the Council qualifying their abstention in this way represent more than one third of the votes weighted in accordance with Article 148(2) of the Treaty establishing the European Community, the decision shall not be adopted.

2. By derogation from the provisions of paragraph 1, the Council shall act by qualified majority:

- when adopting joint actions, common positions or taking any other decision on the basis of a common strategy;

- when adopting any decision implementing a joint action or a common position.

If a member of the Council declares that, for important and stated reasons of national policy, it intends to oppose the adoption of a decision to be taken by qualified majority, a vote shall not be taken. The Council may, acting by a qualified majority, request that the matter be referred to the Council, meeting in the composition of Heads of State or Government, for decision by unanimity.

The votes of the members of the Council shall be weighted in accordance with Article 148(2) of the Treaty establishing the European Community. For their adoption, decisions shall require at least 62 votes in favour, cast by at least 10 members.

This paragraph shall not apply to decisions having military or defence implications.

3. For procedural questions, the Council shall act by a majority of its members.

Article J.14

When it is necessary to conclude an agreement with one or more States or international organizations in implementation of this Title, the Council, acting unanimously, may authorize the Presidency, assisted by the Commission as appropriate, to open negotiations to that effect. Such agreements shall be concluded by the Council acting unanimously on a recommendation from the Presidency. No agreement shall be binding on a Member State whose representative in the Council states that it has to comply with the requirements of its own constitutional procedure; the other members of the Council may agree that the agreement shall apply provisionally to them.

The provisions of this Article shall also apply to matters falling under Title VI.

Article J.15

Without prejudice to Article 151 of the Treaty establishing the European Community, a Political Committee shall monitor the international situation in the areas covered by the common foreign and security policy and contribute to the definition of policies by delivering opinions to the Council at the request of the Council or on its own initiative. It shall also monitor the implementation of agreed policies, without prejudice to the responsibility of the Presidency and the Commission.

Article J.16

The Secretary-General of the Council, High Representative for the common foreign and security policy, shall assist the Council in matters coming within the scope of the common foreign and security policy, in particular through contributing to the formulation, preparation and implementation of policy decisions, and, when appropriate and acting on behalf of the Council at the request of the Presidency, through conducting political dialogue with third parties.

Article J.17

The Commission shall be fully associated with the work carried out in the common foreign and security policy field.

Article J.18

1. The provisions referred to in Articles 137, 138, 139 to 142, 146, 147, 150 to 153, 157 to 163, 191a and 217 of the Treaty establishing the European Community shall apply to the provisions relating to the areas referred to in this Title.

2. Administrative expenditure which the provisions relating to the areas referred to in this Title entail for the institutions shall be charged to the budget of the European Communities.

3. Operational expenditure to which the implementation of those provisions gives rise shall also be charged to the budget of the European Communities, except for such expenditure arising from operations having military or defence implications, and cases where the Council acting unanimously decides otherwise.

In cases where expenditure is not charged to the budget of the European Communities it shall be charged to the Member States in accordance with the gross national product scale, unless the Council acting unanimously decides otherwise. As for expenditure arising from operations having military or defence implications, Member States whose representatives in the Council have made a formal declaration under Article J.13(1), second subparagraph, shall not be obliged to contribute to the financing thereof.

4. The budgetary procedure laid down in the Treaty establishing the European Community shall apply to the expenditure charged to the budget of the European Communities."

(11)   Title VI shall be replaced by the following:

"Title VI

Provisions on police and judicial cooperation in criminal matters

Article K.1

Without prejudice to the powers of the European Community, the Union's objective shall be to provide citizens with a high level of safety within an area of freedom, security and justice by developing common action among the Member States in the fields of police and judicial cooperation in criminal matters and by preventing and combating racism and xenophobia.

That objective shall be achieved by preventing and combating crime, organized or otherwise, in particular terrorism, trafficking in persons and offences against children, illicit drug trafficking and illicit arms trafficking, corruption and fraud, through:

- closer cooperation between police forces, customs authorities and other competent authorities in the Member States, both directly and, through Europol, in accordance with the provisions of Article K.2 and K.4;

- closer cooperation between judicial and other competent authorities of the Member States in accordance with the provisions of Articles K.3(a) to (d) and K.4;

- approximation, where necessary, of rules on criminal matters in the Member States, in accordance with the provisions of Article K.3(e).

Article K.2

1. Common action in the field of police cooperation shall include:

(a) operational cooperation between the competent authorities, including the police, customs and other specialized law enforcement services of the Member States in relation to the prevention, detection and investigation of criminal offences;

(b) the collection, storage, processing, analysis and exchange of relevant information, including information held by law enforcement agencies of reports on suspicious financial transactions, in particular through Europol, subject to appropriate provisions on the protection of personal data;

(c) cooperation and joint initiatives in training, the exchange of liaison officers, secondments, the use of equipment, and forensic research;

(d) the common evaluation of particular investigative techniques in relation to the detection of serious forms of organized crime.

2. The Council shall promote cooperation through Europol and shall in particular, within a period of five years after the date of entry into force of the Treaty of Amsterdam:

(a) enable Europol to facilitate and support the preparation, and to encourage the coordination and carrying out of specific investigative actions by the competent authorities of the Member States, including operational actions of joint teams comprising representatives of Europol in a support capacity;

(b) adopt measures allowing Europol to ask the competent authorities of the Member States to conduct and coordinate their investigations in specific cases and to develop specific expertise which may be put at the disposal of Member States to assist them in investigating cases of organized crime;

(c) promote liaison arrangements between prosecuting/investigating officials specialising in the fight against organised crime in close cooperation with Europol;

(d) establish a research, documentation and statistical network on cross-border crime.

Article K.3

Common action on judicial cooperation in criminal matters shall include:

(a) facilitating and accelerating cooperation between competent ministries and judicial or equivalent authorities of the Member States in relation to proceedings and the enforcement of decisions;

(b) facilitating extradition between Member States;

(c) ensuring compatibility in rules applicable in the Member States, as may be necessary to improve such cooperation;

(d) preventing conflicts of jurisdiction between Member States;

(e) progressively adopting measures establishing minimum rules relating to the constituent elements of criminal acts and to penalties in the fields of organized crime, terrorism and drug trafficking.

Article K.4

The Council shall lay down the conditions and limitations under which the competent authorities referred to in Articles K.2 and K.3 may operate in the territory of another Member State in liaison and in agreement with the authorities of that State.

Article K.5

This Title shall not affect the exercise of the responsibilities incumbent upon Member States with regard to the maintenance of law and order and the safeguarding of internal security.

Article K.6

1. In the areas referred to in this Title, Member States shall inform and consult one another within the Council with a view to coordinating their action. To that end, they shall establish collaboration between the relevant departments of their administrations.

2. The Council shall take measures and promote cooperation, using the appropriate form and procedures as set out in this Title, contributing to the pursuit of the objectives of the Union. To that end, acting unanimously on the initiative of any Member State or of the Commission, the Council may:

(a) adopt common positions defining the approach of the Union to a particular matter;

(b) adopt framework decisions for the purpose of approximation of the laws and regulations of the Member States; framework decisions shall be binding upon the Member States as to the result to be achieved but shall leave to the national authorities the choice of form and methods; they shall not entail direct effect;

(c) adopt decisions for any other purpose consistent with the objectives of this Title, excluding any approximation of the laws and regulations of the Member States. These decisions shall be binding and shall not entail direct effect; the Council, acting by a qualified majority, shall adopt measures necessary to implement those decisions at the level of the Union;

(d) establish conventions which it shall recommend to the Member States for adoption in accordance with their respective constitutional requirements. Member States shall begin the procedures applicable within a time limit to be set by the Council.

Unless they provide otherwise, conventions shall, once adopted by at least half of the Member States, enter into force for those Member States. Measures implementing conventions shall be adopted within the Council by a majority of two thirds of the High Contracting Parties.

3. Where the Council is required to act by a qualified majority, the votes of its members shall be weighted as laid down in Article 148(2) of the Treaty establishing the European Community, and for their adoption, acts of the Council shall require at least 62 votes in favour, cast by at least 10 members.

4. For procedural questions, the Council shall act by a majority of its members.

Article K.7

1. The Court of Justice of the European Communities shall have jurisdiction, subject to the conditions laid down in this Article, to give preliminary rulings on the validity and interpretation of framework decisions and decisions, on the interpretation of conventions established under this Title and on the validity and interpretation of the measures implementing them.

2. By a declaration made at the time of signature of this Treaty or at any time thereafter, any Member State shall be able to accept the jurisdiction of the Court of Justice to give preliminary rulings as specified in paragraph 1.

3. A Member State making a declaration pursuant to paragraph 2 shall specify that either:

(a) any court or tribunal of that State against whose decisions there is no judicial remedy under national law may request the Court of Justice to give a preliminary ruling on a question raised in a case pending before it and concerning the validity or interpretation of an act referred to in paragraph 1 if that court or tribunal considers that a decision on the question is necessary to enable it to give judgement, or

(b) any court or tribunal of that State may request the Court of Justice to give a preliminary ruling on a question raised in a case pending before it and concerning the interpretation or validity of an act referred to in paragraph 1 if that court or tribunal considers that a decision on the question is necessary to enable it to give judgement.

4. Any Member State, whether or not it has made a declaration pursuant to paragraph 2, shall be entitled to submit statements of case or written observations to the Court in cases which arise under paragraph 3.

5. The Court of Justice shall have no jurisdiction to review the validity or proportionality of operations carried out by the police or other law enforcement agencies of a Member State or the exercise of the responsibilities incumbent upon Member States with regard to the maintenance of law and order and the safeguarding of internal security.

6. The Court of Justice shall have jurisdiction to review the legality of framework decisions and decisions in actions brought by a Member State or the Commission on grounds of lack of competence, infringement of an essential procedural requirement, infringement of this Treaty or of any rule of law relating to its application, or misuse of powers. The proceedings provided for in this paragraph shall be instituted within two months of the publication of the measure.

7. The Court of Justice shall have jurisdiction to rule on any dispute between Member States regarding the interpretation or the application of acts adopted under Article K.6(2) whenever such dispute cannot be settled by the Council within six months of its being referred to the Council by one of its members. Moreover, the Court shall have jurisdiction to rule on any dispute between Member States and the Commission regarding the interpretation or the application of conventions established under Article K.6(2)(d).

Article K.8

1. A Coordinating Committee shall be set up consisting of senior officials. In addition to its coordinating role, it shall be the task of the Committee to:

- give opinions for the attention of the Council, either at the Council's request or on its own initiative;

- contribute, without prejudice to Article 151 of the Treaty establishing the European Community, to the preparation of the Council's discussions in the areas referred to in Article K.1.

2. The Commission shall be fully associated with the work in the areas referred to in this Title.

Article K.9

Within international organizations and at international conferences in which they take part, Member States shall defend the common positions adopted under the provisions of this Title.

The provisions of Articles J.8 and J.9 shall apply as appropriate to matters falling under this Title.

Article K.10

Agreements referred to in Article J.14 may cover matters falling under this Title.

Article K.11

1. The Council shall consult the European Parliament before adopting any measure referred to in Article K.6(2)(b), (c) and (d). The European Parliament shall deliver its Opinion within a time-limit which the Council may lay down, which shall not be less than three months. In the absence of an Opinion within that time-limit, the Council may act.

2. The Presidency of the Council and the Commission shall regularly inform the European Parliament of discussions in the areas covered by this Title.

3. The European Parliament may ask questions of the Council or make recommendations to it. Each year, it shall hold a debate on the progress made in the areas referred to in this Title.

Article K.12

1. Member States which intend to establish closer cooperation between themselves may be authorized, subject to Articles K.15 and K.16, to make use of the institutions, procedures and mechanisms laid down by the Treaties provided that the cooperation proposed:

(a) respects the powers of the European Community, and the objectives laid down by this Title;

(b) has the aim of enabling the Union to develop more rapidly into an area of freedom, security and justice.

2. The authorization referred to in paragraph 1 shall be granted by the Council, acting by a qualified majority at the request of the Member States concerned and after inviting the Commission to present its opinion; the request shall also be forwarded to the European Parliament.

If a member of the Council declares that, for important and stated reasons of national policy, it intends to oppose the granting of an authorization by qualified majority, a vote shall not be taken. The Council may, acting by a qualified majority, request that the matter be referred to the Council, meeting in the composition of the Heads of State or Government, for decision by unanimity.

The votes of the members of the Council shall be weighted in accordance with article 148(2) of the Treaty establishing the

European Community. For their adoption, decisions shall require at least 62 votes in favour, cast by at least 10 members.

3. Any Member State which wishes to become a party to cooperation set up in accordance with this Article shall notify its intention to the Council and to the Commission, which shall give an opinion to the Council within three months of receipt of that notification, possibly accompanied by a recommendation for such specific arrangements as it may deem necessary for that Member State to become a party to the cooperation in question. Within four months of the date of that notification, the Council shall decide on the request and on such specific arrangements as it may deem necessary. The decision shall be deemed to be taken unless the Council, acting by a qualified majority, decides to hold it in abeyance; in this case, the Council shall state the reasons for its decision and set a deadline for reexamining it. For the purposes of this paragraph, the Council shall act under the conditions set out in Article K.16.

4. The provisions of Articles K.1 to K.13 shall apply to the closer cooperation provided for by this Article, save as otherwise provided for in this Article and in Articles K.15 and K.16.

The provisions of the Treaty establishing the European Community concerning the powers of the Court of Justice of the European Communities and the exercise of those powers shall apply to paragraphs 1, 2 and 3.

5. This Article is without prejudice to the provisions of the Protocol integrating the Schengen acquis into the framework of the Union.

Article K.13

1. The provisions referred to in Articles 137, 138, 138e, 139 to 142, 146, 147, 148(3), 150 to 153, 157 to 163, 191a and 217 of the Treaty establishing the European Community shall apply to the provisions relating to the areas referred to in this Title.

2. Administrative expenditure which the provisions relating to the areas referred to in this Title entail for the institutions shall be charged to the budget of the European Communities.

3. Operational expenditure to which the implementation of those provisions gives rise shall also be charged to the budget of the European Communities, except where the Council acting unanimously decides otherwise. In cases where expenditure is not charged to the budget of the European Communities it shall be charged to the Member States in accordance with the gross national product scale, unless the Council acting unanimously decides otherwise.

4. The budgetary procedure laid down in the Treaty establishing the European Community shall apply to the expenditure charged to the budget of the European Communities.

Article K.14

The Council, acting unanimously on the initiative of the Commission or a Member State, and after consulting the European Parliament, may decide that action in areas referred to in Article K.1 shall fall under Title IIIa of the Treaty establishing the European Community, and at the same time determine the relevant voting conditions relating to it. It shall recommend the Member States to adopt that decision in accordance with their respective constitutional requirements."

(12) The following new Title shall be inserted:

"Title VIa

Provisions on closer cooperation

Article K.15

1. Member States which intend to establish closer cooperation between themselves may make use of the institutions, procedures and mechanisms laid down by the Treaties provided that the cooperation:

(a) is aimed at furthering the objectives of the Union and at protecting and serving its interests;

(b) respects the principles of the Treaties and the single institutional framework of the Union;

(c) is only used as a last resort, where the objectives of the Treaties could not be attained by applying the relevant procedures laid down therein;

(d) concerns at least a majority of Member States;

(e) does not affect the acquis communautaire and the measures adopted under the other provisions of the Treaties;

(f) does not affect the competences, rights, obligations and interests of those Member States which do not participate therein;

(g) is open to all Member States and allows them to become parties to the cooperation at any time, provided that they comply with the basic decision and with the decisions taken within that framework;

(h) complies with the specific additional criteria laid down in Article 5a of the Treaty establishing the European Community and Article

K.12 of this Treaty, depending on the area concerned and is authorized by the Council in accordance with the procedures laid down therein.

2. Member States shall apply, as far as they are concerned, the acts and decisions adopted for the implementation of the cooperation in which they participate. Member States not participating in such cooperation shall not impede the implementation thereof by the participating Member States.

Article K.16

1. For the purposes of the adoption of the acts and decisions necessary for the implementation of the cooperation referred to in Article K.15, the relevant institutional provisions of the Treaties shall apply. However, while all members of the Council shall be able to take part in the deliberations, only those representing participating Member States shall take part in the adoption of decisions; the qualified majority shall be defined as the same proportion of votes of the Council members concerned weighted in accordance with Article 148(2) of the Treaty establishing the European Community; unanimity shall be constituted by only those Council members concerned.

2. Expenditure resulting from implementation of the cooperation, other than administrative costs entailed for the institutions, shall be borne by the participating Member States, unless the Council, acting unanimously, decides otherwise.

Article K.17

The Council and the Commission shall regularly inform the European Parliament of the development of closer cooperation established on the basis of this Title."

(13)   Article L shall be replaced by the following:

"Article L

The provisions of the Treaty establishing the European Community, the Treaty establishing the European Coal and Steel Community and the Treaty establishing the European Atomic Energy Community concerning the powers of the Court of Justice of the European Communities and the exercise of those powers shall apply only to the following provisions of this Treaty:

(a) provisions amending the Treaty establishing the European Economic Community with a view to establishing the European Community, the Treaty establishing the European Coal and Steel

Community and the Treaty establishing the European Atomic Energy Community;

(b) provisions of Title VI, under the conditions provided for by Articles K.7 and K.12;

(c) Article F(2) with regard to action of the institutions, insofar as the Court has jurisdiction under the Treaties establishing the European Communities and under this Treaty;

(d) Articles L to S."

(14)   In Article N, paragraph 2 shall be deleted and paragraph 1 shall remain without a number.

(15)   In Article O, the first paragraph shall be replaced by the following:

"Any European State which respects the principles set out in Article F(1) may apply to become a member of the Union. It shall address its application to the Council, which shall act unanimously after consulting the Commission and after receiving the assent of the European Parliament, which shall act by an absolute majority of its component members."

ARTICLE 2

The Treaty establishing the European Community shall be amended in accordance with the provisions of this Article.

(1)   In the preamble the following recital shall be added after the eighth existing recital:

"DETERMINED to promote the development of the highest possible level of knowledge for their peoples through a wide access to education and its continuous updating,"

(2)   Article 2 shall be replaced by the following:

"Article 2

The Community shall have as its task, by establishing a common market and an economic and monetary union and by implementing common policies or activities referred to in Articles 3 and 3a, to promote throughout the Community a harmonious, balanced and sustainable development of economic activities, a high level of employment and of social protection, equality between men and women, sustainable and non inflationary growth, a high degree of competitiveness and convergence of economic performance, a high level of protection and improvement of the quality of the environment, the raising of the standard of living and quality of life, and economic and social cohesion and solidarity among Member States."

(3)   Article 3 shall be amended as follows:

(a)   the existing text shall be numbered and become paragraph 1;

(b)   in new paragraph 1 the following new point (i) shall be inserted after point (h); the existing point (i) shall become point (j) and the subsequent points shall be renumbered accordingly;

"(i) the promotion of coordination between employment policies of the Member States with a view to enhancing their effectiveness by developing a coordinated strategy for employment;"

(c)   the following paragraph shall be added:

"2. In all the activities referred to in this Article, the Community shall aim to eliminate inequalities, and to promote equality, between men and women."

(4)   The following Article shall be inserted:

"Article 3c

Environmental protection requirements must be integrated into the definition and implementation of Community policies and activities referred to in Article 3, in particular with a view to promoting sustainable development."

(5)   The following Article shall be inserted:

"Article 5a

1. Member States which intend to establish closer cooperation between themselves may be authorized, subject to Articles K.15 and K.16 of the Treaty on European Union to make use of the institutions, procedures and mechanisms laid down by this Treaty, provided that the cooperation proposed:

(a) does not concern areas which fall within the exclusive competence of the Community;

(b) does not affect Community policies, actions or programmes;

(c) does not concern the citizenship of the Union or discriminate between nationals of Member States;

(d) remains within the limits of the powers conferred upon the Community by this Treaty; and

(e) does not constitute a discrimination or a restriction of trade between Member States and does not distort the conditions of competition between the latter.

2. The authorization referred to in paragraph 1 shall be granted by the Council, acting by a qualified majority on a proposal from the Commission and after consulting the European Parliament.

If a member of the Council declares that, for important and stated reasons of national policy, it intends to oppose the granting of an authorization by qualified majority, a vote shall not be taken. The Council may, acting by a qualified majority, request that the matter be referred to the Council, meeting in the composition of the Heads of State or Government, for decision by unanimity.

Member States which intend to establish closer cooperation as referred to in paragraph 1 may address a request to the Commission, which may submit a proposal to the Council to that effect. In the event of the Commission not submitting a proposal, it shall inform the Member States concerned of the reasons for not doing so.

3. Any Member State which wishes to become a party to cooperation set up in accordance with this Article shall notify its intention to the Council and to the Commission, which shall give an opinion to the Council within three months of receipt of that notification. Within four months of the date of that notification, the Commission shall decide on it and on possible specific arrangements as it may deem necessary.

4. The acts and decisions necessary for the implementation of cooperation activities shall be subject to all the relevant provisions of this Treaty, save as otherwise provided for in this Article and in Articles K.15 and K.16 of the Treaty on European Union.

5. This Article is without prejudice to the provisions of the Protocol integrating the Schengen acquis into the framework of the European Union."

(6)   In Article 6, the second paragraph shall be replaced by the following:

"The Council, acting in accordance with the procedure referred to in Article 189b, may adopt rules designed to prohibit such discrimination."

(7)   The following Article shall be inserted:

"Article 6a

Without prejudice to the other provisions of this Treaty and within the limits of the powers conferred by it upon the Community, the Council, acting unanimously on a proposal from the Commission and after consulting the European Parliament, may take appropriate action to combat discrimination based on sex, racial or ethnic origin, religion or belief, disability, age or sexual orientation."

(8)   The following Article shall be inserted:

"Article 7d

Without prejudice to Articles 77, 90 and 92, and given the place occupied by services of general economic interest in the shared values of the Union as well as their role in promoting social and territorial cohesion, the Community and the Member States, each within their respective powers and within the scope of application of this Treaty, shall take care that such services operate on the basis of principles and conditions which enable them to fulfil their missions."

(9)   Article 8(1) shall be replaced by the following:

"1. Citizenship of the Union is hereby established. Every person holding the nationality of a Member State shall be a citizen of the Union. Citizenship of the Union shall complement and not replace national citizenship."

(10)   Article 8a(2) shall be replaced by the following:

"2. The Council may adopt provisions with a view to facilitating the exercise of the rights referred to in paragraph 1; save as otherwise provided in this Treaty, the Council shall act in accordance with the procedure referred to in Article 189b. The Council shall act unanimously throughout this procedure."

(11)   In Article 8d, the following shall be added as a third paragraph:

"Every citizen of the Union may write to any of the institutions or bodies referred to in this Article or in Article 4 in one of the languages mentioned in Article 248 and have an answer in the same language."

(12)   Article 51 shall be replaced by the following:

"Article 51

The Council shall, acting in accordance with the procedure referred to in Article 189b, adopt such measures in the field of social security as are necessary to provide freedom of movement for workers; to this end, it shall make arrangements to secure for migrant workers and their dependants:

(a) aggregation, for the purpose of acquiring and retaining the right to benefit and of calculating the amount of benefit, of all periods taken into account under the laws of the several countries;

(b) payment of benefits to persons resident in the territories of Member States.

The Council shall act unanimously throughout the procedure referred to in Article 189b."

(13)   Article 56(2) shall be replaced by the following:

"2.   The Council shall, acting in accordance with the procedure referred to in Article 189b, issue directives for the coordination of the abovementioned provisions."

(14)   Article 57(2) shall be replaced by the following:

"2.   For the same purpose, the Council shall, acting in accordance with the procedure referred to in Article 189b, issue directives for the coordination of the provisions laid down by law, regulation or administrative action in Member States concerning the taking-up and pursuit of activities as self-employed persons. The Council, acting unanimously throughout the procedure referred to in Article 189b, shall decide on directives the implementation of which involves in at least one Member State amendment of the existing principles laid down by law governing the professions with respect to training and conditions of access for natural persons. In other cases the Council shall act by qualified majority."

(15)   The following title shall be inserted in Part Three:

"Title IIIa

Visas, asylum, immigration and other policies related to free movement of persons

Article 73i

In order to establish progressively an area of freedom, security and justice, the Council shall adopt:

(a) within a period of five years after the entry into force of the Treaty of Amsterdam, measures aimed at ensuring the free movement of persons in accordance with Article 7a, in conjunction with directly related flanking measures with respect to external borders controls, asylum and immigration, in accordance with the provisions of Article 73j(2) and (3) and Article 73k(1)(a) and (2)(a), and measures to prevent and combat crime in accordance with the provisions of Article K.3(e) of the Treaty on European Union;

(b) other measures in the fields of asylum, immigration and safeguarding the rights of third country nationals, in accordance with the provisions of Article 73k;

(c) measures in the field of judicial cooperation in civil matters as provided for in Article 73m;

(d) appropriate measures to encourage and strengthen administrative cooperation, as provided for in Article 73n;

(e) measures in the field of police and judicial cooperation in criminal matters aimed at a high level of security by preventing and combating crime within the Union in accordance with the provisions of the Treaty on European Union.

Article 73j

The Council, acting in accordance with the procedure referred to in Article 73o, shall, within a period of five years after the entry into force of the Treaty of Amsterdam, adopt:

(1) measures with a view to ensuring, in compliance with Article 7a, the absence of any controls on persons, be they citizens of the Union or nationals of third countries, when crossing internal borders.

(2) measures on the crossing of the external borders of the Member States which shall establish:

(a) standards and procedures to be followed by Member States in carrying out checks on persons at such borders;

(b) rules on visas for intended stays of no more than three months, including:

(i) the list of third countries whose nationals must be in possession of visas when crossing the external borders and those whose nationals are exempt from that requirement;

(ii) the procedures and conditions for issuing visas by Member States;

(iii) a uniform format for visas;

(iv) rules on a uniform visa.

(3) measures setting out the conditions under which the nationals of third countries shall have the freedom to travel within the territory of the Member States during a period of no more than three months.

Article 73k

The Council, acting in accordance with the procedure referred to in Article 73o, shall, within a period of five years after the entry into force of the Treaty of Amsterdam, adopt:

(1) measures on asylum, in accordance with the Convention of 28 July 1951, the Protocol of 31 January 1967 relating to the Status of Refugees and other relevant treaties, within the following areas:

(a) criteria and mechanisms for determining which Member State is responsible for considering an application for asylum submitted by a third country national in one of the Member States,

(b) minimum standards on the reception of asylum seekers in Member States,

(c) minimum standards with respect to the qualification of third country nationals as refugees,

(d) minimum standards on procedures in Member States for granting or withdrawing refugee status;

(2) measures on refugees and displaced persons within the following areas:

(a) minimum standards for giving temporary protection to displaced persons from third countries who cannot return to their country of origin and for persons who otherwise need international protection,

(b) promoting a balance of effort between Member States in receiving and bearing the consequences of receiving refugees and displaced persons;

(3) measures on immigration policy within the following areas:

(a) conditions of entry and residence, and standards on procedures for the issue by Member States of long term visas and residence permits, including those for the purpose of family reunion,

(b) illegal immigration and illegal residence, including repatriation of illegal residents;

(4) measures defining the rights and conditions under which nationals of third countries who are legally resident in a Member State may reside in other Member States.

Measures adopted by the Council pursuant to points 3 and 4 shall not prevent any Member State from maintaining or introducing in the areas concerned national provisions which are compatible with this Treaty and with international agreements.

Measures to be adopted pursuant to points 2(b), 3(a) and 4 shall not be subject to the five year period referred to above.

Article 73l

1. This Title shall not affect the exercise of the responsibilities incumbent upon Member States with regard to the maintenance of law and order and the safeguarding of internal security.

2. In the event of one or more Member States being confronted with an emergency situation characterised by a sudden inflow of nationals from a third country and without prejudice to paragraph 1, the Council may, acting by qualified majority on a proposal from

the Commission, adopt provisional measures of a duration not exceeding six months for the benefit of the Member States concerned.

Article 73m

Measures in the field of judicial cooperation in civil matters having cross-border implications, to be taken in accordance with Article 73o and insofar as necessary for the proper functioning of the internal market, shall include:

(a) improving and simplifying:

- the system for cross-border service of judicial and extrajudicial documents;

- cooperation in the taking of evidence;

- the recognition and enforcement of decisions in civil and commercial cases, including extrajudicial cases;

(b) promoting the compatibility of the rules applicable in the Member States concerning the conflict of laws and of jurisdiction;

(c) eliminating obstacles to the good functioning of civil proceedings, if necessary by promoting the compatibility of the rules on civil procedure applicable in the Member States.

Article 73n

The Council, acting in accordance with the procedure referred to in Article 73o, shall take measures to ensure cooperation between the relevant departments of the administrations of the Member States in the areas covered by this Title, as well as between those departments and the Commission.

Article 73o

1. During a transitional period of five years following the entry into force of the Treaty of Amsterdam, the Council shall act unanimously on a proposal from the Commission or on the initiative of a Member State and after consulting the European Parliament.

2. After this period of five years:

- the Council shall act on proposals from the Commission; the Commission shall examine any request made by a Member State that it submit a proposal to the Council;

- the Council, acting unanimously after consulting the European Parliament, shall take a decision with a view to making all or parts of the areas covered by this Title governed by the procedure referred to in Article 189b and adapting the provisions relating to the powers of the Court of Justice.

3. By derogation from paragraphs 1 and 2:

- measures referred to in Article 73j(2)(b) (i) and (iii) shall, from the entry into force of the Treaty of Amsterdam, be adopted by the Council acting by a qualified majority on a proposal from the Commission and after consulting the European Parliament;

- measures referred to in Article 73j(2)(b) (ii) and (iv) shall, after a period of five years following the entry into force of the Treaty of Amsterdam, be adopted by the Council acting in accordance with the procedure referred to in Article 189b.

Article 73p

1. The provisions of Article 177 shall apply to this Title under the following circumstances and conditions: where a question on the interpretation of this Title or on the validity or interpretation of acts of the institutions of the Community based on this Title is raised in a case pending before a court or a tribunal of a Member State against whose decisions there is no judicial remedy under national law, that court or tribunal shall, if it considers that a decision on the question is necessary to enable it to give judgement, request the Court of Justice to give a ruling thereon.

2. In any event, the Court of Justice shall not have jurisdiction to rule on any measure or decision taken pursuant to Article 73j(1) relating to the maintenance of law and order and the safeguarding of internal security.

3. The Council, the Commission or a Member State may request the Court of Justice to give a ruling on a question of interpretation of this Title or of acts of the institutions of the Community based on this Title. The ruling given by the Court of Justice in response to such a request shall not apply to judgements of courts or tribunals of the Member States which have become res judicata.

Article 73q

The application of this Title shall be subject to the provisions of the Protocol on the position of the United Kingdom and Ireland and to the Protocol on the position of Denmark, without prejudice to the Protocol on the application of certain aspects of Article 7a of the Treaty establishing the European Community to the United Kingdom and to Ireland."

(16)   In Article 75(1), the introductory part shall be replaced by the following:

"1. For the purpose of implementing Article 74, and taking into account the distinctive features of transport, the Council shall, acting in accordance with the procedure referred to in Article 189b and after consulting the Economic and Social Committee and the Committee of the Regions, lay down:"

(17) In Article 100a, paragraphs 3, 4 and 5 shall be replaced by the following:

"3. The Commission, in its proposals envisaged in paragraph 1 concerning health, safety, environmental protection and consumer protection, will take as a base a high level of protection, taking account in particular of any new development based on scientific facts. Within their respective powers, the European Parliament and the Council will also seek to achieve this objective.

4. If, after the adoption by the Council or by the Commission of a harmonization measure, a Member State deems it necessary to maintain national provisions on grounds of major needs referred to in Article 36, or relating to the protection of the environment or the working environment, it shall notify the Commission of these provisions as well as the grounds for maintaining them.

5. Moreover, without prejudice to the previous subparagraph, if, after the adoption by the Council or by the Commission of a harmonization measure, a Member State deems it necessary to introduce national provisions based on new scientific evidence relating to the protection of the environment or the working environment on grounds of a problem specific to that Member State arising after the adoption of the harmonization measure, it shall notify the Commission of the envisaged provisions as well as the grounds for introducing them.

6. The Commission shall, within six months of the notifications as referred to in paragraphs 4 and 5, approve or reject the national provisions involved after having verified that they are not a means of arbitrary discrimination or a disguised restriction on trade between Member States and that they shall not constitute an obstacle to the functioning of the internal market.

In the absence of a decision by the Commission within this period the national provisions referred to in paragraphs 4 and 5 shall be deemed to have been approved.

When justified by the complexity of the matter and in the absence of danger for human health, the Commission may notify the Member State concerned that the period referred to in this paragraph may be extended for a further period of up to six months.

7. When, pursuant to paragraph 6, a Member State is authorized to maintain or introduce national provisions derogating from a

harmonization measure, the Commission shall immediately examine whether to propose an adaptation to that measure.

8. When a Member State raises a specific problem on public health in a field which has been the subject of prior harmonization measures, it shall bring it to the attention of the Commission which shall immediately examine whether to propose appropriate measures to the Council.

9. By way of derogation from the procedure laid down in Articles 169 and 170, the Commission and any Member State may bring the matter directly before the Court of Justice if it considers that another Member State is making improper use of the powers provided for in this Article.

10. The harmonization measures referred to above shall, in appropriate cases, include a safeguard clause authorizing the Member States to take, for one or more of the non-economic reasons referred to in Article 36, provisional measures subject to a Community control procedure."

(18)   Articles 100c and 100d shall be repealed.

(19)   The following Title shall be inserted after Title VI:

"Title VIa

Employment

Article 109n

Member States and the Community shall, in accordance with this Title, work towards developing a coordinated strategy for employment and particularly for promoting a skilled, trained and adaptable workforce and labour markets responsive to economic change with a view to achieving the objectives defined in Article B of the Treaty on European Union and in Article 2 of this Treaty.

Article 109o

1. Member States, through their employment policies, shall contribute to the achievement of the objectives referred to in Article 109n in a way consistent with the broad guidelines of the economic policies of the Member States and of the Community adopted pursuant to Article 103(2).

2. Member States, having regard to national practices related to the responsibilities of management and labour, shall regard promoting employment as a matter of common concern and shall coordinate their action in this respect within the Council, in accordance with the provisions of Article 109q.

242

Article 109p

1. The Community shall contribute to a high level of employment by encouraging cooperation between Member States and by supporting and, if necessary, complementing their action. In doing so, the competences of the Member States shall be respected.

2. The objective of a high level of employment shall be taken into consideration in the formulation and implementation of Community policies and activities.

Article 109q

1. The European Council shall each year consider the employment situation in the Community and adopt conclusions thereon, on the basis of a joint annual report by the Council and the Commission.

2. On the basis of the conclusions of the European Council, the Council, acting by a qualified majority on a proposal from the Commission and after consulting the European Parliament, the Economic and Social Committee, the Committee of the Regions and the Employment Committee referred to in Article 109s, shall each year draw up guidelines which the Member States shall take into account in their employment policies. These guidelines shall be consistent with the broad guidelines adopted pursuant to Article 103(2).

3. Each Member State shall provide the Council and the Commission with an annual report on the principal measures taken to implement its employment policy in the light of the guidelines for employment as referred to in paragraph 2.

4. The Council, on the basis of the reports referred to in paragraph 3 and having received the views of the Employment Committee shall each year carry out an examination of the implementation of the employment policies of the Member States in the light of the guidelines for employment. The Council, acting by a qualified majority on a recommendation from the Commission, may, if it considers it appropriate in the light of that examination, make recommendations to Member States.

5. On the basis of the results of that examination, the Council and the Commission shall make a joint annual report to the European Council on the employment situation in the Community and on the implementation of the guidelines for employment.

Article 109r

The Council, acting in accordance with the procedure referred to in Article 189b and after consulting the Economic and Social

Committee and the Committee of the Regions, may adopt incentive measures designed to encourage cooperation between Member States and to support their action in the field of employment through initiatives aimed at developing exchanges of information and best practices, providing comparative analysis and advice as well as promoting innovative approaches and evaluating experiences, in particular by recourse to pilot projects.

Those measures shall not include harmonization of the laws and regulations of the Member States.

Article 109s

The Council, after consulting the European Parliament, shall establish an Employment Committee with advisory status to promote coordination between Member States on employment and labour market policies. The tasks of the Committee shall be:

- to monitor the employment situation and employment policies in the Member States and the Community;

- without prejudice to Article 151, to formulate opinions at the request of either the Council or the Commission or on its own initiative, and to contribute to the preparation of the Council proceedings referred to in Article 109q.

In fulfilling its mandate, the Committee shall consult the social partners.

The Member States and the Commission shall each appoint two members of the Committee."

(20) In Article 113, the following paragraph shall be added:

"5. The Council, acting unanimously on a proposal from the Commission and after consulting the European Parliament, may extend the application of paragraphs 1 to 4 to international negotiations and agreements on services and intellectual property insofar as they are not covered by these paragraphs."

(21) The following Title shall be inserted after Title VII:

"Title VIIa

Customs cooperation

Article 116

Within the scope of application of this Treaty, the Council, acting in accordance with the procedure referred to in Article 189b, shall take measures in order to strengthen customs cooperation between Member States and between the latter and the Commission. These measures shall not concern the application of national criminal law and the national administration of justice."

(22)   Articles 117 to 120 shall be replaced by the following:

"Article 117

The Community and the Member States, having in mind fundamental social rights such as those set out in the European Social Charter signed at Turin on 18 October 1961 and in the 1989 Community Charter of the Fundamental Social Rights of Workers, shall have as their objectives the promotion of employment, improved living and working conditions, so as to make possible their harmonization while the improvement is being maintained, proper social protection, dialogue between management and labour, the development of human resources with a view to lasting high employment and the combating of exclusion.

To this end the Community and the Member States shall implement measures which take account of the diverse forms of national practices, in particular in the field of contractual relations, and the need to maintain the competitiveness of the Community economy.

They believe that such a development will ensue not only from the functioning of the common market, which will favour the harmonization of social systems, but also from the procedures provided for in this Treaty and from the approximation of provisions laid down by law, regulation or administrative action."

Article 118

1. With a view to achieving the objectives of Article 117, the Community shall support and complement the activities of the Member States in the following fields:

-    improvement in particular of the working environment to protect workers' health and safety;

-    working conditions;

-    the information and consultation of workers;

-    the integration of persons excluded from the labour market, without prejudice to Article 127;

-    equality between men and women with regard to labour market opportunities and treatment at work.

2. To this end, the Council may adopt, by means of directives, minimum requirements for gradual implementation, having regard to the conditions and technical rules obtaining in each of the Member

States. Such directives shall avoid imposing administrative, financial and legal constraints in a way which would hold back the creation and development of small and medium-sized undertakings.

The Council shall act in accordance with the procedure referred to in Article 189b after consulting the Economic and Social Committee and the Committee of the Regions.

The Council, acting in accordance with the same procedure, may adopt measures designed to encourage cooperation between Member States through initiatives aimed at improving knowledge, developing exchanges of information and best practices, promoting innovative approaches and evaluating experiences in order to combat social exclusion.

3. However, the Council shall act unanimously on a proposal from the Commission, after consulting the European Parliament, the Economic and Social Committee and the Committee of the Regions in the following areas:

- social security and social protection of workers;

- protection of workers where their employment contract is terminated;

- representation and collective defence of the interests of workers and employers, including co-determination, subject to paragraph 6;

- conditions of employment for third-country nationals legally residing in Community territory;

- financial contributions for promotion of employment and job-creation, without prejudice to the provisions relating to the Social Fund.

4. A Member State may entrust management and labour, at their joint request, with the implementation of directives adopted pursuant to paragraphs 2 and 3.

In this case, it shall ensure that, no later than the date on which a directive must be transposed in accordance with Article 189, management and labour have introduced the necessary measures by agreement, the Member State concerned being required to take any necessary measure enabling it at any time to be in a position to guarantee the results imposed by that directive.

5. The provisions adopted pursuant to this Article shall not prevent any Member State from maintaining or introducing more stringent protective measures compatible with the Treaty.

6. The provisions of this Article shall not apply to pay, the right of association, the right to strike or the right to impose lock-outs.

Article 118a

1. The Commission shall have the task of promoting the consultation of management and labour at Community level and shall take any relevant measure to facilitate their dialogue by ensuring balanced support for the parties.

2. To this end, before submitting proposals in the social policy field, the Commission shall consult management and labour on the possible direction of Community action.

3. If, after such consultation, the Commission considers Community action advisable, it shall consult management and labour on the content of the envisaged proposal. Management and labour shall forward to the Commission an opinion or, where appropriate, a recommendation.

4. On the occasion of such consultation, management and labour may inform the Commission of their wish to initiate the process provided for in Article 118b. The duration of the procedure shall not exceed nine months, unless the management and labour concerned and the Commission decide jointly to extend it.

Article 118b

1. Should management and labour so desire, the dialogue between them at Community level may lead to contractual relations, including agreements.

2. Agreements concluded at Community level shall be implemented either in accordance with the procedures and practices specific to management and labour and the Member States or, in matters covered by Article 118, at the joint request of the signatory parties, by a Council decision on a proposal from the Commission.

The Council shall act by qualified majority, except where the agreement in question contains one or more provisions relating to one of the areas referred to in Article 118(3), in which case it shall act unanimously.

Article 118c

With a view to achieving the objectives of Article 117 and without prejudice to the other provisions of this Treaty, the Commission shall encourage cooperation between the Member States and facilitate the coordination of their action in all social policy fields under this chapter, particularly in matters relating to:

- employment;

- labour law and working conditions;

- basic and advanced vocational training;

- social security;

- prevention of occupational accidents and diseases;

- occupational hygiene;

- the rights of association and collective bargaining between employers and workers.

To this end, the Commission shall act in close contact with Member States by making studies, delivering opinions and arranging consultations both on problems arising at national level and on those of concern to international organizations.

Before delivering the opinions provided for in this Article, the Commission shall consult the Economic and Social Committee.

Article 119

1. Each Member State shall ensure that the principle of equal pay for male and female workers for equal work or work of equal value is applied.

2. For the purpose of this Article, 'pay' means the ordinary basic or minimum wage or salary and any other consideration, whether in cash or in kind, which the worker receives directly or indirectly, in respect of his employment, from his employer.

Equal pay without discrimination based on sex means:

(a) that pay for the same work at piece rates shall be calculated on the basis of the same unit of measurement;

(b) that pay for work at time rates shall be the same for the same job.

3. The Council, acting in accordance with the procedure referred to in Article 189b, and after consulting the Economic and Social Committee, shall adopt measures to ensure the application of the principle of equal opportunities and equal treatment of men and women in matters of employment and occupation, including the principle of equal pay for equal work or work of equal value.

4. With a view to ensuring full equality in practice between men and women in working life, the principle of equal treatment shall not prevent any Member State from maintaining or adopting measures providing for specific advantages in order to make it easier

for the underrepresented sex to pursue a vocational activity or to prevent or compensate for disadvantages in professional careers.

Article 119a

Member States shall endeavour to maintain the existing equivalence between paid holiday schemes.

Article 120

The Commission shall draw up a report each year on progress in achieving the objectives of Article 117, including the demographic situation in the Community. It shall forward the report to the European Parliament, the Council and the Economic and Social Committee.

The European Parliament may invite the Commission to draw up reports on particular problems concerning the social situation."

(23)   Article 125 shall be replaced by the following:

"Article 125

The Council, acting in accordance with the procedure referred to in Article 189b and after consulting the Economic and Social Committee and the Committee of the Regions, shall adopt implementing decisions relating to the European Social Fund."

(24)   Article 127(4) shall be replaced by the following:

"4. The Council, acting in accordance with the procedure referred to in Article 189b and after consulting the Economic and Social Committee and the Committee of the Regions, shall adopt measures to contribute to the achievement of the objectives referred to in this Article, excluding any harmonisation of the laws and regulations of the Member States."

(25)   Article 128(4) shall be replaced by the following:

"4. The Community shall take cultural aspects into account in its action under other provisions of this Treaty, in particular in order to respect and to promote the diversity of its cultures."

(26)   Article 129 shall be replaced by the following:

"Article 129

1. A high level of human health protection shall be ensured in the definition and implementation of all Community policies and activities.

Community action, which shall complement national policies, shall be directed towards improving public health, preventing human illness and diseases, and obviating sources of danger to human health.

Such action shall cover the fight against the major health scourges, by promoting research into their causes, their transmission and their prevention, as well as health information and education.

The Community shall complement the Member States' action in reducing drugs related health damage, including information and prevention.

2. The Community shall encourage cooperation between the Member States in the areas referred to in this Article and, if necessary, lend support to their action.

Member States shall, in liaison with the Commission, coordinate among themselves their policies and programmes in the areas referred to in paragraph 1. The Commission may, in close contact with the Member States, take any useful initiative to promote such coordination.

3. The Community and the Member States shall foster cooperation with third countries and the competent international organizations in the sphere of public health.

4. The Council, acting in accordance with the procedure referred to in Article 189b, after consulting the Social and Economic Committee and the Committee of the Regions shall contribute to the achievement of the objectives referred to in this Article through adopting:

(a) measures setting high standards of quality and safety of organs and substances of human origin, blood and blood derivatives; these measures shall not prevent any Member State from maintaining or introducing more stringent protective measures;

(b) by way of derogation from Article 43, measures in the veterinary and phytosanitary fields which have as their direct objective the protection of public health;

(c) incentive measures designed to protect and improve human health, excluding any harmonization of the laws and regulations of the Member States.

The Council, acting by a qualified majority on a proposal from the Commission, may also adopt recommendations for the purposes set out in this Article.

5. Community action in the field of public health shall fully respect the responsibilities of the Member States for the organization and delivery of health services and medical care. In particular, measures referred to in paragraph 4(a) shall not affect national provisions on the donation or medical use of organs and blood."

(27)   Article 129a shall be replaced by the following:

"Article 129a

1. In order to promote the interests of consumers and to ensure a high level of consumer protection, the Community shall contribute to protecting the health, safety and economic interests of consumers, as well as to promoting their right to information, education and to organize themselves in order to safeguard their interests.

2. Consumer protection requirements shall be taken into account in defining and implementing other Community policies and activities.

3. The Community shall contribute to the attainment of the objectives referred to in paragraph 1 through:

(a) measures adopted pursuant to Article 100a in the context of the completion of the internal market;

(b) measures which support, supplement and monitor the policy pursued by the Member States.

4. The Council, acting in accordance with the procedure referred to in Article 189b and after consulting the Economic and Social Committee, shall adopt the measures referred to in paragraph 3(b).

5. Measures adopted pursuant to paragraph 4 shall not prevent any Member State from maintaining or introducing more stringent protective measures. Such measures must be compatible with this Treaty. The Commission shall be notified of them."

(28)   In the first subparagraph of Article 129c(1), the first part of the third indent shall be replaced by the following:

"- may support projects of common interest supported by Member States, which are identified in the framework of the guidelines referred to in the first indent, particularly through feasibility studies, loan guarantees or interest-rate subsidies;".

(29)   In Article 129d, the third paragraph shall be replaced by the following:

"The Council acting in accordance with the procedure referred to in Article 189b and after consulting the Economic and Social Committee and the Committee of the Regions, shall adopt the other measures provided for in Article 129c(1)."

(30)   In Article 130a, the second paragraph shall be replaced by the following:

"In particular, the Community shall aim at reducing disparities between the levels of development of the various regions and the backwardness of the least favoured regions or islands, including rural areas."

(31) In Article 130e, the first paragraph shall be replaced by the following:

"Implementing decisions relating to the European Regional Development Fund shall be taken by the Council, acting in accordance with the procedure referred to in Article 189b and after consulting the Economic and Social Committee and the Committee of the Regions."

(32) In Article 130i(1), the first subparagraph shall be replaced by the following:

"1. A multiannual framework programme, setting out all the activities of the Community, shall be adopted by the Council, acting in accordance with the procedure referred to in Article 189b after consulting the Economic and Social Committee."

(33) Article 130o shall be replaced by the following:

"Article 130o

The Council, acting by qualified majority on a proposal from the Commission and after consulting the European Parliament and the Economic and Social Committee, shall adopt the provisions referred to in Article 130n.

The Council, acting in accordance with the procedure referred to in Article 189b and after consulting the Economic and Social Committee, shall adopt the provisions referred to in Articles 130j, 130k and 130l. Adoption of the supplementary programmes shall require the agreement of the Member States concerned."

(34) Article 130r(2) shall be replaced by the following:

"2. Community policy on the environment shall aim at a high level of protection taking into account the diversity of situations in the various regions of the Community. It shall be based on the precautionary principle and on the principles that preventive action should be taken, that environmental damage should as a priority be rectified at source and that the polluter should pay.

In this context, harmonisation measures answering the environmental protection requirements shall include, where appropriate, a safeguard clause allowing Member States to take provisional meansures, for non-economic environmental reasons, subject to a Community inspection procedure."

(35) Article 130s shall be amended as follows:

(a) Paragraph 1 shall be replaced by the following:

"1. The Council, acting in accordance with the procedure referred to in Article 189b and after consulting the Economic and Social Committee and the Committee of the Regions, shall decide what action is to be taken by the Community in order to achieve the objectives referred to in Article 130r."

(b) The introductory part of paragraph 2 shall be replaced by the following:

"2. By way of derogation from the decision-making procedure provided for in paragraph 1 and without prejudice to Article 100a, the Council, acting unanimously on a proposal from the Commission and after consulting the European Parliament, the Economic and Social Committee and the Committee of the Regions, shall adopt:"

(c) The first subparagraph of paragraph 3 shall be replaced by the following:

"3. In other areas, general action programmes setting out priority objectives to be attained shall be adopted by the Council, acting in accordance with the procedure referred to in Article 189b and after consulting the Economic and Social Committee and the Committee of the Regions."

(36)   Article 130w(1) shall be replaced by the following:

"1. Without prejudice to the other provisions of this Treaty, the Council, acting in accordance with the procedure referred to in Article 189b, shall adopt the measures necessary to further the objectives referred to in Article 130u. Such measures may take the form of multiannual programmes."

(37)   In Article 137, the following paragraph shall be added:

"The number of Members of the European Parliament shall not exceed seven hundred."

(38)   Article 138 shall be amended as follows:

(a) in paragraph 3, the first subparagraph shall be replaced by the following:

"3. The European Parliament shall draw up a proposal for elections by direct universal suffrage in accordance with a uniform procedure in all Member States or in accordance with principles common to all Member States.";

(b) the following paragraph shall be added:

"4. The European Parliament shall, after seeking an opinion from the Commission and with the approval of the Council acting unanimously, lay down the regulations and general conditions governing the performance of the duties of its Members."

(39)   Article 151 shall be replaced by the following:

"Article 151

1. A committee consisting of the Permanent Representatives of the Member States shall be responsible for preparing the work of the Council and for carrying out the tasks assigned to it by the Council. The Committee may adopt procedural decisions in cases provided for in the Council's Rules of Procedure.

2. The Council shall be assisted by a General Secretariat, under the responsibility of a Secretary-General, High Representative for the common foreign and security policy, who shall be assisted by a Deputy Secretary-General responsible for the running of the General Secretariat. The Secretary-General and the Deputy Secretary-General shall be appointed by the Council acting unanimously.

The Council shall decide on the organization of the General Secretariat.

3. The Council shall adopt its Rules of Procedure.

For the purpose of applying Article 191a(3), the Council shall elaborate in these Rules the conditions under which the public shall have access to Council documents. For the purpose of this paragraph, the Council shall define the cases in which it is to be regarded as acting in its legislative capacity, with a view to allowing greater access to documents in those cases, while at the same time preserving the effectiveness of its decision-making process. In any event, when the Council acts in its legislative capacity, the results of votes and explanations of vote as well as statements in the minutes shall be made public."

(40)   In Article 158(2) the first and second subparagraphs shall be replaced by the following:

"2. The governments of the Member States shall nominate by common accord the person they intend to appoint as President of the Commission; the nomination shall be approved by the European Parliament.

The governments of the Member States shall, by common accord with the nominee for President, nominate the other persons whom they intend to appoint as Members of the Commission."

(41)   In Article 163, the following paragraph shall be inserted as the first paragraph:

"The Commission shall work under the political guidance of its President."

(42)   In Article 173, the third paragraph shall be replaced by the following:

"The Court of Justice shall have jurisdiction under the same conditions in actions brought by the European Parliament, by the Court of Auditors and by the ECB for the purpose of protecting their prerogatives."

(43)   Article 188c shall be amended as follows:

(a) The second subparagraph of paragraph 1 shall be replaced by the following:

"The Court of Auditors shall provide the European Parliament and the Council with a statement of assurance as to the reliability of the accounts and the legality and regularity of the underlying transactions which shall be published in the Official Journal of the European Communities."

(b) The first subparagraph of paragraph 2 shall be replaced by the following:

"2. The Court of Auditors shall examine whether all revenue has been received and all expenditure incurred in a lawful and regular manner and whether the financial management has been sound. In doing so, it shall report in particular on any cases of irregularity."

(c) Paragraph 3 shall be replaced by the following:

"3. The audit shall be based on records and, if necessary, performed on the spot in the other institutions of the Community, on the premises of any body which manages revenue or expenditure on behalf of the Community and in the Member States, including on the premises of any natural or legal person in receipt of payments from the budget. In the Member States the audit shall be carried out in liaison with national audit bodies or, if these do not have the necessary powers, with the competent national departments. The Court of Auditors and the national audit bodies of the Member States shall cooperate in a spirit of trust while maintaining their independence. These bodies or departments shall inform the Court of Auditors whether they intend to take part in the audit.

The other institutions of the Community, any bodies managing revenue or expenditure on behalf of the Community, any natural or legal person in receipt of payments from the budget, and the national audit bodies or, if these do not have the necessary powers, the competent national departments, shall forward to the Court of

Auditors, at its request, any document or information necessary to carry out its task."

In respect of the European Investment Bank's activity in managing Community expenditure and revenue, the Court's rights of access to information held by the Bank shall be governed by an agreement between the Court, the Bank and the Commission. In the absence of an agreement, the Court shall nevertheless have access to information necessary for the audit of Community expenditure and revenue managed by the Bank."

(44)   Article 189b shall be replaced by the following:

"Article 189b

1. Where reference is made in this Treaty to this Article for the adoption of an act, the following procedure shall apply.

2. The Commission shall submit a proposal to the European Parliament and the Council.

The Council, acting by a qualified majority after obtaining the Opinion of the European Parliament,

-   if it approves all the amendments contained in the European Parliament's Opinion, may adopt the proposed act thus amended;

-   if the European Parliament does not propose any amendments, may adopt the proposed act;

-   shall otherwise adopt a common position and communicate it to the European Parliament. The Council shall inform the European Parliament fully of the reasons which led it to adopt its common position. The Commission shall inform the European Parliament fully of its position.

If, within three months of such communication, the European Parliament:

(a) approves the common position or has not taken a decision, the act in question shall be deemed to have been adopted in accordance with that common position;

(b) rejects, by an absolute majority of its component members, the common position, the proposed act shall be deemed not to have been adopted;

(c) proposes amendments to the common position by an absolute majority of its component members, the amended text shall be forwarded to the Council and to the Commission, which shall deliver an opinion on those amendments;

3. If, within three months of the matter being referred to it, the Council, acting by a qualified majority, approves all the amendments of the European Parliament, the act in question shall be deemed to have been adopted in the form of the common position thus amended; however, the Council shall act unanimously on the amendments on which the Commission has delivered a negative opinion. If the Council does not approve all the amendments, the President of the Council, in agreement with the President of the European Parliament, shall within six weeks convene a meeting of the Conciliation Committee.

4. The Conciliation Committee, which shall be composed of the members of the Council or their representatives and an equal number of representatives of the European Parliament, shall have the task of reaching agreement on a joint text, by a qualified majority of the members of the Council or their representatives and by a majority of the representatives of the European Parliament. The Commission shall take part in the Conciliation Committee's proceedings and shall take all the necessary initiatives with a view to reconciling the positions of the European Parliament and the Council. In fulfilling this task, the Conciliation Committee shall address the common position on the basis of the amendments proposed by the European Parliament.

5. If, within six weeks of its being convened, the Conciliation Committee approves a joint text, the European Parliament, acting by an absolute majority of the votes cast, and the Council, acting by a qualified majority, shall each have a period of six weeks from that approval in which to adopt the act in question in accordance with the joint text. If either of the two institutions fails to approve the proposed act within that period, it shall be deemed not to have been adopted.

6. Where the Conciliation Committee does not approve a joint text, the proposed act shall be deemed not to have been adopted.

7. The periods of three months and six weeks referred to in this Article shall be extended by a maximum of one month and two weeks respectively at the initiative of the European Parliament or the Council."

(45)   The following Article shall be inserted:

"Article 191a

1. Any citizen of the Union, and any natural or legal person residing or having its registered office in a Member State, shall have a right of access to European Parliament, Council and Commission

documents, subject to the principles and the conditions to be defined in accordance with paragraphs 2 and 3.

2. General principles and limits on grounds of public or private interest governing this right of access to documents shall be determined by the Council, acting in accordance with the procedure referred to in Article 189b within two years of the entry into force of the Treaty of Amsterdam.

3. Each institution referred to above shall elaborate in its own rules of procedure specific provisions regarding access to its documents."

(46)   In Article 198, the following paragraph shall be added:

"The Economic and Social Committee may be consulted by the European Parliament."

(47)   In Article 198a, the third paragraph shall be replaced by the following:

"The members of the Committee and an equal number of alternative members shall be appointed for four years by the Council acting unanimously on proposals from the respective Member States. Their term of office shall be renewable. No member of the Committee shall at the same time be a Member of the European Parliament."

(48)   In Article 198b the second paragraph shall be replaced by the following:

"It shall adopt its Rules of Procedure."

(49)   Article 198c shall be amended as follows:

(a)   the first paragraph shall be replaced by the following:

"The Committee of the Regions shall be consulted by the Council or by the Commission where this Treaty so provides and in all other cases, in particular those which concern cross-border cooperation, in which one of these two institutions considers it appropriate."

(b)   after the existing third paragraph, the following paragraph shall be inserted:

"The Committee of the Regions may be consulted by the European Parliament."

(50)   In Article 205, the first paragraph shall be replaced by the following:

"The Commission shall implement the budget, in accordance with the provisions of the regulations made pursuant to Article 209, on its own responsibility and within the limits of the appropriations, having regard to the principles of sound financial management. Member States shall cooperate with the Commission to ensure that the budget appropriations are used in accordance with the principles of sound financial management."

(51)   Article 206(1) shall be replaced by the following:

"1. The European Parliament, acting on a recommendation from the Council which shall act by a qualified majority, shall give a discharge to the Commission in respect of the implementation of the budget. To this end, the Council and the European Parliament in turn shall examine the accounts and the financial statement referred to in Article 205a, the annual report by the Court of Auditors together with the replies of the institutions under audit to the observations of the Court of Auditors, the statement of assurance referred to in Article 188c(1), second subparagraph and any relevant special reports by the Court of Auditors."

(52)   Article 209a shall be replaced by the following:

"Article 209a

1. The Community and the Member States shall counter fraud and any other illegal activities affecting the financial interests of the Community through measures to be taken in accordance with this Article, which shall act as a deterrent and be such as to afford effective protection in the Member States.

2. Member States shall take the same measures to counter fraud affecting the financial interests of the Community as they take to counter fraud affecting their own financial interests.

3. Without prejudice to other provisions of this Treaty, the Member States shall coordinate their action aimed at protecting the financial interests of the Community against fraud. To this end they shall organize, together with the Commission, close and regular cooperation between the competent authorities.

4. The Council, acting in accordance with the procedure referred to in Article 189b, after consulting the Court of Auditors, shall adopt the necessary measures in the fields of the prevention of and fight against fraud affecting the financial interests of the Community with a view to affording effective and equivalent protection in the Member States. These measures shall not concern the application of national criminal law and the national administration of justice.

5. The Commission, in cooperation with Member States, shall each year submit to the Council and to the European Parliament a report on the measures taken for the implementation of this Article."

(53)   The following Article shall be inserted:

"Article 213a

1. Without prejudice to the provisions of Article 5 of the Protocol on the Statute of the European System of Central Banks and of the European Central Bank, the Council, acting in accordance with the procedure referred to in Article 189b, shall adopt measures for the production of statistics where necessary for the performance of the activities of the Community.

2. The production of Community statistics shall conform to impartiality, reliability, objectivity, scientific independence, cost-effectiveness and statistical confidentiality; it shall not entail excessive burdens on economic operators."

(54)   The following Article shall be inserted:

"Article 213b

1. From 1 January 1999, Community acts on the protection of individuals with regard to the processing of personal data and the free movement of such data shall apply to the institutions and bodies set up by, or on the basis of, this Treaty.

2. Before the date referred to in paragraph 1, the Council, acting in accordance with the procedure referred to in Article 189b, shall establish an independent supervisory body responsible for monitoring the application of such Community acts to Community institutions and bodies and shall adopt any other relevant provisions as appropriate."

(55)   Article 227(2) shall be replaced by the following:

"2. The provisions of this Treaty shall apply to the French overseas departments, the Azores, Madeira and the Canary Islands.

However, taking account of the structural social and economic situation of the French overseas departments, the Azores, Madeira and the Canary Islands, which is compounded by their remoteness, insularity, small size, difficult topography and climate, economic dependence on a few products, the permanence and combination of which severely restrain their development, the Council, acting by a qualified majority on a proposal from the Commission and after consulting the European Parliament, shall adopt specific measures aimed, in particular, at laying down the conditions of application of the present Treaty to those regions, including common policies.

The Council shall, when adopting the relevant measures referred to in the previous subparagraph, take into account areas such as customs and trade policies, fiscal policy, free zones, agriculture and fisheries

260

policies, conditions for supply of raw materials and essential consumer goods, State aids and conditions of access to structural funds and to horizontal Community programmes.

The Council shall adopt the measures referred to in the second subparagraph taking into account the special characteristics and constraints of the outermost regions without undermining the integrity and the coherence of the Community legal order, including the internal market and common policies."

(56)   Article 228 shall be amended as follows:

(a) the second subparagraph of paragraph 1 shall read as follows:

"In exercising the powers conferred upon it by this paragraph, the Council shall act by a qualified majority, except in the cases where the first subparagraph of paragraph 2 provides that the Council shall act unanimously."

(b) paragraph 2 shall be replaced by the following:

"2. Subject to the powers vested in the Commission in this field, the signing, which may be accompanied by a decision on provisional application before entry into force, and the conclusion of the agreements shall be decided on by the Council, acting by a qualified majority on a proposal from the Commission. The Council shall act unanimously when the agreement covers a field for which unanimity is required for the adoption of internal rules and for the agreements referred to in Article 238.

By way of derogation from the rules laid down in paragraph 3, the same procedures shall apply for a decision to suspend the application of an international agreement, and for the purpose of establishing the positions to be adopted on behalf of the Community in a body set up by an agreement based on Article 238, when that body is called upon to adopt decisions having legal effects, with the exception of decisions supplementing or amending the institutional framework of the agreement.

The European Parliament shall be immediately and fully informed on any decision under this paragraph concerning the provisional application or the suspension of agreements, or the establishment of the Community position in a body set up by an agreement based on Article 238."

(57)   The following Article shall be inserted:

"Article 236

1. Where a decision has been taken to suspend voting rights of a Member State in accordance with Article F.1(2) of the Treaty on

European Union, these voting rights shall also be suspended with regard to this Treaty.

2. Moreover, where the existence of a serious and persistent breach by a Member State of the principles mentioned in Article F(1) of the Treaty on European Union has been determined in accordance with Article F.1(1) of that Treaty, the Council, acting by a qualified majority, may decide to suspend certain of the rights deriving from the application of this Treaty to the State in question. In doing so, the Council shall take into account the possible consequences of such a suspension on the rights and obligations of natural and legal persons.

The obligations of the Member State concerned under this Treaty shall in any case continue to be binding on that State.

3. The Council, acting by a qualified majority, may decide subsequently to vary or revoke measures taken in accordance with paragraph 2 in response to changes in the situation which led to their being imposed.

4. When taking decisions referred to in paragraphs 2 and 3, the Council shall act without taking into account the votes of the representative of the government of the Member State concerned. By way of derogation from Article 148(2) a qualified majority shall be defined as the same proportion of the weighted votes of the members of the Council concerned as laid down in Article 148(2).

The provisions of this paragraph shall also apply in the event of voting rights being suspended in accordance with paragraph 1. In such cases, a decision requiring unanimity shall be taken without the vote of the representative of the government of the Member State concerned."

(58)   Protocol (No. 14) on Social Policy and the Agreement on social policy attached thereto shall be repealed.

(59)   Protocol (No. 16) on the Economic and Social Committee and the Committee of the Regions shall be repealed.

ARTICLE 3

This Article amends the Treaty establishing the European Coal and Steel Community in accordance with the above amendments to the Treaty establishing the European Community.

......

ARTICLE 4

This Article amends the Treaty establishing the European Atomic Energy Community in accordance with the above amendments to the Treaty establishing the European Community.

......

ARTICLE 5

The Act concerning the election of the representatives of the European Parliament by direct universal suffrage annexed, to the Council Decision of 20 September 1976 shall be amended in accordance with the provisions of this Article.

(1)   In Article 2, the following paragraph shall be added:

"In the event of amendments to this Article, the number of representatives elected in each Member State must ensure appropriate representation of the peoples of the States brought together in the Community.".

(2)   In Article 6(1), the following indent shall be inserted after the fifth indent:

-     "member of the Committee of the Regions,".

(3)   Article 7(2) shall be replaced by the following:

"2. Pending the entry into force of a uniform electoral procedure or a procedure based on common principles and subject to the other provisions of this Act, the electoral procedure shall be governed in each Member State by its national provisions."

(4)   Article 11 shall be replaced by the following:

"Pending the entry into force of the uniform electoral procedure or the procedure based on common principles referred to in Article 7, the European Parliament shall verify the credentials of representatives. For this purpose it shall take note of the results declared officially by the Member States and shall rule on any disputes which may arise out of the provisions of this Act other than those arising out of the national provisions to which the Act refers."

(5)   Article 12(1) shall be replaced by the following:

"1. Pending the entry into force of the uniform electoral procedure or the procedure based on common principles referred to in Article 7 and subject to the other provisions of this Act, each Member State shall lay down appropriate procedures for filling any seat which falls vacant during the five-year term of office referred to in Article 3 for the remainder of that period ."

PART TWO

PROVISIONS ON THE SIMPLIFICATION OF THE TREATIES

ARTICLE 6

The Treaty establishing the European Community shall be amended in accordance with the provisions of this Article for the purpose of deleting lapsed provisions of the Treaty and adapting in consequence the text of certain of its provisions.

.....

ARTICLES 7, 8, 9, 10 and 11

These Articles have similar functions with regard to the European Coal and Steel Community, Euratom, and other instruments of the EU.

......

PART THREE

GENERAL AND FINAL PROVISIONS

ARTICLE 12

1. The articles, titles and sections of the Treaty on European Union and of the Treaty establishing the European Community, as amended by the provisions of this Treaty, shall be renumbered in accordance with the table of equivalences set out in the Annex to this Treaty, which shall form an integral part thereof.

2. The cross references to articles, titles and sections in the Treaty on European Union and in the Treaty establishing the European Community, as well as between them, shall be adapted in consequence. The same shall apply as regards references to articles, titles and sections of those treaties contained in other Community treaties.

3. The references to the articles of the Treaties referred to in paragraph 2 contained in other acts shall be understood as references to the articles of the Treaties as renumbered pursuant to paragraph 1 and, respectively, to the paragraphs of the said articles, as renumbered by certain provisions of Article 6.

4. References, contained in other instruments or acts, to paragraphs of articles of the Treaties referred to in Articles 7 and 8 shall be understood as referring to those paragraphs as renumbered by certain provisions of the said Articles 7 and 8.

ARTICLE 13

This Treaty is concluded for an unlimited period.

ARTICLE 14

1. This Treaty shall be ratified by the High Contracting Parties in accordance with their respective constitutional requirements. The instruments of ratification shall be deposited with the Government of the Italian Republic.

2. This Treaty shall enter into force on the first day of the second month following that in which the instrument of ratification is deposited by the last signatory State to fulfil that formality.

ARTICLE 15

This Treaty, drawn up in a single original in the Danish, Dutch, English, Finnish, French, German, Greek, Irish, Italian, Portuguese, Spanish and Swedish languages, the texts in each of these languages being equally authentic, shall be deposited in the archives of the government of the Italian Republic, which will transmit a certified copy to each of the governments of the other signatory States.

IN WITNESS WHEREOF the undersigned Plenipotentiaries have signed this Treaty.

Done at Amsterdam on the .... in the year one thousand nine hundred and ninety-seven.

ANNEX

TABLES OF EQUIVALENCES REFERRED TO IN ARTICLE 11 OF THE TREATY OF AMSTERDAM

A. TREATY ON EUROPEAN UNION

Title 1

Article A	Article 1
Article B	Article 2
Article C	Article 3
Article D	Article 4
Article E	Article 5
Article F	Article 6
Article F.1	Article 7
Title II	
Article G	Article 8
Title III	
Article H	Article 9
Title IV	
Article I	Article 10
Title V	
Article J.1	Article 11
Article J.2	Article 12
Article J.3	Article 13
Article J.4	Article 14
Article J.5	Article 15
Article J.6	Article 16
Article J.7	Article 17
Article J.8	Article 18
Article J.9	Article 19
Article J.10	Article 20
Article J.11	Article 21
Article J.12	Article 22
Article J.13	Article 23
Article J.14	Article 24
Article J.15	Article 25
Article J.16	Article 26
Article J.17	Article 27
Article. J.18	Article 28

B. Treaty establishing the European Community

PROTOCOLS

A. Protocol annexed to the Treaty on European Union

PROTOCOL ON ARTICLE J.7 OF THE TREATY ON EUROPEAN UNION

THE HIGH CONTRACTING PARTIES,

BEARING IN MIND the need to implement fully the provisions of Article J.7(1), second subparagraph, and (3) of the Treaty on European Union,

BEARING IN MIND that the policy of the Union in accordance with Article J.7 shall not prejudice the specific character of the security and defence policy of certain Member States and shall respect the obligations of certain Member States, which see their common defence realized in NATO, under the North Atlantic Treaty and be compatible with the common security and defence policy established within that framework,

HAVE AGREED UPON the following provision, which is annexed to the Treaty on European Union,

The European Union shall draw up, together with the Western European Union, arrangements for enhanced cooperation between them, within a year from the entry into force of this Protocol.

B. Protocols annexed to the Treaty on European Union and the Treaty establishing the European Community

PROTOCOL INTEGRATING THE SCHENGEN ACQUIS INTO THE FRAMEWORK OF THE EUROPEAN UNION

THE HIGH CONTRACTING PARTIES,

NOTING that the Agreements on the gradual abolition of checks at common borders signed by some Member States of the European Union in Schengen on 14 June 1985 and on 19 June 1990, as well as related agreements and the rules adopted on the basis of these agreements, are aimed at enhancing European integration and, in particular, at enabling the European Union to develop more rapidly into an area of freedom, security and justice,

DESIRING to incorporate the above mentioned agreements and rules into the framework of the European Union,

CONFIRMING that the provisions of the Schengen acquis are applicable only if and as far as they are compatible with the European Union and Community law,

TAKING INTO ACCOUNT the special position of Denmark,

TAKING INTO ACCOUNT the fact that Ireland and the United Kingdom of Great Britain and Northern Ireland are not parties to and have not signed the abovementioned agreements; that provision should, however, be made to allow those Member States to accept some or all of the provisions thereof,

RECOGNIZING that, as a consequence, it is necessary to make use of the provisions of the Treaty on European Union and of the Treaty establishing the European Community concerning closer cooperation between some Member States and that those provisions should only be used as a last resort,

TAKING INTO ACCOUNT the need to maintain a special relationship with the Republic of Iceland and the Kingdom of Norway, both States having confirmed their intention to become bound by the provisions mentioned above, on the basis of the Agreement signed in Luxembourg on 19 December 1996,

HAVE AGREED UPON the following provisions, which shall be annexed to the Treaty on European Union and the Treaty establishing the European Community,

ARTICLE 1

The Kingdom of Belgium, the Kingdom of Denmark, the Federal Republic of Germany, the Hellenic Republic, the Kingdom of Spain, the French Republic, the Italian Republic, the Grand Duchy of Luxembourg, the Kingdom of the Netherlands, the Republic of Austria, the Portuguese Republic, the Republic of Finland and the Kingdom of Sweden, signatories to the Schengen Agreements, are authorized to establish closer cooperation among themselves within the scope of those agreements and related provisions, as they are listed in the Annex to this Protocol, hereinafter referred to as the "Schengen acquis". This cooperation shall be conducted within the institutional and legal framework of the European Union and with respect for the relevant provisions of the Treaty on European Union and of the Treaty establishing the European Community.

ARTICLE 2

1. From the date of entry into force of this Protocol, the Schengen acquis, including the decisions of the Executive Committee established by the Schengen agreements which have been adopted before this date, shall immediately apply to the thirteen Member States referred to in Article 1, without prejudice to the provisions of paragraph 2. From the same date, the Council will substitute itself for the said Executive Committee.

The Council, acting by the unanimity of its Members referred to in Article 1, shall take any measure necessary for the implementation of this paragraph. The Council, acting unanimously, shall determine, in conformity with the relevant provisions of the Treaties, the legal basis for each of the provisions or decisions which constitute the Schengen acquis.

With regard to such provisions and decisions and in accordance with that determination, the Court of Justice of the European Communities shall exercise the powers conferred upon it by the relevant applicable provisions of the Treaties. In any event, the Court of Justice shall have no jurisdiction on measures or decisions relating to the maintenance of law and order and the safeguarding of internal security.

As long as the measures referred to above have not been taken and without prejudice to Article 5(2), the provisions or decisions which constitute the Schengen acquis shall be regarded as acts based on Title VI of the Treaty on European Union.

2. The provisions of paragraph 1 shall apply to the Member States which have signed accession protocols to Schengen from the dates decided by the Council, acting with the unanimity of its Members mentioned in Article 1, unless the conditions for the accession of any of those States to the Schengen acquis are met before the date of the entry into force of this Protocol.

ARTICLE 3

Following the determination referred to in Article 2(1), second subparagraph, Denmark shall maintain the same rights and obligations in relation to the other [signatories parties] to the Schengen agreements, as before the said determination with regard to those parts of the Schengen acquis that are determined to have a legal basis in Title IIIa of the Treaty establishing the European Community.

With regard to those parts of the Schengen acquis that are determined to have legal base in Title VI of the Treaty on European Union, Denmark shall continue to have the same rights and obligations as the other [signatories parties] to the Schengen agreements.

ARTICLE 4

Ireland and the United Kingdom of Great Britain and Northern Ireland, which are not bound by the Schengen acquis, may at any time request to take part in some or all of the provisions of this acquis.

The Council shall decide on the request with the unanimity of its members referred to in Article 1 and of the representative of the Government of the State concerned.

ARTICLE 5

1. Proposals and initiatives to build upon the Schengen acquis shall be subject to the relevant provisions of the Treaties.

In this context, where either Ireland or the United Kingdom or both have not notified the President of the Council in writing within a reasonable period that they wish to take part, the authorization referred to in Articles 5a of the Treaty establishing the European Community or Article K.12 of the Treaty on European Union shall be deemed to have been granted to the Members States referred to in Article 1 and to Ireland or the United Kingdom where either of them wishes to take part in the areas of cooperation in question.

2. The relevant provisions of the Treaties referred to in the first subparagraph of paragraph 1 shall apply even if the Council has not adopted the measures referred to in Article 2(1), second subparagraph.

ARTICLE 6

The Republic of Iceland and the Kingdom of Norway shall be associated with the implementation of the Schengen acquis and its further development on the basis of the Agreement signed in Luxembourg on 19 December 1996. Appropriate procedures shall be agreed to that effect in an Agreement to be concluded with those States by the Council, acting by the unanimity of its Members mentioned in Article 1. Such Agreement shall include provisions on the contribution of Iceland and Norway to any financial consequences resulting from the implementation of this Protocol.

A separate Agreement shall be concluded with the abovementioned countries by the Council, acting unanimously, for the establishment of rights and obligations between Ireland and the United Kingdom of Great Britain and Northern Ireland on the one hand, and Iceland and Norway on the other, in domains of the Schengen acquis which apply to these States.

ARTICLE 7

The Council shall, acting by a qualified majority, adopt the modalities for the integration of the Schengen Secretariat into the General Secretariat of the Council.

ARTICLE 8

For the purposes of the negotiations for the admission of new Member States into the European Union, the Schengen acquis and further measures taken by the institutions within its scope shall be regarded as an acquis which must be accepted in full by all States candidates for admission.

ANNEX

SCHENGEN ACQUIS

1. The Agreement, signed in Schengen on 14 June 1985, between the Governments of the States of the Benelux Economic Union, the Federal Republic of Germany and the French Republic on the gradual abolition of checks at their common borders.

2. The Convention, signed in Schengen on 19 June 1990, between the Kingdom of Belgium, the Federal Republic of Germany, the French Republic, the Grand Duchy of Luxembourg and the Kingdom of Netherlands, implementing the Agreement on the gradual abolition of checks at their common borders, signed in Schengen on 14 June 1985, with related Final Act and common declarations.

3. The Accession Protocols and Agreements to the 1985 Agreement and the 1990 Implementation Convention with Italy (signed in Paris on 27 November 1990), Spain and Portugal (both signed in Bonn on 25 June 1991), Greece (signed in Madrid on 6 November 1992), Austria (signed in Brussels on 28 April 1995) and Denmark, Finland and Sweden (all signed in Luxembourg on 19 December 1996), with related Final Acts and declarations.

4. Decisions and declarations adopted by the Executive Committee established by the 1990 Implementation Convention, as well as acts adopted for the implementation of the Convention by the organs upon which the Executive Committee has conferred decision making powers.

PROTOCOL ON THE APPLICATION OF CERTAIN ASPECTS OF ARTICLE 7A OF THE TREATY ESTABLISHING THE EUROPEAN COMMUNITY TO THE UNITED KINGDOM AND TO IRELAND

THE HIGH CONTRACTING PARTIES,

DESIRING to settle certain questions relating to the United Kingdom and Ireland,

HAVING REGARD to the existence for many years of special travel arrangements between the United Kingdom and Ireland,

HAVE AGREED UPON the following provisions, which shall be annexed to the Treaty on European Union and to the Treaty establishing the European Community,

ARTICLE 1

The United Kingdom shall be entitled, notwithstanding Article 7a of the Treaty establishing the European Community, any other provision of that Treaty or of the Treaty on European Union, any measure adopted under those Treaties, or any international agreement concluded by the Community or by the Community and its Member States with one or more third States, to exercise at its frontiers with other Member States such controls on persons seeking to enter the United Kingdom as it may consider necessary for the purpose:

(a) of verifying the right to enter the United Kingdom of citizens of States which are Contracting Parties to the Agreement on the European Economic Area and of their dependants exercising rights conferred by Community law, as well as citizens of other States on whom such rights have been conferred by an agreement by which the United Kingdom is bound; and

(b) of determining whether or not to grant other persons permission to enter the United Kingdom.

Nothing in Article 7a of the Treaty establishing the European Community or in any other provision of these Treaties or in any measure adopted under them shall prejudice the right of the United Kingdom to adopt or exercise any such controls. References to the United Kingdom in this Article shall include territories for whose external relations the United Kingdom is responsible.

ARTICLE 2

The United Kingdom and Ireland may continue to make arrangements between themselves relating to the movement of persons between their territories ("the common travel area"), while fully respecting the rights of persons referred to in Article 1(a) of this Protocol. Accordingly, as long as they maintain such arrangements, the provisions of Article 1 of this Protocol shall apply to Ireland under the same terms and conditions as for the United Kingdom. Nothing in Article 7a of the Treaty establishing the European Community, in any other provision of the Treaties referred to above or in any measure adopted under them, shall affect any such arrangements.

ARTICLE 3

The other Member States shall be entitled to exercise at their frontiers or at any point of entry into their territory such controls on persons seeking to enter their territory from the United Kingdom or any territories whose external relations are under its responsibility for the same purposes stated in Article 1 of this Protocol, or from Ireland as long as the provisions of Article 1 of this Protocol apply to Ireland.

Nothing in Article 7a of the Treaty establishing the European Community or in any other provision of these treaties or in any measure adopted under them shall prejudice the right of the other Member States to adopt or exercise any such controls.

PROTOCOL ON THE POSITION OF THE UNITED KINGDOM AND IRELAND

THE HIGH CONTRACTING PARTIES,

DESIRING to settle certain questions relating to the United Kingdom and Ireland,

HAVING REGARD to the Protocol on the application of certain aspects of Article 7a of the Treaty establishing of the European Community to the United Kingdom and to Ireland,

HAVE AGREED UPON the following provisions which shall be annexed to the Treaty establishing the European Community and the Treaty on European Union,

ARTICLE 1

Subject to Article 3, the United Kingdom and Ireland shall not take part in the adoption by the Council of proposed measures pursuant to Title IIIa of the Treaty establishing the European Community. By way of derogation from Article 148(2) of the Treaty establishing the European Community, a qualified majority shall be defined as the same proportion of the weighted votes of the members of the Council concerned as laid down in the said Article 148(2). The unanimity of the members of the Council, with the exception of the representatives of the governments of the United Kingdom and Ireland, shall be necessary for decisions of the Council which must be adopted unanimously.

ARTICLE 2

In consequence of Article 1 and subject to Articles 3, 4 and 6, none of the provisions of Title IIIa of the Treaty establishing the European Community, no measure adopted pursuant to that Title, no provision of any international agreement concluded by the Community pursuant to that Title, and no decision of the Court of Justice interpreting any such provision or measure shall be binding upon or applicable in the United Kingdom or Ireland; and no such provision, measure or decision shall in any way affect the competences, rights and obligations of those States; and no such provision, measure or decision shall in any way affect the acquis communautaire nor form part of Community law as they apply to the United Kingdom or Ireland.

ARTICLE 3

1. The United Kingdom or Ireland may notify the President of the Council in writing, within three months after a proposal or initiative has been presented to the Council pursuant to Title IIIa of the Treaty establishing the European Community, that it wishes to take part in the adoption and application of any such proposed measure, whereupon that State shall be entitled to do so. By way of derogation from Article 148(2) of the Treaty establishing the European Community, a qualified

majority shall be defined as the same proportion of the weighted votes of the members of the Council concerned as laid down in the said Article 148(2).

The unanimity of the members of the Council, with the exception of a member which has not made such a notification, shall be necessary for decisions of the Council which must be adopted unanimously. A measure adopted under this paragraph shall be binding upon all Member States which took part in its adoption.

2. If after a reasonable period of time a measure referred to in paragraph 1 cannot be adopted with the United Kingdom or Ireland taking part, the Council may adopt such measure in accordance with Article 1 without the participation of the United Kingdom or Ireland. In that case Article 2 applies.

ARTICLE 4

The United Kingdom or Ireland may at any time after the adoption of a measure by the Council pursuant to Title IIIa of the Treaty establishing the European Community notify its intention to the Council and to the Commission that it wishes to accept that measure. In that case, the procedure provided for in Article 5a(3) of the Treaty establishing the European Community shall apply mutatis mutandis.

ARTICLE 5

A Member State which is not bound by a measure adopted pursuant to Title IIIa of the Treaty establishing the European Community shall bear no financial consequences of that measure other than administrative costs entailed for the institutions.

ARTICLE 6

Where, in cases referred to in this Protocol, the United Kingdom or Ireland is bound by a measure adopted by the Council pursuant to Title IIIa of the Treaty establishing the European Community, the relevant provisions of that Treaty, including Article 73p, shall apply to that State in relation to that measure.

ARTICLE 7

Articles 3 and 4 shall be without prejudice to the Protocol integrating the Schengen acquis into the framework of the European Union.

ARTICLE 8

Ireland may notify the President of the Council in writing that it no longer wishes to be covered by the terms of this Protocol. In that case, the normal Treaty provisions will apply to Ireland.

PROTOCOL ON THE POSITION OF DENMARK

THE HIGH CONTRACTING PARTIES,

RECALLING the Decision of the Heads of State or Government, meeting within the European Council at Edinburgh on 12 December 1992, concerning certain problems raised by Denmark on the Treaty on European Union,

HAVING NOTED the position of Denmark with regard to Citizenship, Economic and Monetary Union, Defence Policy and Justice and Home Affairs as laid down in the Edinburgh Decision,

BEARING IN MIND Article 3 of the Protocol integrating the Schengen acquis into the framework of the European Union,

HAVE AGREED UPON the following provisions, which shall be annexed to the Treaty establishing the European Community and to the Treaty on European Union,

PART I

ARTICLE 1

Denmark shall not take part in the adoption by the Council of proposed measures pursuant to Title IIIa of the Treaty establishing the European Community. By way of derogation from Article 148(2) of the Treaty establishing the European Community, a qualified majority shall be defined as the same proportion of the weighted votes of the members of the Council concerned as laid down in the said Article 148(2). The unanimity of the members of the Council, with the exception of the representative of the government of Denmark, shall be necessary for the decisions of the Council which must be adopted unanimously.

ARTICLE 2

None of the provisions of Title IIIa of the Treaty establishing the European Community, no measure adopted pursuant to that Title, no provision of any international agreement concluded by the Community pursuant to that Title, and no decision of the Court of Justice interpreting any such provision or measure shall be binding upon or applicable in Denmark; and no such provision, measure or decision shall in any way affect the competences, rights and obligations of Denmark; and no such provision, measure or decision shall in any way affect the acquis communautaire nor form part of Community law as they apply to Denmark.

ARTICLE 3

Denmark shall bear no financial consequences of measures referred to in Article 1, other than administrative costs entailed for the institutions.

ARTICLE 4

Articles 1, 2 and 3 shall not apply to measures determining the third countries whose nationals must be in possession of a visa when crossing the external borders of the Member States, or measures relating to a uniform format for visas.

ARTICLE 5

1. Denmark shall decide within a period of 6 months after the Council has decided on a proposal or initiative to build upon the Schengen acquis under the provisions of Title IIIa of the Treaty establishing the European Community, whether it will implement this decision in its national law. If it decides to do so, this decision will create an obligation under international law between Denmark and the other Member States referred to in Article 1 of the Protocol integrating the Schengen acquis into the framework of the European Union as well as with Ireland or the United Kingdom if those Member States take part in the areas of cooperation in question.

2. If Denmark decides not to implement a decision of the Council as referred to in paragraph 1, the Member States referred to in Article 1 of the Protocol integrating the Schengen acquis into the framework of the European Union will consider appropriate measures to be taken.

PART II

ARTICLE 6

With regard to measures adopted by the Council in the field of Articles J.3(1) and J.7 of the Treaty on European Union, Denmark does not participate in the elaboration and the implementation of decisions and actions of the Union which have defence implications, but will not prevent the development of closer cooperation between Member States in this area. Therefore Denmark shall not participate in their adoption. Denmark shall not be obliged to contribute to the financing of operational expenditure arising from such measures.

PART III

ARTICLE 7

At any time Denmark may, in accordance with its constitutional requirements, inform other Member States that it no longer wishes to avail itself of all or part of this Protocol. In that event, Denmark will apply in full all relevant measures then in force taken within the framework of the European Union.

C. Protocols annexed to the Treaty establishing the European Community

PROTOCOL ON ASYLUM FOR NATIONALS OF MEMBER STATES OF THE EUROPEAN UNION

THE HIGH CONTRACTING PARTIES;

WHEREAS pursuant to the provisions of Article F(2) of the Treaty on European Union the Union shall respect fundamental rights as guaranteed by the European Convention for the Protection of Human Rights and Fundamental Freedoms signed in Rome on 4 November 1950';

WHEREAS the Court of Justice of the European Communities has jurisdiction to ensure that in the interpretation and application of Article F(2) of the Treaty on European Union the law is observed by the European Community;

WHEREAS pursuant to Article O of the Treaty on European Union any European State, when applying to become a Member of the Union, must respect the principles set out in Article F(1) of the Treaty on European Union,

BEARING IN MIND that Article 236 of the Treaty establishing the European Community establishes a mechanism for the suspension of certain rights in the event of a serious and persistent breach by a Member State of those principles;

RECALLING that each national of a Member State, as a citizen of the Union, enjoys a special status and protection which shall be guaranteed by the Member States in accordance with the provisions of Part Two of the Treaty establishing the European Community;

BEARING IN MIND that the Treaty establishing the European Community establishes an area without internal frontiers and grants every citizen of the Union the right to move and reside freely within the territory of the Member States;

RECALLING that the question of extradition of nationals of Member States of the Union is addressed in the European Convention on Extradition of 13 December 1957 and the Convention of 27 September 1996 based on Article K.3 of the Treaty on European Union concerning extradition between the Member States of the European Union;

WISHING to prevent the institution of asylum being resorted to for purposes alien to those for which it is intended;

WHEREAS this Protocol respects the finality and the objectives of the Convention relating to the Status of Refugees of 28 July 1951;

HAVE AGREED UPON the following provisions which shall be annexed to the Treaty establishing the European Community,

SOLE ARTICLE

Given the level of protection of fundamental rights and freedoms by the Member States of the European Union, Member States shall be regarded as constituting safe countries of origin in respect of each other for all legal and practical purposes in relation to asylum matters. Accordingly, any application for asylum made by a national of a Member State may be taken into consideration or declared admissible for processing by another Member State only in the following cases:

(a) if the Member State of which the applicant is a national proceeds after the entry into force of this Treaty, availing itself of the provisions of Article 15 of the Convention for the Protection of Human Rights and Fundamental Freedoms, to take measures derogating in its territory from its obligations under that Convention;

(b) if the procedure referred to in Article F.1(1) of the Treaty on European Union, has been initiated and until the Council takes a decision in respect thereof;

(c) if the Council, acting on the basis of Article F.1(1) of the Treaty on European Union, has determined, in respect of the Member State of which the applicant is a national, the existence of a serious and persistent breach by that Member State of the principles mentioned in Article F(1);

(d) if a Member State should so decide unilaterally in respect of the application of a national of another Member State; in that case the Council shall be immediately informed; the application shall be dealt with on the basis of the presumption that it is manifestly unfounded without affecting in any way, whatever the cases may be, the decision-making power of the Member State.

PROTOCOL ON THE APPLICATION OF THE PRINCIPLE OF SUBSIDIARITY AND PROPORTIONALITY

THE HIGH CONTRACTING PARTIES;

DETERMINED to establish the conditions for the application of the principles of subsidiarity and proportionality enshrined in Article 3b of the Treaty establishing the European Community with a view to defining more precisely the criteria for applying them and to ensure their strict observance and consistent implementation by all institutions;

WISHING to ensure that decisions are taken as closely as possible to the citizens of the Union;

TAKING ACCOUNT of the Interinstitutional Agreement of 28 October 1993 between the European Parliament, the Council and the Commission on procedures for implementing the principle of subsidiarity;

HAVE CONFIRMED that the conclusions of the Birmingham European Council on 16 October 1992 and the overall approach to the application of the subsidiarity principle agreed by the European Council meeting in Edinburgh on 11-12 December 1992 will continue to guide the action of the Union's institutions as well as the development of the application of the principle of subsidiarity, and, for this purpose, have agreed on the following provisions which shall be annexed to the Treaty establishing the European Community:

(1) In exercising the powers conferred on it, each institution shall ensure that the principle of subsidiarity is complied with. It shall also ensure compliance with the principle of proportionality, according to which any action by the Community shall not go beyond what is necessary to achieve the objectives of the Treaty.

(2) The application of the principles of subsidiarity and proportionality shall respect the general provisions and the objectives of the Treaty, particularly as regards the maintaining in full of the acquis communautaire and the institutional balance; it shall not affect the principles developed by the Court of Justice regarding the relationship between national and Community law, and it should take into account Article F(4) of the Treaty on European Union, according to which "the Union shall provide itself with the means necessary to attain its objectives and carry through its policies".

(3) The principle of subsidiarity does not call into question the powers conferred on the European Community by the Treaty, as interpreted by the Court of Justice. The criteria referred to in the second paragraph of Article 3b shall relate to areas for which the Community does not have exclusive competence. The principle of subsidiarity provides a guide as to how those powers are to be exercised at the Community level.

Subsidiarity is a dynamic concept and should be applied in the light of the objectives set out in the Treaty. It allows Community action within the limits of its powers to be expanded where circumstances so require, and conversely, to be restricted or discontinued where it is no longer justified.

(4) For any proposed Community legislation, the reasons on which it is based shall be stated with a view to justifying that it complies with the principles of subsidiarity and proportionality; the reasons for concluding that a Community objective can be better achieved by the Community must be substantiated by qualitative or, wherever possible, quantitative indicators.

(5) For Community action to be justified, both aspects of the subsidiarity principle shall be met: the objectives of the proposed action cannot be sufficiently achieved by Member States' action in the framework of their national constitutional system and can therefore be better achieved by action on the part of the Community.

The following guidelines should be used in examining whether the abovementioned condition is fulfilled:

– the issue under consideration has transnational aspects which cannot be satisfactorily regulated by action by Member States;

– actions by Member States alone or lack of Community action would conflict with the requirements of the Treaty (such as the need to correct distortion of competition or avoid disguised restrictions on trade or strengthen economic and social cohesion) or would otherwise significantly damage Member States' interests;

– action at Community level would produce clear benefits by reason of its scale or effects compared with action at the level of the Member States.

(6) The form of Community action shall be as simple as possible, consistent with satisfactory achievement of the objective of the measure and the need for effective enforcement. The Community shall legislate only to the extent necessary. Other things being equal, directives should be preferred to regulations and framework directives to detailed measures. Directives as provided for in Article 189, while binding upon each Member State to which they are addressed as to the result to be achieved, shall leave to the national authorities the choice of form and methods.

(7) Regarding the nature and the extent of Community action, Community measures should leave as much scope for national decision as possible, consistent with securing the aim of the measure and observing the requirements of the Treaty. While respecting Community law, care should be taken to respect well established national

arrangements and the organization and working of Member States legal systems. Where appropriate and subject to the need for proper enforcement, Community measures should provide Member States with alternative ways to achieve the objectives of the measures.

(8) Where the application of the principle of subsidiarity leads to no action being taken by the Community, Member States are required in their action to comply with the general rules laid down in Article 5 of the Treaty, by taking all appropriate measures to ensure fulfilment of their obligations under the Treaty and by abstaining from any measure which could jeopardize the attainment of the objectives of the Treaty.

(9) Without prejudice to its right of initiative, the Commission should:

– except in cases of particular urgency or confidentiality, consult widely before proposing legislation and, wherever appropriate, publish consultation documents;

– justify the relevance of its proposals with regard to the principle of subsidiarity; whenever necessary, the explanatory memorandum accompanying a proposal will give details in this respect. The financing of Community action in whole or in part from the Community budget shall require an explanation;

– take duly into account the need for any burden, whether financial or administrative, falling upon the Community, national governments, local authorities, economic operators and citizens, to be minimized and proportionate to the objective to be achieved;

– submit an annual report to the European Council, the Council and the European Parliament on the application of Article 3b of the Treaty. This annual report shall also be sent to the Committee of the Regions and to the Economic and Social Committee.

(10) The European Council shall take account of the Commission report referred to in the fourth indent of point 9 within the report on the progress achieved by the Union which it is required to submit to the European Parliament in accordance with Article D of the Treaty on European Union.

(11) While fully observing the procedures applicable, the European Parliament and the Council shall, as an integral part of the overall examination of Commission proposals, consider their consistency with Article 3b. This concerns the original Commission proposal as well as amendments which the European Parliament and the Council envisage making to the proposal.

(12) In the course of the procedures referred to in Articles 189b and 189c, the European Parliament shall be informed of the Council's position on the application of Article 3b, by way of a statement of the

reasons which led the Council to adopt its common position. The Council shall inform the European Parliament of the reasons on the basis of which all or part of a Commission proposal is deemed to be inconsistent with Article 3b of the Treaty.

(13) Compliance with the principle of subsidiarity shall be reviewed in accordance with the rules laid down by the Treaty.

PROTOCOL ON EXTERNAL RELATIONS OF THE MEMBER STATES WITH REGARD TO THE CROSSING OF EXTERNAL BORDERS

THE HIGH CONTRACTING PARTIES,

TAKING INTO ACCOUNT the need of the Member States to ensure effective controls at their external borders, in cooperation with third countries where appropriate,

HAVE AGREED UPON the following provisions, which shall be annexed to the Treaty establishing the European Community,

The provisions on the measures on the crossing of external borders included in Article 73j(2) of Title IIIa shall be without prejudice to the competence of Member States to negotiate or conclude agreements with third countries as long as they respect Community law and other relevant international agreements.

PROTOCOL ON THE SYSTEM OF PUBLIC BROADCASTING IN THE MEMBER STATES

THE HIGH CONTRACTING PARTIES;

CONSIDERING that the system of public broadcasting in the Member States is directly related to the democratic, social and cultural needs of each society and to the need to preserve media pluralism;

HAVE AGREED UPON the following interpretative provisions, which shall be annexed to the Treaty establishing the European Community,

The provisions of the Treaty establishing the European Community shall be without prejudice to the competence of Member States to provide for the funding of public service broadcasting in so far as such funding is granted to broadcasting organizations for the fulfilment of the public service remit as conferred, defined and organized by each Member State, and that such funding does not affect trading conditions and competition in the Community to an extent which would be contrary to the common interest, while the realization of the remit of that public service shall be taken into account.

PROTOCOL ON IMPROVED PROTECTION AND RESPECT FOR THE WELFARE OF ANIMALS

THE HIGH CONTRACTING PARTIES;

DESIRING to ensure improved protection and respect for the welfare of animals as sentient beings;

HAVE AGREED UPON the following provision which shall be annexed to the Treaty establishing the European Community,

In formulating and implementing the Community's agriculture, transport, internal market and research policies, the Community and the Member States shall pay full regard to the welfare requirements of animals, while respecting the legislative or administrative provisions and customs of the Member States relating in particular to religious rites, cultural traditions and regional heritage.

D. Protocols annexed to the Treaty on European Union and the Treaty establishing the European Community

PROTOCOL ON THE INSTITUTIONS WITH THE PROSPECT OF ENLARGEMENT OF THE EUROPEAN UNION

THE HIGH CONTRACTING PARTIES,

HAVE AGREED UPON the following provisions, which shall be annexed to the Treaty on European Union and to the Treaties establishing the European Communities,

ARTICLE 1

At the date of entry into force of the first enlargement of the Union, notwithstanding Article 157(1) of the Treaty establishing the European Community, Article 9(1) of the Treaty establishing the European Coal and Steel Community and Article 126(1) of the Treaty establishing the European Atomic Energy Community, the Commission shall comprise one national of each of the Member States, provided that, by that date, the weighting of the votes in the Council has been modified, whether by reweighting of the votes or by dual majority, in a manner acceptable to all Member States, taking into account all relevant elements, notably compensating those Member States which give up the possibility of nominating a second member of the Commission.

ARTICLE 2

At least one year before the membership of the European Union exceeds twenty, a conference of representatives of the governments of Member States shall be convened in order to carry out a comprehensive review of the provisions of the Treaties on the composition and functioning of the institutions.

PROTOCOL ON THE LOCATION OF THE SEATS OF THE INSTITUTIONS AND OF CERTAIN BODIES AND DEPARTMENTS OF THE EUROPEAN COMMUNITIES

THE REPRESENTATIVES OF THE GOVERNMENTS OF THE MEMBER STATES,

HAVING REGARD to Article 216 of the Treaty establishing the European Community, Article 77 of the Treaty establishing the European Coal and Steel Community and Article 189 of the Treaty establishing the European Atomic Energy Community,

HAVING REGARD to the Treaty on European Union,

RECALLING AND CONFIRMING the Decision of 8 April 1965, and without prejudice to the decisions concerning the seat of future institutions, bodies and departments,

HAVE AGREED UPON the following provisions, which shall be annexed to the Treaty on European Union and the Treaties establishing the European Communities,

SOLE ARTICLE

(a) The European Parliament shall have its seat in Strasbourg where the 12 periods of monthly plenary sessions, including the budget session, shall be held. The periods of additional plenary sessions shall be held in Brussels. The committees of the European Parliament shall meet in Brussels. The General Secretariat of the European Parliament and its departments shall remain in Luxembourg.

(b) The Council shall have its seat in Brussels. During the months of April, June and October, the Council shall hold its meetings in Luxembourg.

(c) The Commission shall have its seat in Brussels. The departments listed in Articles 7, 8 and 9 of the Decision of 8 April 1965 shall be established in Luxembourg.

(d) The Court of Justice and the Court of First Instance shall have their seats in Luxembourg.

(e) The Court of Auditors shall have its seat in Luxembourg.

(f) The Economic and Social Committee shall have its seat in Brussels.

(g) The Committee of the Regions shall have its seat in Brussels.

(h) The European Investment Bank shall have its seat in Luxembourg.

(i) The European Monetary Institute and the European Central Bank shall have their seat in Frankfurt.

(j) Europol shall have its seat in The Hague.

PROTOCOL ON THE ROLE OF NATIONAL PARLIAMENTS IN THE EUROPEAN UNION

THE HIGH CONTRACTING PARTIES,

RECALLING that scrutiny by individual national parliaments of their own government in relation to the activities of the Union is a matter for the particular constitutional organization and practice of each Member State,

DESIRING, however, to encourage greater involvement of national parliaments in the activities of the European Union and to enhance their ability to express their views on matters which may be of particular interest to them,

HAVE AGREED UPON the following provisions, which shall be annexed to the Treaty on European Union and the Treaties establishing the European Communities,

I. Information for national Parliaments of Member States

1. All Commission consultation documents (green and white papers and communications) shall be promptly forwarded to national parliaments of the Member States.

2. Commission proposals for legislation as defined by the Council in accordance with Article 151 of the Treaty establishing the European Community, shall be made available in good time so that the Government of each Member State may ensure that its own national parliament receives them as appropriate.

3. A six-week period shall elapse between a legislative proposal or a proposal for a measure to be adopted under Title VI of the Treaty on European Union being made available in all languages to the European Parliament and the Council by the Commission and the date when it is placed on a Council agenda for decision either for the adoption of an act or for adoption of a common position pursuant to Article 189b or 189c, subject to exceptions on grounds of urgency, the reasons for which shall be stated in the act or common position.

II. The Conference of European Affairs Committees

4. The Conference of European Affairs Committees, hereinafter referred to as COSAC, established in Paris on 16-17 November 1989, may make any contribution it deems appropriate for the attention of the institutions of the European Union, in particular on the basis of draft legal texts which Representatives of Governments of the Member States may decide by common accord to forward to it, in view of the nature of its subject matter.

5. COSAC may examine any legislative proposal or initiative in relation to the establishment of an area of freedom, security and justice

which might have a direct bearing on the rights and freedoms of individuals. The European Parliament, the Council and the Commission shall be informed of any contribution made by COSAC under this paragraph.

6. COSAC may address to the European Parliament, the Council and the Commission any contribution which it deems appropriate on the legislative activities of the Union, notably in relation to the application of the principle of subsidiarity, the area of freedom, security and justice as well as questions regarding fundamental rights.

7. Contributions made by COSAC shall in no way bind national parliaments or prejudge their position.

Declarations

A. Declarations relating to the Treaty on European Union

(1) DECLARATION ON ENHANCED COOPERATION BETWEEN THE EUROPEAN UNION AND THE WESTERN EUROPEAN UNION

With a view to enhanced cooperation between the European Union and the Western European Union, the Conference invites the Council to seek the early adoption of appropriate arrangements for the security clearance of the personnel of the General Secretariat of the Council.

(2) DECLARATION RELATING TO WESTERN EUROPEAN UNION

The Conference notes the following Declaration, adopted by the Council of Ministers of the Western European Union on 22 July 1997.

DECLARATION OF WESTERN EUROPEAN UNION ON THE ROLE OF WESTERN EUROPEAN UNION AND ITS RELATIONS WITH THE EUROPEAN UNION AND WITH THE ATLANTIC ALLIANCE

Introduction

1. The WEU Member States agreed at Maastricht in 1995 on the need to develop a genuine European Security and Defence Identity (ESDI) and to assume a greater European responsibility for defence matters. In the light of the Treaty of Amsterdam, they reaffirm the importance of continuing and strengthening these efforts. WEU is an integral part of the development of the European Union providing the Union with access to an operational capability, notably in the context of the Petersberg tasks and is an essential element of the development of the ESDI within the Atlantic Alliance in accordance with the Paris Declaration and with the decisions taken by NATO ministers in Berlin.

2. Today the WEU Council brings together all the Member States of the European Union and all the European Members of the Atlantic Alliance in accordance with their respective status. The Council also brings together those States with the Central and Eastern European States linked to the European Union by an Association Agreement and that are applicants for accession to both the European Union and the Atlantic Alliance. WEU is thus establishing itself as a genuine framework for

dialogue and cooperation among European on wider European security and defence issues.

3. In this context, WEU none of Title V of the Treaty of Amsterdam regarding the EU's common foreign and security policy, in particular Articles J.3.1, J.7 and the Protocol to Article J.7.

A. WEU's relations with the European Union: accompanying the implementation of the Treaty of Amsterdam

4. In the "Declaration on the Role of the Western European Union and its Relations with the European Union and with the Atlantic Alliance" of 10 December 1991, WEU Member States set as their objective "to build up WEU in stages as the defence component of the European Union". They today reaffirm this aim as developed by the Treaty of Amsterdam.

5. When the Union avails itself of WEU, WEU will elaborate and implement decisions and actions of the EU which have defence implications.

In elaborating and implementing decisions and actions of the EU for which the Union avails itself of WEU, WEU will act consistently with guidelines established by the European Council.

WEU supports the Union in framing the defence aspects of the European Union Common Foreign and Security Policy as set out in Article J.7 of the Treaty on European Union.

6. WEU confirms that when the European Union avails itself of WEU to elaborate and implement decisions of the Union on the tasks referred to in Article J.7.2. of the Treaty on European Union, all Member States of the Union shall be entitled to participate fully in the tasks in question in accordance with Article J.7.3. of the Treaty on European Union.

WEU will develop the role of the Observers in WEU in line with provisions contained in Article J.7.3 and will adopt the necessary practical arrangements to allow all Member States of the EU contributing to the tasks undertaken by WEU at the request of the EU to participate fully and on an equal footing in planning and decision-taking in the WEU.

7. Consistent with the Protocol on Article J.7 of the Treaty on European Union, WEU shall draw up, together with the European Union, arrangements for enhanced cooperation between them. In this regard, a range of measures, on some of which work is already in hand in WEU, can be taken forward now, such as:

- arrangements for improving the coordination of the consultation and decision-making processes of the respective Organisations, in particular in crisis situations:

- holding of joint meetings of the relevant bodies of the two Organisations;

- harmonisation as much as possible of the sequence of the Presidencies of WEU and the EU, as well as the administrative rules and practices of the two Organisations;

- close coordination of the work of the staff of the Secretariat-General of the WEU and the General Secretariat of the Council of the EU, including through the exchange and secondment of personnel;

- arrangements to allow the relevant bodies of the EU, including its Policy Planning and Early Warning Unit, to draw on the resources of WEU's Planning Cell, Situation Centre and Satellite Centre;

- cooperation in the field of armaments, as appropriate, within the framework of the WEAG, as the European forum for armaments cooperation, the EU and WEU in the context of rationalisation of the European armaments market and the establishment of a European Armaments Agency;

- practical arrangements for ensuring cooperation with the European Commission reflecting its role in the CFSP as defined in the revised Treaty on European Union;

- improved security arrangements with the European Union.

B. Relations between WEU and NATO in the framework of the development of an ESDI within the Atlantic Alliance

8. The Atlantic Alliance continues to be the basis of collective defence under the North Atlantic Treaty. It remains the essential forum for consultation among Allies and the framework in which they agree on policies bearing on their security and defence commitments under the Washington Treaty. The Alliance has embarked on a process of adaptation and reform so that is can more effectively carry out the full range of its missions. This process is aimed at strengthening and renewing the transatlantic partnership, including building an ESDI within the Alliance.

9. WEU is an essential element of the development of the European Security and Defence identity within the Atlantic Alliance and will accordingly continue its efforts to strengthen institutional practical cooperation with NATO.

10. In addition to its support for the common defence enshrined in Article 5 of the Washington Treaty and Article V of the modified Brussels Treaty, WEU takes an active role in conflict prevention and crisis management as provided for in the Petersberg Declaration. In this context, WEU undertakes to perform its role to the full, respecting the full transparency and complementarity between the two Organisations.

11. WEU affirms that this identity will be grounded on sound military principles and supported by appropriate military planning and will permit the creation of militarily coherent and effective forces capable of operating under the political control and strategic direction of WEU.

12. To this end, WEU will develop in cooperation with NATO, in particular in the following fields:

- mechanisms for consultation between WEU and NATO in the context of a crisis.

- WEU's active involvement in the NATO defence planning process;

- operational links between WEU and NATO for the planning, preparation and conduct of operations using NATO assets and capabilities under the political control and strategic direction of WEU, including:

- military planning, conducting by NATO in coordination with WEU, and exercises;

- a framework agreement on the transfer, monitoring and return of NATO assets and capabilities;

- liaison between WEU and NATO in the context of European command arrangements.

This cooperation will continue to evolve, also taking account of the adaptation of the Alliance.

C. WEU's operational role in the development of the ESDI

13. WEU will develop its role as the European politico-military body for crisis management, by using the assets and capabilities made available by WEU nations on a national or multinational basis, and having recourse, when appropriate, to Nato's assets and capabilities under arrangements being worked out. In this context, WEU will also support the UN and OSCE in their crisis management tasks.

WEU will contribute, in the framework of Article J.7 of the Treaty on European Union, to the progressive framing of a common defence policy and carry forward its concrete implementation through the further development of its own operational role.

14. To this end, WEU will take forward work in the following fields:

• WEU has developed crisis management mechanisms and procedures which will be updated as WEU gains experience through exercises and operations. The implementation of Petersberg missions calls for flexible modes of action geared to the diversity of crisis situations and making optimum use of the available capabilities including through recourse to a national headquarters, which might be one provided by a framework nation, or to a multinational headquarters answerable to WEU or to NATO assets and capabilities;

• WEU has already worked out Preliminary Conclusions on the Formulation of a Common European Defence Policy which is an initial contribution on the objectives, scope and means of a common European defence policy.

WEU will continue this work on the basis in particular of the Paris Declaration and taking account of the relevant elements of the decisions of WEU and NATO summits and ministerial meetings since Birmingham. It will focus on the following fields:

- definition of principles for the use of armed forces of the WEU States for WEU Petersberg operations in pursuit of common European security interests;

- organisation of operational means for Petersberg tasks, such as generic and contingency planning and exercising, preparation and interoperability of forces, including through participation in the NATO defence planning process, as appropriate;

- strategic mobility on the basis of its current work;

- defence intelligence, through its Planning Cell, Situation Centre and Satellite Centre;

• WEU has adopted many measures to strengthen its operational role (Planning Cell, Situation Centre, Satellite Centre). The improvement of the functioning of the military components at WEU Headquarters and the establishment, under the Council's authority, of a military committee will represent a further enhancement of structures which are important for the successful preparation and conduct of WEU operations;

• with the aim of opening participation in all its operations to Associate Members and Observer States, WEU will also examine the necessary modalities to allow Associate Members and Observer States to participate fully in accordance with their status in all operations undertaken by WEU;

- WEU recalls that Associate Members take part on the same basis as full members in operations to which they contribute, as well as in relevant exercise and planning. WEU will also examine the question of participation of the Observers as fully as possible in accordance with their status in planning and decision-taking within WEU in all operations to which they contribute;

- WEU will, in consultation where appropriate with the relevant bodies, examine the possibilities for maximum participation in its activities by Associate Members and Observer States in accordance with their status. It will address in particular activities in the fields of armaments, space and military studies;

- WEU will examine how to strengthen the Associate Partners' participation in an increasing number of activities.

(3) DECLARATION ON THE ABOLITION OF THE DEATH PENALTY

With reference to Article F(2) of the Treaty on European Union, the Conference recalls that Protocol No. 6 to the European Convention for the Protection of Human Rights and Fundamental Freedoms signed in Rome on 4 November 1950, and which has been signed and ratified by a large majority of Member States, provides for the abolition of the death penalty.

In this context, the Conference notes the fact that since the signature of the abovementioned Protocol on 28 April 1983, the death penalty has been abolished in most of the Member States of the Union and has not been applied in any of them.

(4) DECLARATION RELATING TO ARTICLES J.14 AND K.10

The provisions of Articles J.14 and K.10 of the Treaty on European Union and any agreements resulting from them shall not imply any transfer of competence from the Member States to the Union.

(5) DECLARATION ON ARTICLE J.15

The Conference agrees that Member States shall ensure that the Political Committee referred to in Article J.15 of the Treaty on European Union is able to meet at any time, in the event of international crises or other urgent matters, at very short notice at Political Director or deputy level.

(6) DECLARATION ON ARTICLE K.2

Action in the field of police cooperation under Article K.2 of the Treaty on European Union, including activities of Europol, shall be subject to appropriate judicial review by the competent national authorities in accordance with rules applicable in each Member State.

(7) DECLARATION ON ARTICLE K.3(E)

The Conference agrees that the provisions of Article K.3(e) of the Treaty on European Union shall not have the consequence of obliging a Member State whose legal system does not provide for minimum sentences to adopt them.

(8) DECLARATION ON ARTICLE K.6(2)

The Conference agrees that initiatives for measures referred to in Article K.6(2) of the Treaty on European Union and acts adopted by the Council thereunder shall be published in the Official Journal of the European Communities, in accordance with the relevant rules of procedure of the Council and the Commission.

(9) DECLARATION RELATING TO ARTICLE K.7

The Conference notes that Member States may, when making a declaration pursuant to Article K.7(2) of the Treaty on European Union, reserve the right to make provisions in their national law to the effect that, where a question relating to the validity or interpretation of an act referred to in Article K.7(1) is raised in a case pending before a national court or tribunal against whose decision there is no judicial remedy under national law, that court or tribunal will be required to refer the matter to the Court of Justice.

(10)   DECLARATION ON THE STATUS OF CHURCHES AND NON CONFESSIONAL ORGANIZATIONS

The European Union will respect and does not prejudice the status under national law of churches and religious associations or communities in the Member States.

The European Union will equally respect the status of philosophical and non confessional organizations.

(11)   DECLARATION ON THE ESTABLISHMENT OF A POLICY PLANNING AND EARLY WARNING UNIT

The Conference agrees that:

1. A policy planning and early warning unit, shall be established in the General Secretariat of the Council under the responsibility of its Secretary-General, High Representative for the CFSP. Appropriate cooperation shall be established with the Commission in order to ensure

full coherence with the Union's external economic and development policies.

2. The tasks of the unit shall include the following:

(a) monitoring and analysing developments in areas relevant to the CFSP;

(b) providing assessments of the Union's foreign and security policy interests and identifying areas where the CFSP could focus in future;

c) providing timely assessments and early warning of events or situations which may have significant repercussions for the Union's foreign and security policy, including potential political crises;

(d) producing, at the request of either the Council or the Presidency or on its own initiative, argued policy options papers to be presented under the responsibility of the Presidency as a contribution to policy formulation in the Council, and which may contain analyses, recommendations and strategies for the CFSP.

3. The unit shall consist of personnel drawn from the General Secretariat, the Member States, the Commission and the WEU.

4. Any Member State or the Commission may make suggestions to the unit for work to be undertaken.

5. Member States and the Commission shall assist the policy planning process by providing, to the fullest extent possible, relevant information, including confidential information.

B. Declarations relating to the Treaty establishing the European Community

(12) DECLARATION ON ENVIRONMENTAL IMPACT ASSESSMENTS

The Conference notes that the Commission undertakes to prepare environmental impact assessment studies when making proposals which may have significant environmental implications.

(13) DECLARATION ON ARTICLE 7D

The provisions of Article 7d of the Treaty establishing the European Community on public services shall be implemented with full respect for the jurisprudence of the Court of Justice, inter alia as regards the principles of equality of treatment, quality and continuity of such services.

(14) DECLARATION ON THE SIMPLIFICATION OF ARTICLE 44

The repeal of Article 44 of the Treaty establishing the European Community, which contains a reference to a natural preference between Member States in the context of fixing minimum prices during the transitional period, has no effect on the principle of Community preference as defined by the case law of the Court of Justice.

(15) DECLARATION ON THE PRESERVATION OF THE LEVEL OF PROTECTION AND SECURITY PROVIDED BY THE SCHENGEN ACQUIS

The Conference agrees that measures to be adopted by the Council, which will have the effect of replacing provisions on the abolition of checks at common borders contained in the 1990 Schengen Convention, should provide at least the same level of protection and security as under the aforementioned provisions of the Schengen Convention.

(16) DECLARATION ON ARTICLE 73J(2)(B)

The Conference agrees that foreign policy considerations of the Union and the Member States shall be taken into account in the application of Article 73j(2)(b) of the Treaty establishing the European Community.

(17) DECLARATION ON ARTICLE 73K

Consultations shall be established with the United Nations High Commissioner for Refugees and other relevant international organisations on matters relating to asylum policy.

(18) DECLARATION ON ARTICLE 73K(3)(A)

The Conference agrees that Member States may negotiate and conclude agreements with third countries in the domains covered by Article 73k(3)(a) of the Treaty establishing the European Community as long as such agreements respect Community law.

(19) DECLARATION ON ARTICLE 73L(1)

The Conference agrees that Member States may take into account foreign policy considerations when exercising their responsibilities under Article 73l(1) of the Treaty establishing the European Community.

(20) DECLARATION ON ARTICLE 73M

Measures adopted pursuant to Article 73m shall not prevent any Member State from applying its constitutional rules relating to freedom of the press and freedom of expression in other media.

(21) DECLARATION REGARDING PERSONS WITH A DISABILITY

The Conference agrees that, in drawing up measures under Article 100a of the Treaty establishing the European Community, the institutions of the Community shall take account of the needs of persons with a disability.

(22) DECLARATION ON ARTICLE 73O

The Conference agrees that the Council will examine the elements of the decision referred to in Article 73o(2), second indent, of the Treaty establishing the European Community before the end of the five year period referred to in Article 73o with a view to taking and applying this decision immediately after the end of that period.

(23) DECLARATION ON INCENTIVE MEASURES REFERRED TO IN ARTICLE 109R

The Conference agrees that the incentive measures referred to in Article 109r of the Treaty establishing the European Community should always specify the following:

– the grounds for taking them based on an objective assessment of their need and the existence of an added value at Community level;

– their duration, which should not exceed five years;

– the maximum amount for their financing, which should reflect the incentive nature of such measures.

(24) DECLARATION ON ARTICLE 109R

It is understood that any expenditure under Article 109r of the Treaty establishing the European Community will fall within Heading 3 of the financial perspectives.

(25) DECLARATION ON ARTICLE 118

It is understood that any expenditure under Article 118 of the Treaty establishing the European Community will fall within Heading 3 of the financial perspectives.

(26) DECLARATION ON ARTICLE 118(2)

The High Contracting Parties note that in the discussions on Article 118(2) of the Treaty establishing the European Community it was agreed that the Community does not intend, in laying down minimum requirements for the protection of the safety and health of employees, to discriminate in a manner unjustified by the circumstances against employees in small and medium-sized undertakings.

(27) DECLARATION ON ARTICLE 118B(2)

The High Contracting Parties declare that the first of the arrangements for application of the agreements between management and labour at Community level - referred to in Article 118b(2) of the Treaty establishing the European Community - will consist in developing, by collective bargaining according to the rules of each Member State, the content of the agreements, and that consequently this arrangement implies no obligation on the Member States to apply the agreements directly or to work out rules for their transposition, nor any obligation to amend national legislation in force to facilitate their implementation.

(28) DECLARATION ON ARTICLE 119(4)

When adopting measures referred to in Article 119(4) of the Treaty establishing the European Community, Member States should, in the first instance, aim at improving the situation of women in working life.

(29) DECLARATION ON SPORT

The Conference emphasizes the social significance of sport, in particular its role in forging identity and bringing people together. The Conference therefore calls on the bodies of the European Union to listen to sports associations when important questions affecting sport are at issue. In this connection, special consideration should be given to the particular characteristics of amateur sport.

(30) DECLARATION ON ISLAND REGIONS

The Conference recognizes that island regions suffer from structural handicaps linked to their island status, the permanence of which impairs their economic and social development.

The Conference accordingly acknowledges that Community legislation must take account of these handicaps and that specific measures may be taken, where justified, in favour of these regions in order to integrate them better into the internal market on fair conditions.

(31) DECLARATION RELATING TO COUNCIL DECISION OF 13 JULY 1987

The Conference calls on the Commission to submit to the Council by the end of 1998 at the latest a proposal to amend the Council decision of 13 July 1987 laying down the procedures for the exercise of implementing powers conferred on the Commission.

(32) DECLARATION ON THE ORGANIZATION AND FUNCTIONING OF THE COMMISSION

The Conference notes the Commission's intention to prepare a reorganization of tasks within the college in good time for the Commission which will take up office in 2000, in order to ensure an optimum division between conventional portfolios and specific tasks.

In this context, it considers that the President of the Commission must enjoy broad discretion in the allocation of tasks within the College, as well as in any reshuffling of those tasks during a Commission's term of office.

The Conference also notes the Commission's intention to undertake in parallel a corresponding reorganization of its departments. It notes in particular the desirability of bringing external relations under the responsibility of a Vice-President.

(33) DECLARATION ON ARTICLE 188C(3)

The Conference invites the Court of Auditors, the European Investment Bank and the Commission to maintain in force the present Tripartite Agreement. If a succeeding or amending text is required by any party, they shall endeavour to reach agreement on such a text having regard to their respective interests.

(34) DECLARATION ON RESPECT FOR TIME LIMITS UNDER THE CO-DECISION PROCEDURE

The Conference calls on the European Parliament, the Council and the Commission to make every effort to ensure that the co-decision procedure operates as expeditiously as possible. It recalls the importance of strict respect for the deadlines set out in Article 189b of the Treaty establishing the European Community and confirms that recourse, provided for in paragraph 7 of that Article, to extension of the periods in question should be considered only when strictly necessary. In no case should the actual period between the second reading by the European Parliament and the outcome of the Conciliation Committee exceed nine months.

(35) DECLARATION ON ARTICLE 191A(1)

The Conference agrees that the principles and conditions referred to in Article 191a(1) of the Treaty establishing the European Community will allow a Member State to request the Commission or the Council not to communicate to third parties a document originating from that State without its prior agreement.

(36) DECLARATION ON THE OVERSEAS COUNTRIES AND TERRITORIES

The Conference recognizes that the special arrangements for the association of the OCTs under Part Four of the Treaty establishing the European Community were designed for countries and territories that were numerous, covered vast areas and had large populations. The arrangements have changed little since 1957.

The Conference notes that there are today only 20 OCTs and that they are extremely scattered island territories with a total population of approximately 900 000. Moreover, most OCT lag far behind in structural terms, a fact linked to their particularly severe geographical and economic handicaps. In these circumstances, the special arrangements for association as they were conceived in 1957 can no longer deal effectively with the challenges of OCT development.

The Conference solemnly restates that the purpose of association is to promote the economic and social development of the countries and territories and to establish close economic relations between them and the Community as a whole.

The Conference invites the Council, acting in accordance with the provisions of Article 136 of the Treaty establishing the European Community, to review the association arrangements by February 2000, with the fourfold objective of:

– promoting the economic and social development of the OCTs more effectively;

– developing economic relations between the OCTs and the European Union;

– taking greater account of the diversity and specific characteristics of the individual OCTs, including aspects relating to freedom of establishment;

– ensuring that the effectiveness of the financial instrument is improved.

(37) DECLARATION ON PUBLIC CREDIT INSTITUTIONS IN GERMANY

The Conference notes the Commission's opinion to the effect that the Community's existing competition rules allow services of general economic interest provided by public credit institutions existing in Germany and the facilities granted to them to compensate for the costs connected with such services to be taken into account in full. In this context, the way in which Germany enables local authorities to carry out their task of making available in their regions a comprehensive and efficient financial infrastructure is a matter for the organization of that Member State. Such facilities may not adversely affect the conditions of competition to an extent beyond that required in order to perform these particular tasks and which is contrary to the interests of the Community.

The Conference recalls that the European Council has invited the Commission to examine whether similar cases exist in the other Member States, to apply as appropriate the same standards on similar cases and to inform the ECOFIN Council.

(38) DECLARATION ON VOLUNTARY SERVICE ACTIVITIES

The Conference recognizes the important contribution made by voluntary service activities to developing social solidarity.

The Community will encourage the European dimension of voluntary organizations with particular emphasis on the exchange of information and experiences as well as on the participation of the young and the elderly in voluntary work.

(39) DECLARATION ON THE QUALITY OF THE DRAFTING OF COMMUNITY LEGISLATION

The Conference notes that the quality of the drafting of Community legislation is crucial if it is to be properly implemented by the competent national authorities and better understood by the public and in business circles. It recalls the conclusions on this subject reached by the Presidency of the European Council in Edinburgh on 11 and 12 December 1992, as well as the Council Resolution on the quality of drafting of Community legislation adopted on 8 June 1993 (Official Journal of the European Communities, No C 166, 17.6.1993, p. 1).

The Conference considers that the three institutions involved in the procedure for adopting Community legislation, the European Parliament, the Council and the Commission, should lay down guidelines on the quality of drafting of the said legislation. It also stresses that Community legislation should be made more accessible and welcomes in this regard the adoption and first implementation of an accelerated working method for official codification of legislative texts, established by the Interinstitutional Agreement of 20 December 1994 (Official Journal of the European Communities, No C 293, 8.11.1995, p. 2).

Therefore, the Conference declares that the European Parliament, the Council and the Commission ought to:

– establish by common accord guidelines for improving the quality of the drafting of Community legislation and follow those guidelines when considering proposals for Community legislation or draft legislation, taking the internal organizational measures they deem necessary to ensure that these guidelines are properly applied;

– make their best efforts to accelerate the codification of legislative texts.

C. Declaration relating to the Treaty establishing the European Coal and Steel Community

(40) DECLARATION CONCERNING THE PROCEDURE FOR CONCLUDING INTERNATIONAL AGREEMENTS BY THE EUROPEAN COAL AND STEEL COMMUNITY

......

D. Declaration relating to the Treaty on European Union and the Treaties establishing the European Communities

(41) DECLARATION ON THE CONSOLIDATION OF THE TREATIES

The High Contracting Parties agreed that the technical work begun during the course of this Intergovernmental Conference shall continue as speedily as possible with the aim of drafting a consolidation of all the relevant Treaties, including the Treaty on European Union.

They agreed that the final results of this technical work, which shall be made public for illustrative purposes under the responsibility of the Secretary-General of the Council, shall have no legal value.

E. Declarations relating to protocols

(42) DECLARATION RELATING TO THE PROTOCOL ON THE APPLICATION OF THE PRINCIPLES OF SUBSIDIARITY AND PROPORTIONALITY

The High Contracting Parties confirm, on the one hand, Declaration No 19 annexed to the Treaty establishing the European Community on the implementation of Community law and, on the other, the conclusions of the Essen European Council stating that the administrative implementation of Community law shall in principle be the responsibility of the Member States in accordance with their constitutional arrangements. This shall not affect the supervisory, monitoring and implementing powers of the Community Institutions as provided under Article 145 and 155 of the Treaty establishing the European Community.

(43) DECLARATION ON ARTICLE 2 OF THE PROTOCOL INTEGRATING THE SCHENGEN ACQUIS INTO THE FRAMEWORK OF THE EUROPEAN UNION

The High Contracting Parties agree that the Council shall adopt all the necessary measures referred to in Article 2 of the Protocol integrating the Schengen acquis into the framework of the European Union upon the date of entry into force of this Treaty. To that end, the necessary preparatory work shall be undertaken in due time in order to be completed prior to that date.

(44) DECLARATION ON ARTICLE 4 OF THE PROTOCOL INTEGRATING THE SCHENGEN ACQUIS INTO THE FRAMEWORK OF THE EUROPEAN UNION

The High Contracting Parties undertake to make all efforts in order to make action among all Member States possible in the domains of the Schengen acquis, in particular whenever Ireland and the United Kingdom of Great Britain and Northern Ireland have accepted some or all of the provisions of that acquis in accordance with Article 4 of the Protocol integrating the Schengen acquis into the framework of the European Union.

(45) DECLARATION ON ARTICLE 5 OF THE PROTOCOL INTEGRATING THE SCHENGEN ACQUIS INTO THE FRAMEWORK OF THE EUROPEAN UNION

The High Contracting Parties agree to make all efforts in order to make action among all Member States possible in the domains of the Schengen acquis, in particular whenever Ireland and the United Kingdom of Great Britain and Northern Ireland have accepted some or all of the provisions of that acquis in accordance with Article 4 of the Protocol integrating the Schengen acquis into the framework of the European Union.

(46) DECLARATION ON ARTICLE 6 OF THE PROTOCOL INTEGRATING THE SCHENGEN ACQUIS INTO THE FRAMEWORK OF THE EUROPEAN UNION

The High Contracting Parties agree to take all necessary steps so that the Agreements referred to in Article 6 of the Protocol integrating the Schengen acquis into the framework of the European Union may enter into force on the same date as the date of entry into force of the Treaty of Amsterdam.

(47) DECLARATION RELATING TO THE PROTOCOL ON ASYLUM FOR NATIONALS OF MEMBER STATES OF THE EUROPEAN UNION

The Protocol on asylum for nationals of Member States of the European Union does not prejudice the right of each Member State to take the organisational measures it deems necessary to fulfil its obligations under the Geneva Convention relating to the status of refugees of 28 July 1951.

(48) DECLARATION RELATING TO SUBPARAGRAPH (D) OF THE SOLE ARTICLE OF THE PROTOCOL ON ASYLUM FOR NATIONALS OF MEMBER STATES OF THE EUROPEAN UNION

The Conference declares that, while recognising the importance of the Resolution of the Ministers of the Member States of the European Communities responsible for immigration of 30 November/1 December 1992 on manifestly unfounded applications for asylum and of the Resolution of the Council of 9/10 March 1995 on minimum guarantees for asylum procedures, the question of abuse of asylum procedures and appropriate rapid procedures to dispense with manifestly unfounded applications for asylum should be further examined with a view to introducing new improvements in order to accelerate these procedures.

(49) DECLARATION RELATING TO THE PROTOCOL ON THE INSTITUTIONS WITH THE PROSPECT OF ENLARGEMENT OF THE EUROPEAN UNION

Until the entry into force of the first enlargement it is agreed that the decision of the Council of 29 March 1994 ("the Ioannina Compromise") will be extended and, by that date, a solution for the special case of Spain will be found.

F. Declaration relating to the Treaty of Amsterdam

(50) DECLARATION ON ARTICLE 10 OF THE TREATY OF AMSTERDAM

The Treaty of Amsterdam repeals lapsed provisions of the Treaty establishing the European Community, the Treaty establishing the European Coal and Steel Community and the Treaty establishing the European Atomic Energy Community as they were in force before the entry into force of the Treaty of Amsterdam and adapts certain of their provisions, including the insertion of certain provisions of the Treaty establishing a single Council and a single Commission of the European

Communities and the Act concerning the election of the representatives of the European Parliament by direct universal suffrage. Those operations do not affect the "acquis communautaire".

Declarations of which the Conference took note

(1) DECLARATION BY AUSTRIA AND LUXEMBOURG ON CREDIT INSTITUTIONS

Austria and Luxembourg consider that the Declaration on public credit institutions in Germany also applies to credit institutions in Austria and Luxembourg with a comparable organisational structure.

(2) DECLARATION BY DENMARK ON ARTICLE K.14

Article K.14 of the Treaty on European Union requires that unanimity of all members of the Council of the European Union, i.e. all Member States, for the adoption of any decision to apply the provisions in the new Title III(a) of the Treaty establishing the European Community on visas, asylum, immigration and other policies related to free movement of persons to action in areas referred to in Article K.1. Moreover, any unanimous decision of the Council, before coming into force, will have to be adopted in each Member State, in accordance with its constitutional requirements. In Denmark, such adoption will, in the case of a transfer of sovereignty, as defined in the Danish constitution, require either a majority of five sixths of members of the Folketing or both a majority of the members of the Folketing and a majority of voters in a referendum.

(3) DECLARATION BY GERMANY, AUSTRIA AND BELGIUM ON SUBSIDIARITY

It is taken for granted by the German, Austrian and Belgian governments that action by the European Community in accordance with the principle of subsidiarity not only concerns the Member States but also their entities to the extent that they have their own law-making powers conferred on them under national constitutional law.

(4) DECLARATION BY IRELAND ON ARTICLE 3 OF THE PROTOCOL ON THE POSITION OF THE UNITED KINGDOM AND IRELAND

Ireland declares that it intends to exercise its right under Article 3 of the Protocol on the position of the United Kingdom and Ireland to take part in the adoption of measures pursuant to Title IIIa of the Treaty establishing the European Community to the maximum extent compatible with the maintenance of its Common Travel Area with the

United Kingdom. Ireland recalls that its participation in the Protocol on the application of certain aspects of Article 7a of the Treaty establishing the European Community reflects its wish to maintain its common travel Area with the United Kingdom in order to maximise freedom of movement into and out of Ireland.

(5) DECLARATION BY BELGIUM ON THE PROTOCOL ON ASYLUM FOR NATIONALS OF MEMBER STATES OF THE EUROPEAN UNION

In approving this Protocol, Belgium declares that in accordance with its obligations under the 1951 Geneva Convention and the 1967 New York Protocol, it shall, in accordance with the provision set out in point (d) of the sole Article of that Protocol, carry out an individual examination of any asylum request made by a national of another Member State.

(6) DECLARATION BY BELGIUM

—

(7) DECLARATION BY FRANCE CONCERNING THE SITUATION OF THE OVERSEAS DEPARTMENTS IN THE LIGHT OF THE PROTOCOL INTEGRATING THE SCHENGEN ACQUIS INTO THE FRAMEWORK OF THE EUROPEAN UNION

France considers that the implementation of the Protocol integrating the Schengen acquis into the framework of the European Union does not affect the geographical scope of the Convention implementing the Schengen Agreement of 14 June 1985 signed in Schengen on 19 June 1990, as it is defined by Article 138, first paragraph, of that convention.

(8) DECLARATION BY GREECE CONCERNING THE DECLARATION ON THE STATUS OF CHURCHES AND NON CONFESSIONAL ORGANISATIONS

With reference to the Declaration on the status of churches and non-confessional organisations, Greece recalls the Joint Declaration on Mount Athos annexed to the Final Act of the Treaty of Accession of Greece to the European Communities.